THE CHRONICLES OF FLEETWOOD HOUSE

by

A. J. SHIRREN

LONDON

Printed for the Author
by
Barnes Printers

1951

The Chronicles of Fleetwood House by H. J. Shirren who lived in Stoke Newington, England, was published for the author in London in 1951. It is now out of print and the plates have been destroyed.

This special limited edition of 500 copies of which this is no. 429 has been made possible by the kind permission of Mr. Shirren's sister, Mrs. Moira Durno of Truro, Cornwall England and through the gift by Mr. Charles Green Fleetwood of Houston, Texas of a copy of the original book.

Published for the University of Houston Foundation by The Gulf Publishing Company, Houston, Texas U.S.A.

Pacesetter Press
A Division of Gulf Publishing Company
Houston, Texas

ACKNOWLEDGMENTS

This is an attempt to bring together as much information as possible about Fleetwood House and the persons who have lived in it. Several residents were very important personages in their day and something of the historical background has been filled in to save the reader from referring to other books. The Fleetwood family has been dealt with in some detail as references to it are very scattered. There is clearly scope for a full length book on the three Fleetwood brothers by a first-rate historian of the seventeenth century. While the writer has been fortunate in fiinding much new information and in correcting some of the errors of previous writers, yet, as Mark Noble in the preface to his great book on the Cromwell family says, "it is an unhappiness that accompanies researches of this kind, that they cannot be complete; nor is it possible scarce, to prevent mistakes occurring." It is, however, a happiness also; there always remains something for another writer to do, something for another researcher to discover. For every doubtful point there is surely a manuscript letter or other document lying somewhere awaiting discovery which will solve the problem. Many of the illustrations have never appeared before, and will be of interest to those who still have some regard for the old days.

It is very pleasant to be able to record the assistance and interest given and shown by many persons during the preparation of this little book. I am greatly indebted to the Marquess of Lothian and the Earl Beauchamp for the great trouble they took to have certain letters and miniatures photographed from their collections at Melbourne Hall and Madresfield Court respectively. Dr. G. Ahlström, Director of the Swedish Institute for Cultural Relations, kindly obtained the portraits of George Fleetwood and Charles XII from Sweden and supplied information relating to the Fleetwoods and Thomas Cooke. Mr. Robert W. Ramsey, author of "Henry Ireton," and three other distinguished books on Cromwell's family circle, gave up an afternoon to discuss various points relating to the Fleetwood family, and indicated where a fine portrait of Charles Fleetwood was to be found. Professor E. R. Vincent, already the author of "Byron, Hobhouse and Foscolo," and now engaged on another book on Foscolo's career in England, which will deal with his association with the Fleetwood House school, supplied very helpful information, including a copy of William Allen's letter to Foscolo.

It goes without saying that, as always, the Officers at the British Museum, the Public Record Office, the National Portrait Gallery, the Library of the Society of Friends, the Commonwealth Relations Office, and the Bank of England, have provided invaluable assistance. The following also kindly troubled to answer queries and were helpful in many different ways: The Librarians of Chelsea, Leicester, Melton Mowbray, Stepney, and Stoke Newington; the Reverend E.

John Collinson of Laleham; Mr. E. A. P. Jenkins, Land Agent at Blenheim Palace, Mr. R. P. Bateman, M.B.E., the Reverend Arthur M. Dutton, formerly Vicar of Buckminster, Canon J. F. Winter of Aldwincle, the Reverend C. M. S. Clarke of Melton Mowbray, the Reverend W. Oriel James, Minister of the Congregational Church at Melton Mowbray, Lady Cradock-Hartopp, Miss Louisa Hack, Mr. H. K. Barker, Ll.B., Clerk of the Melton Mowbray U.D.C., and Mr. C. D. Morley, Secretary to the Council of the Stock Exchange. With regard to the portraits, etc., acknowledgment is made under the list of illustrations. The passages relating to Sir John Coke and Charles Fleetwood from the Earl of Clarendon's works are quoted by kind permission of the Clarendon Press, which holds a perpetual copyright in those works.

A. J. S.

Stoke Newington, 1950.

ILLUSTRATIONS

(Between pp. 168 – 169)

20. Letter from Charles Fleetwood to Oliver Cromwell.
S.P. 18/123. No. 7 (i). By kind permission of the Public Record Office.

21. Charles or George Fleetwood (?). Miniature by David Des Granges.
By kind permission of the Rt. Hon. the Earl Beauchamp.

22. Mrs. Lucy Hutchinson.
By kind permission of the Trustees of the British Museum.

23. Charles Fleetwood's Monument in Bunhill Fields.
By kind permission of " Illustrated London News."

24. Dr. John Owen, by John Riley.
By kind permission of the Trustees of the National Portrait Gallery.

25. Lady Mary Fauconberg, *after C. Janssen.*
By kind permission of the Trustees of the British Museum.

26. The Dunbar Medal.
By kind permission of the Trustees of the British Museum.

27. Dr. Isaac Watts.
By kind permission of the Trustees of the National Portrait Gallery.

28. The Watts Window at Freeby.
Photograph by Heawood & Son, Melton Mowbray.

29. Title page of Miss Elizabeth Fleetwood's funeral sermon, preached by John Asty.
By kind permission of the Librarian, Stoke Newington.

30. Signatures of Isaac Watts, Thomas Gunston, Sir Nathaniel Gould and Thomas Cooke.

31. Title page of Sir Nathaniel Gould's " An Essay on the Public Debts."
By kind permission of the Trustees of the British Museum.

32. Charles XII of Sweden.
By kind permission of Svenska Portrattarkivet.

33. Postscript of Letter from the East India Company to Warren Hastings, showing the signature of Joseph Hurlock.
By kind permission of the Trustees of the British Museum.

34. The Perrott Monument in Laleham Church.
Photograph by G. Cattley, Staines.

35. The Countess of Albany.
By kind permission of the Trustees of the National Portrait Gallery.

36. Vittorio Alfieri.
By kind permission of the Trustees of the British Museum.

37. Lord Byron, by T. Phillips.
By kind permission of the Trustees of the National Portrait Gallery.

38. John Cam Hobhouse.
By kind permission of the Trustees of the British Museum.

39. Title page of the " Illustrations " from Hobhouse's presentation copy to the Countess of Jersey, in the author's possession.

40. Ugo Foscolo, by Filippo Pistrucci.
By kind permission of the Cambridge University Press. The original is at Cambridge.

41. Letter from William Allen to Ugo Foscolo.
By kind permission of the Labronica Library, Leghorn.

42. William Allen.
By kind permission of the Librarian, Stoke Newington.

43. Fleetwood House.
By kind permission of the Librarian, Stoke Newington.

44. Letter from Susanna Corder to Thomas Thompson.
By kind permission of the Librarian of the Society of Friends.

45. Fleetwood House.
By kind permission of the Librarian, Stoke Newington.

46. Plasterwork from a Fleetwood House ceiling.
By kind permission of the Librarian, Stoke Newington.

47. Plasterwork from a Fleetwood House ceiling.
By kind permission of the Librarian, Stoke Newington.

48. The Fleetwood Cabinet.
By kind permission of the National Gallery of Ireland and of the National Museum of Ireland.

49. The Fleetwood Cabinet.
By kind permission of the National Gallery of Ireland and of the National Museum of Ireland.

50. (a) Seventeenth century seal, showing the arms of the Fleetwoods of Aldwincle; (b) the arms of the Hartopps.
By kind permission of the Librarian, Stoke Newington.

Note.—The first edition of Robinson's " History of Stoke Newington " had a very badly executed engraved portrait of Charles Fleetwood (omitted from the second edition) which seems to have been copied from the miniature by David Des Granges (No. 21), now at Madresfield Court and which is more likely to be a portrait of George Fleetwood. According to the British Museum Catalogue portrait No. 19 is of Bridget Fleetwood. It is, however, almost identical with the portrait of her sister, Lady Mary Fauconberg, at " Chequers." The National Portrait Gallery has a large group of 135 figures—" The Anti-Slavery Society Convention of 1840," by B. R. Haydon. William Allen is shown prominently in the foreground, dressed in much the same manner as in the portrait now reproduced (No. 42).

" Then every eye the stately fabric drew
To every part; for all were fair to view:
The powerful chief the far-famed work descried,
And heard the public voice that waked his pride.
Pleased he began—' About, above, below,
What more can wealth command, or science show?
Here taste and grandeur join with massy strength,
Slow comes perfection, but it comes at length.
Still must I grieve: these halls and towers sublime,
Like vulgar domes, must feel the force of time;
And, when decay'd, can future days repair
What I in these have made so strong and fair?
My future heirs shall want of power deplore,
When time destroys what Time can not restore.' "

—George Crabbe.

From " Belvoir Castle "

THE CHRONICLES OF FLEETWOOD HOUSE.

I

The great house later to be known as Fleetwood House, which once stood on the northern side of Stoke Newington Church Street, was in all probability built either during the closing years of the reign of James I, or the opening years of the reign of his son, Charles I. It is strange that no evidence has been forthcoming as to how and when it came to be built, but from what is known of its architectural style this was predominantly Jacobean. The Leicestershire family of Hartopp had been steadily advancing in wealth and importance during the reigns of Elizabeth and James I, and doubtless it became necessary for Sir Edward Hartopp, the first Baronet, to build for himself a house conveniently close to London in which to live during the ever increasing periods that his affairs compelled him to spend in town. He became a Member of Parliament for Leicestershire in 1628, and his determination to embark on a parliamentary career may well have been the deciding factor in causing him to acquire a town house in addition to one in the country. It was an age for the building of great houses, which were often big enough to be occupied by more than one branch of the same family. Generally such houses constituted self-contained units comprising gardens, brewhouse, dairy and bakehouse, and employing miniature armies of servants to satisfy the needs of the family and their friends, and the enormous demands of hospitality. Sir Simonds d'Ewes, writing of his grandfather, describes a typical squire of the period, and no doubt the Hartopps, important Lords of the Manor on their Leicestershire estates, fitted the description well enough. " Sound and sure he was of his word, true and faithful to his friend, somewhat choleric yet apt to forgive, cheerful in his journey or at his meals, of a sound and deep judgment with a strong memory, giving good examples to his neighbours by his constant hospitality, earnest he was and sincere in the rightful cause of his client, pitiful in the relief of the distressed and merciful to the poor."

It is often overlooked that the first part of the seventeenth century during which Fleetwood House was built, must have been a period of uncertainty, in many ways similar to the times in which we now live. The clear Elizabethan sky was being rapidly overcast with the clouds of religious and political differences. Eventually the storm broke with a civil war that was to bring the King to the scaffold, and to set father against son and brother against brother. Of Sir Miles Fleetwood's two sons who remained in England, William was to side with the King, and Charles was to become one of Cromwell's greatest generals. It was Charles' residence in the house that gave it its name. Jacobean poets and dramatists, such as John Donne and Webster, reflected this growing sense of fear and alarm which was perhaps not consciously apparent to the ordinary person. When the war did come, although on the whole fought with typical English restraint, it provided examples of conduct which have since become only too familiar. At the seige of Colchester, where later we shall find Dr. Owen officiating as chaplain to Lord Fairfax, it was alleged that " dum-dum " bullets had been used, relatives of leaders of the defence were arrested to weaken their determination to resist, bows and arrows reappeared as weapons of war to shoot propaganda pamphlets into the town, ration cards were issued, popular preachers reassured the combatants of the righteousness of their cause, and in case this did not avail there were quack astrologers to foretell survival in the coming battle. When the garrison finally capitulated its leaders, Lucas and Lisle, were shot contrary to all the rules of war.

On the continent the terrible Thirty Years War had broken out in 1618, when Elizabeth, daughter of James I, and her husband lost the throne of Bohemia. This was a war due as much to religious as civil causes as was the war in England. In it George Fleetwood, Charles' elder brother and second son of Sir Miles, was to win fame and honour at the side of Gustavus Adolphus, and to be rewarded with a Swedish baronetcy at the hand of the beautiful Queen Christina. The story of Elizabeth of Bohemia, this " Princess resplendent in darkness, whose virtues were born within the chance, but without the power of Fortune,"* shows that something of the chivalry of the middle ages had lingered on, and only required a spark to set it once more alight. Christian, the Halberstadter of Brunswick, one of the most brutal mercenary soldiers of the age, who in the ordinary course of events would have fought for the side that paid him most, fell under her spell, and went into battle with her glove in his helmet, took as his motto " Tout pour Dieu et ma très chère reine," and signed his letters to her, " Your most humblest, most constant, most faithful, most affectionate and most obedient slave, who loves you, and will love you infinitely and incessantly till death." Sir Henry Wotton was about 55 when, in the language of the platonic idealism and rococo chivalry of the times he became her " servant." In an earlier age he would have described himself as her " knight."

He was to immortalise his Princess and himself in one of the most exquisite lyrics ever written. Already in 1621 James Howell was writing, " the Lady Elizabeth is called, for her winning Princely comportment, the Queen of Hearts." Perhaps the secret of her charm lay in her attitude to life, shown in a letter to Sir Thomas Roe : — " Though I have cause enough to be sad, yet I am still of my wild humour to be as merry as I can in spite of fortune." And during her long exile Sir Henry Wotton was to lament : — " Shall I die without seeing again my royal mistress ? " Remnants of feudalism were also still to be found, which may explain the Hartopps' support of the

* Sir Henry Wotton.

cause of parliament. The great family of Manners, Earls of Rutland, of Belvoir Castle, dominated the neighbourhood in which the Hartopps' country estates were situated, and although both Sir Edward Hartopp and his son had been favoured by James I and Charles I, the adherence of Belvoir Castle to the side of parliament may have had much to do with their decision to follow the example of their traditional overlord. Religious feelings also must have influenced their decision.

4

The Hartopp family was one of considerable position in the county of Leicestershire, and its various branches held the manors of Buckminster, Freeby, Burton Lazars, Little Dalby, Welby and Braunston which are situated in that part of the county which lies towards Lincoln and Rutland. Little Dalby has the distinction of being the village in which Stilton cheese was first made by a Mrs. Orton about 1730. " At first," says Nichols, " it was supposed that it could be made only from the milk of those cows which fed in one close, now called Orton's close; but this was afterwards found to be an error." Defoe in his " Tour thro' Great Britain " mentioned Stilton cheese, " which is called our English Parmesan, and is sometimes brought to table so full of Mites or Maggots, that they use a spoon to eat them." The Hartopps owned a large Elizabethan house in a good park situated on high ground above the village.

Burton Lazars took its name from the leper hospital built by Roger de Mowbray for the Order of St. Augustine. The Master of this hospital was the head of all the lazar-houses in England. The air and water were regarded as particularly beneficial, and cattle were driven there from surrounding districts whenever there was an outbreak of cattle sickness. Buckminster, which is particularly associated with the main branch of the Hartopp family, stands high up in the Lincolnshire Wolds and is a most picturesque village.

The first Hartopp to appear on record is Ralph, who lived in the reign of Richard II, and married a daughter of one Alexander Mayne. Early in the reign of Henry VII the manor of Braunston was granted to the family, and tradition points out the site of their ancient manor house. Walter Devereux, an adherent of Richard III, had previously held this manor, but was slain with his master at the battle of Bosworth, and his estates forfeited to the Crown.*

Valentine Hartopp (died 1633) during the course of his life held both Little Dalby and Burton Lazars, the second of which was also held by Sir Edward (1572-1654), the first Baronet, during part of his life. Valentine's grandson, Sir Thomas Hartopp, bought the manorial rights for his branch of the family in 1660. It must be this Sir Thomas Hartopp, whose name is linked with Samuel Oates, the father of the notorious Titus Oates, and himself almost as big a scoundrel as his son who did so much to discredit the nonconformist cause. " Abel Barker to his much honoured friend Sir Thomas Hartopp, Knight, at Leicester. Sending a declaration concerning one Samuel Oates, a weaver, ' who preacheth constantly in this country,' for the consideration of the judges who may see fit to issue a warrant for his arrest and conveyance to the Assizes at Okeham. Hambleton, March 19, 1646/47." Oates was an Anabaptist and a leading light at Lamb's Church in Bell Alley, Coleman Street, At one service

he informed the congregation " That the doctrine of God's eternal
Election and Predestination was a damnable Doctrine and Error," and
seems to have openly contradicted the preacher whenever he disagreed
with anything he said. Mr. Lamb used to send his brethren out
preaching and baptizing, which was called " Dipping " as it meant
total immersion. It was customary to dip the candidates stark naked
in a river at night. Oates seems to have been very successful in making
converts among young women, and it is recorded that " where Oates
hath been dipping, that it was spoken of by many, that some young
women who having beene married divers yeeres and never were with
child, now since theer dipping are proved with child." It was after
an expedition to Essex, about which a minister complains, " Oates
hath been sowing his tares, boolimong, and wild oates in these parts
these last five weeks, hath seduced hundreds and dipped many in
Bocking river, and when that's done he hath a feast in the night, and
at the end of that the Lord's Supper," that Sir Thomas Hartopp was
written to. In 1660 when Charles II returned Oates deserted his
sect, joined the Church of England and obtained a living.

Another branch of the family established itself in the fine Elizabethan Manor house at Little Dalby under George Hartopp. One
of his sons, Thomas Hartopp (1628-1723) settled at Antwerp and
of him it is related that being . . . .

" a gentleman of remarkable strength and courage, upon witnessing
a prize fight in which the combatants did not acquit themselves
to the satisfaction of the spectators, he was so offended thereat, that
he got upon the stage, and challenging them, encountered no less
than five, one after another, whom he entirely disabled, whereby
he gained very great applause; and being of a comely personage
and stature, a lady of quality and fortune fell so much in love with
him, that she sent him word, she was at his service, if he was
disposed to marry; and he embracing the offer settled there, served
the king of Spain in his armies, and his son was afterwards a colonel
in the emperor's service, and governor of Liege in Brabant, where
he is buried in the chapel of Ter Cluyse under a monument with
the following inscription: ' Cygist messire Thomas Hartopp,
d'ancienne et noble famille d'Engleterre; en son vivant colonel d'un
regiment d'infanterie au service de S.M. Imperiale et Catholique,
gouverneur de la ville et dependences de Liege. Il y deceda le
20 Juin, 1723, et laissa deux fitz de noble dame Marie-Constance
Van Hove sa compagne, laquelle fit dresser ce memoire. Priez
Dieu pour le repos eternel de son ame.' "

On 26th November, 1655, Major General Whalley, William
Hartopp and nine others wrote to Thurloe, Cromwell's secretary,
from Leicester : —

" We desire to be ever thankful to the Lord for continuing the good
hand of providence over us, so lately manifested to us in directing
his highness, and induing him with so much wisdom and vigilancy,
as under himself to discover and frustrate the destructive designs
of our implacable enemies and to provide so well for the peace of

this Commonwealth. We hope we shall not be wanting to contribute our best assistance in our places to so good a work being thereunto called; and to the end our endeavours may be the more effectual we desire you to send us the examinations and other proofs that you have against Sir Robert Shirly and Sir Kenelme Digby, or any other that you know have had their hands in these late designs and insurrections, that have estates in this county (if there be any such) and we doubt not to give his highness a good account of what he hath entrusted."

The William Hartopp signing this letter was the Squire of Little Dalby (1625-1677), and it is interesting to find this link—although not of a friendly nature—with Sir Kenelm Digby, one of the most picturesque and fascinating characters of the seventeenth century.

William Hartopp, the son of Thomas and Ellen Hartopp of Burton Lazars, married Eleanor, daughter of . . . Adcock, and was the father of two sons with whom we are particularly concerned, Thomas and Edward. He died on 22nd September, 1586, and was buried at Melton Mowbray. Thomas, his eldest son, succeeded him, and in 1596 he was granted a coat of arms: —

> Sable, a chevron between three otters ermine;
> *Crest*: On a wreath, out of a ducal coronet or
> a pelican argent, vulning herself proper.

In 1598 he obtained the manor of Freeby by exchange with the Earl of Rutland. His coat of arms and crest now became: —

> Sable, a chevron between three otters argent
> (The later baronets bore the chevron ermine)
> *Crest*: Out of a coronet or a demi-pelican with
> wings endorsed argent, vulning herself gules.

He married Dorothy, daughter of Roger Cave, but died without issue. His brother, Edward, second son of William Hartopp, succeeded to the family estates.

Edward Hartopp was born in 1572 and was ninth in descent from Ralph Hartopp. He is said to have served under Robert Dudley, Earl of Leicester, in the Netherlands. As he was only thirteen at the time no doubt he acted as page to one of the noblemen of Leicester's entourage. William of Orange had been assassinated at Delft in 1584 and Queen Elizabeth decided to make a stand against the power of Spain. The expeditionary force sailed from Harwich on 8th December, 1585, and disembarked at Flushing. Leicester on arrival enjoyed an enormous personal success and on arriving at Amsterdam "was received with sundry sortes of great fishes, as whales and others of great hugeness which towed his ships to the landing stages." Such pageantry must have made a memorable impression on the mind of a young boy. Leicester was even offered "the absolute government of the whole provinces," to the great displeasure of Queen Elizabeth. The expedition, however, ended in ignominious failure and withdrawal, the gallant death of Sir Philip Sidney at Zutphen alone conferring upon it a kind of afterglow of glory.

Probably in the year 1607 Edward Hartopp married Mary Dryden,* and in the following year his eldest son, Edward, was born, the first of nine children. In 1617 he was High Sheriff for Leicestershire, and at about the same time purchased the manor of Buckminster from the Cave family. His elder brother, Thomas, on whose death he inherited Freeby, had been married to Dorothy Cave. On 3rd December, 1619, King James I created him a baronet. In 1622 he is recorded as giving £20 to the contribution to assist the King's son-in-law, Frederick the Elector Palatine, husband of Elizabeth, who had lost the throne of Bohemia and the Palatinate on the outbreak of the Thirty Years' War.

In 1628 he was elected Member of Parliament for Leicestershire, and no doubt it then became necessary to consider acquiring a house in London, or somewhere conveniently nearby. Although the origin of the house, once standing on the present site of Fleetwood Street, is shrouded in mystery, it can be stated with some confidence that Sir Edward Hartopp, the first baronet, chose the site and put the builders to work. The house was a magnificent one of red brick containing over sixty rooms with superb panelling and massive Jacobean staircases. One of the rooms had its ceiling ornamented with coats of arms, from the presence of which it is reasonably possible to date the completion of the building operations. Edward, the eldest son of the first baronet, had been born in 1608, and married Mary, daughter of Sir John Coke, about 1634. Coke asked his friend, Kenrick Edisbury, to make enquiries about Edward Hartopp as a suitable husband for his daughter and received this reply:—" I spake with Mr. Valentine, the minister, touching Mr. Hartopp of whom he

*See Addenda, 15.

gives a singular good report. He affects his studies and a country
life, seldom drinks any wine, and when he was his pupil he would not
drink strong beer. He is no gamester." At any rate his first child,
John, was born and died in 1635, and a second son, Edward, who did
not live long, was born in the following year. A third son, also
christened John, who lived to be the third baronet, was born in 1637.
As the arms of Coke of Melbourne—gules, three crescents and a
canton or—together with his crest—a sun in splendour or—were done
in plaster work on this ceiling the building of the house was surely
completed by 1634 or 1635. Sir John Coke was employed in government affairs at this time in London, and it is probable that he visited
his daughter and saw his own coat of arms on the ceiling. Later on
he was to end his days in his house at Tottenham, no great distance
away, and was, therefore, no doubt at least an occasional visitor to
Stoke Newington.

★

Sir John Coke (1563-1644) was one of the eleven children of
Richard Coke of Trusley, near Derby, and began life with only an
annuity of £40. He went to Trinity College, Cambridge, and then
entered the service of Lord Burghley and became deputy-treasurer of
the Navy. In 1605 he married Marie Powell. He now spent some
years in the country farming, and acting as auditor of the accounts of
Sir Fulke Greville's estates. In 1618 he was appointed one of a
Commission to examine the state of the Navy. In the following year
this became a permanent board. Eliot says, "the rest of the Commissioners were but cyphers unto him." James I rewarded his industry
by a grant of £300 a year. In February, 1624, he lost his wife, but
married again, before the end of the year, Joan, daughter of Sir John
Lee and widow of Sir John Gore, both of whom were Aldermen of
London. Mary, who married Sir Edward Hartopp, the second Baronet,
was the daughter of Coke's first wife and was no doubt named after
her mother.

Coke's marriage to Marie Powell had been a love match, and it
remained so until the end. Only a short while before her death he
had written:—" This only let me tell you, that you are daily in my
heart and dearest affection and in my prayers. That I esteem you as
myself and will ever impart unto you all the comforts and blessings
which God bestoweth on us. That no woman shall have more cause
to be confident in the love and care and tenderness of a husband than
you will find whilst I live . . . ."

When Prince Rupert first came over to the Court of Charles I from
Holland his mother, Elizabeth of Bohemia, wrote:—" Good Mr.
Secretary Coke, I must now send my son to kiss the King his uncle's
hand, but withal recommend him to your care, that you will continue
your love to me, and show it by your care of my son this bearer.
Rupert can so well inform you of all things as I need not take the
pains to do it, especially being in haste, the wind being now good,

which he has stayed for this fortnight at the least. I have commanded
him to be diligent in waiting and serving his uncle. I hope he will
do it, for he goeth with a great deal of zeale and affection to him. I
again entreat you to show your love to me in him and so believe me,
Ever your affectionate friend, Elizabeth,"

Clarendon's references to Coke are hostile, or at any rate reflect the
views of those who were intriguing to push him out of office.
Eventually "the Queen's Side," that is those with Catholic leanings
who surrounded Henrietta Maria, were to succeed and to replace him
with Sir Henry Vane. Coke was too staunch a protestant to be popular
with them. All, however, acknowledged his honesty. Fulke Greville
ended a letter, " Farewell honest and honourable Secretary," while
Lord Cottington said of him to Sir Henry Vane: —" You will find
yourself very well with Secretary Coke: certainly he is an honest and
able man."

Clarendon in his " History of the Rebellion " says that Coke " was
a man of a very narrow education, and a narrower nature; having
continued long in the university of Cambridge where he had gotten
Latin learning enough; and afterwards in the country in the condition
of a private gentleman till after he was fifty years of age; when, upon
some reputation he had for industry and diligence, he was called to
some painful employment in the office of the navy, which he discharged
well; and afterwards to be master of requests, and then to be secretary
of state, which he enjoyed to a great age: and was a man rather
unadorned with parts of vigour and quickness, and unendowed with
any notable virtues, than notorious for any weakness or defect of
understanding, than transported with any vicious inclinations, appetite
to money only excepted. His cardinal perfection was industry, and
his most eminent infirmity covetousness. His long experience had
informed him well of the state and affairs of England; but of foreign
transactions, or of the common interest of Christian princes he was
entirely ignorant and undiscerning."

Whether Coke was " covetous " or not he certainly acquired his
wealth in an honest way, which is more than can be said for many
of the officials of the period. No stigma attaches to his public or
private character. Before the outbreak of the Civil War he was a
strong supporter of an absolute monarchy, and he set out his views in
a remarkable speech at Oxford in 1636, which is printed in Archbishop
Laud's history of his chancellorship of Oxford University. At the
same time he was a staunch protestant and in Prynne's pamphlet,
" Rome's Masterpiece," is described as " a most bitter hater of the
jesuits, from whom he intercepted access to the King." After the
outbreak of the war he seems to have become a supporter of the
parliamentary cause for we find him writing to the Earl of Essex, the
parliament's general: —" My elder son and I live together with our
wives and families, and we humbly desire your protection to free us
from being molested by such troops and companies as shall pass this
way. I assure your Excellency my heart is faithful and my prayers

assiduous for the prosperity of the parliament, wherein consisteth the welfare of this church and state." In the Historical Manuscripts Commission's volumes of the Coke papers at Melbourne Hall this letter appears only as a draft without the name of the person to whom it was addressed. It may well be that his sympathies still lay with the King, and that this letter was simply written to try and preserve his property from marauding soldiers. It was also in his house that Baxter planned his " Saints' Everlasting Rest." One of Coke's sons, John, supported Cromwell and another, Thomas, the King, and as we shall see his son-in-law, Sir Edward Hartopp, was active on the parliament side. In 1638 Coke was a member of a committee for Scotch affairs and favoured peace rather than war. Clarendon takes the opportunity of dealing him another blow, " Secretary Coke, who had all the dispatches upon his hand, was near eighty years of age; a man of gravity, who never had quickness from his cradle; who loved the church well enough as it was twenty years before; and understood nothing that had been done in Scotland, and thought that nothing that was or could be done there worth such a journey as the King had put himself to."

At the end of the first Scotch war the King's affairs were going so badly that some action had to be taken, and as usual in such political predicaments it was decided to find a scapegoat. To quote Clarendon once more: —" The King himself was very melancholic, and quickly discerned that he had lost reputation at home and abroad; and those counsellors who had been most faulty, either through want of courage, or wisdom (for at that time few of them wanted fidelity) never afterwards recovered spirit enough to do their duty, but gave themselves up to those who had so much overwitted them; every man shifting the fault from himself and finding some friend to excuse him; and it being yet necessary, that so infamous a matter should not be covered with absolute oblivion, it fell to secretary Coke's turn (for whom nobody cared) who was then near fourscore years of age, to be made the sacrifice; and, upon pretence, that he had omitted the writing what he ought to have done, and inserted some what he ought not to have done he was put out of office."

Coke wrote to his son John, that he found " both a gracious countenance and profession that no offence is taken against me, and so much expression of good opinion and good will towards me both in court and city that I could never withdraw myself with a more favourable aspect." He now retired to his Derbyshire property at Melbourne.

After his retirement he must have found life rather dull, but old colleagues, friends and relatives sent him news of affairs. Charles's I second campaign against the Scots was a gloomy fiasco and resulted in the Scots crossing the Tyne at Newburn. His son-in-law, Sir Edward Hartopp, wrote to tell him of this: —

" I presume you have already heard how far the Scots are marched into England, but the number of their army variously reported. Whereas it was said they have ransacked and burned

Newcastle, it is absolutely contradicted . . . For my Lord Willoughby sent a man to Durham to be truly informed, and partly, if there was need, to remove his son which is with the Bishop. He came this afternoon, and related that the beginning of the skirmish was there. The Scots, having marched as far as Newcastle without any resistance, and might have taken the town, they refused to do it . . . But perceiving some of our troops of horse and some companies of foot in the field, put them close in battle array and planted nine field pieces undiscovered upon a little hill nearby. When they had this done . . . a Scot galloping from his company, brandished his sword about his head, which an impatient Welshman spying, gave spurs to his horse and in the encounter slew him. Upon which occasion companies on either side was sent forth, but the field pieces of the Scots galled our horse and slew many of them; upon which disadvantage the remnant of the horse was commanded to interpose, whilst the foot fled clear away. . . . My Lord of Carnarvon fought madly, like himself, for being forsaken by his countrymen, he made good the place while he had any powder and shot, and after threw his pistols at them: then drawing his sword, fought manfully till he was relieved . . . I forgot to let you know the Scots do no hurt in their march, but pay very well for whatsoever they have in the country."

As the war increased in violence, Melbourne became unsafe as a residence, and Coke wrote to Sir Edward for advice as to where to seek shelter. He thought he might go to the Danvers at Swithland. Sir Edward, however, replied: —

"I am exceedingly sorry you cannot find a more quiet repose at Melbourne, but you will also find it very difficult in these parts. I am confident you will find neither security nor accommodation at Swithland. And being the general opinion and conclusion that the main armies on both sides are drawing into these parts for the enlargement of their quarters, I question whether Leicester will be convenient for you."

The next day Coke received a letter sent from Swithland by Elizabeth Danvers, in which she says: —

"I am heartily sorry the times are such as constrain you to remove from Melbourne at this unseasonable time of the year, and I am as sorry I cannot accomplish your desire in having you at Swithland by reason all my goods but some few for my children's needful use are at Leicester, and because of my uncertain stay and dangerous fetching of coals I am very ill-provided of fuel and other necessaries to entertain Your Honour at Swithland; and the great house at Leicester is so full, having three families besides myself in it, and being very unquiet because it is so near the street. But if Your Honour please to come to Leicester I think the Newark the safest and quietest place in Leicester and Mr. Wadland's house the fittest, because the judges lie there every assizes . . . ."

As a result Coke undertook the last long journey he was to make from Derbyshire to his house at Tottenham at the great age of eighty-one. He did not long survive, dying on the 8th September, 1644. Thus died "the last Elizabethan," a capable and honest public servant, who had carried on the fine traditions learnt in the service of England's greatest Queen.

Perhaps his best epitaph is the account he wrote of himself in a letter addressed to the Duke of Buckingham, but for some reason never sent: —

"Howsoever I am valued my descent is not base. I was not bred in servile or illiberal trades, the University (i.e. Cambridge) was my nurse, I have travelled many countries, where I saw peace and war. I am acquainted with books, and no stranger to the Courts and affairs of the world. And though those know who know me best that I ever affected a private course of life, yet I never refused any service whatsoever to give God, my prince, and my country a good account of my time; nor ever made the public a step to private ends, nor set profit or honour in the first place of my heart, as the common fashion is."

It is interesting to note that the dates of Sir John Coke's birth and death are only known from a note written by Sir John Hartopp, the third Baronet, on the authority of a memorandum he had inherited from his uncle, Sir John Coke the younger.

★

Mary Coke, and her brothers and sisters, must have had a happy childhood. This was passed at Hall Court near Much Marcle in Herefordshire. Coke purchased the property in 1606, pulled down the old house and built a new one. Its position must have pleased his wife, for her parents, the Powells, lived only four miles away at Preston Court, and she could visit her old home whenever she wished. On 30th October, 1605, she wrote from Preston Court: —

"To my loving husband Mr. John Coke give this. I sent a short notice to you this week mentioning the receipt of your letters and things sent by Dobs, the carrier, which now I may show more plainly that he sent the wicker basket hither to the house on Wednesday after you despatched from thence. My gown and hat I like very well, and they are very fit for me, but considering our foul and dirty weather though my walks be very few I am loath to carry so much gold at my skirt into the dirt about the house which maketh me wear my gown seldomer than I would do. I do acknowledge your kindness and care in sending it so quickly and getting it so well made ... The piece of silk you sent me doth serve me well. I have the pintado and gold lace and do defer the making of my kirtle till I hear from you. Now I am speaking of these things I may tell you that you need buy no cradle for I am told that I may have one here within 4 or 5 miles ... I thank God, I can certify you that I am in health and comfort, and do spend part of my time in making baby's clothes, and yet I cannot but think that we are not in our own place whiles we are so far asunder, which being so let me put you in mind as I do myself that we keep our minds one, as though we were together, and I pray God to sanctify this absence to us ..."

Coke was an indulgent husband and father and there are frequent references to his children in the letters he wrote to his wife when public affairs took him away from home: —

" It shall, I assure you, add earnestness to my prayers that God will be pleased to take charge of you and our little one, and supply in it those comforts which are defective in me."

" In the meantime I have bought your gown cloth, and for the children, which I purpose, God willing, to send by Dobbs this next Saturday . . . . "

" I pray you take order that Mr. Mease may not want to keep him warm lest . at his first day and change of air he find inconvenience in his health. Let your maids look his lodging be warm. For his diet I doubt not but such part as your board affordeth will content him, and I hope you will find him sober and honest and able to profit our children and be good company for us."

" And for the children a crawel coife and 2 green masks . . . ."

Mr. Mease, alas, proved far from satisfactory as a tutor.

In Coke's accounts, which he paid for the year 1625, appears this item: — " 2 pairs of stockings for your daughters—5s. 0d."

As Coke became more and more occupied with affairs of state he decided to find a house in London for his family. He did so in 1623, at St. John's Gate, Clerkenwell. His wife had been suffering for some time from a pain in her side, and it was not long after moving from Hall Court that she died in giving birth to twins, one of whom also died. The following sad account is preserved among Coke's papers: —

"a cradle for Dorothy	5	0
a box for Dorothy	2	6
a coffin for Peter	3	4
To the bearers for carrying Peter to the church	4	0
To the comfit maker at the Christening	3	0
For my wife's funeral		
For a rich coffin for my wife	6	6
2 dozen torches	16	0
A pound of wax lights	2	6
To the eight bearers	1 0	0
Paid to the minister for preaching at the baptising of my daughter, Dorothy	1 0	0
For 2 unlaced bands and cuffs bought at the Exchange	1 0	0 "

Coke never went to Hall Court again, where he had spent such happy times. It was sold in 1628.

In the early autumn of 1624 Coke married again. His second

wife was Joan Gore, widow of Alderman William Gore, and daughter of Sir Robert Lee, a former Lord Mayor of London. He seems to have married her as much to provide a home for his children as for any other reason. This she did as she was a kindly woman, and her own children were brought up with Coke's. She wrote to Sir John in September, 1625: —" . . . it is no small comfort to me sweet husband to hear of your good health . . . and my prayers shall not be slack for your health and happy return . . . My son Elways came home the Monday after you went, and he hath had one fit of the ague, but not great. All the rest of our children are in good health, I thank God, and the maids that were sick are about the house. Our town is very clear, and all our friends in good health and remember their services unto you, Mr. Fish, Mr. Latimore, my son Elways and daughters . . . I rest your ever loving wife." On 26th June, 1628, she wrote to her husband, ". . . My sister Carey and your daughter Mary is in good health, and all the rest of us, God be thanked . . ." Mary seems to have passed an uneventful childhood, and there is no mention of illness in her parents' letters. The death of her mother had probably been her first great grief. In 1631 Coke began to think of finding a husband for his daughter, and on 26th February, 1631-2, he received a letter from Christopher Fulwood: —

"Mr. Gilbert tells me that Sir Thomas Burdett hath sold so much of his land as he hath paid all his debts and left a thousand per annum still, and besides hath some of the moneys upon the sale left. He thinks if it be your pleasure a fitting time to let somewhat be spoken touching a match between his son and your daughter, Mistress Mary, for he thinks no great portion will be now stood upon."

Fulwood was a relative of Francis Fulwood, whom Coke's sister, Mary, had married. Nothing came of the marriage proposal. On 22nd May, 1633, Richard Poole concluded a letter to Sir John Coke with these words, ". . . My Lord Bishop of Bristol* and Mrs. Carey remember their love. Mistress Mary and Mr. Thomas their duty."

Richard Poole was Coke's clerk, and Mrs. Carey his sister, Dorothy. Her death is described in a memorandum dated 1st February, 1634, among Coke's papers. She left him the remainder of the lease of her house in Drury Lane "to her brother Sir John Coke, to whose daughter Mary she shewed herself rather a mother than an aunt."

In a letter to Coke dated 13th January, 1625, Valentine Carey, Bishop of Exeter, had written: —" My family are in good health. I reckon your daughter for one of the number . . . ." Mary was evidently then staying with her aunt. Thomas Coke, writing to his brother, John, in October, 1633, gave what he considered the cause of Dorothy Carey's illness: —" My Aunt Carey hath been this month sore visited; we much doubt of her recovery. I think the principal cause of her sickness was grief for my cousin Ernestus Carey his misdemeanour, who hath lately married some filthy drab in the bishopric of Durham, worse than nought, and brought her to London to the undoing of himself and all his fortunes . . . ."

*Sir John Coke's brother, George, was Bishop of Bristol. Valentine Carey (or Cary) Bishop of Exeter, had died in 1626 at his house in Drury Lane.

On 27th May, 1633, John Coke, the younger, wrote to his father regarding the lady he wished to marry, and gave an indirect description of his sister: —

"I desired Sir Henry Willoughby to give me leave to have some speech with his daughter . . . she is a gentlewoman of a good person in my eye, and of a pretty sweet disposition; not tall, about my sister Mary's height, and proportion or rather not altogether so tall, something pale and of few words, those civil and discreet . . . ."

Elizabeth Willoughby was not Sir Henry Willoughby's daughter, but the widow of his son. Her father was Timothy Pusey of Selston Hall, Nottinghamshire. She was not at first attracted to John Coke, but after a long courtship he finally won her. The marriage was a successful one, and she gave much happiness to Sir John Coke and to his son. On 10th November, 1630, Thomas Burrye wrote to Sir John Coke: —"I have been sick, my first journey abroad shall be to Sir E. Hartopp's, at which time your honour shall receive satisfaction . . . ." This is a reference to the father of Edward Hartopp, who, as we have seen, became Mary's husband in 1634. On 28th April, 1635, James Mayo wrote from Drury Lane (perhaps Dorothy Carey's old house) to Sir John Coke, the younger, at Selston, Nottinghamshire: —

"Let this letter be left at Sir Edward Hartopp's to be sent accordingly.

With Mr. Witherings' advice I have bought you—

	£	s	d
A riding suit and coat, the cloth is in grain, dyed in the wool, 5 yards at 26s.	6	16	6
A riding suit and coat, the plush (very good) 7 yards at 22s.	7	14	0
A riding suit and coat, satin 3½ yards at 14s.	2	9	0
To the Tailor (he hath used you ill)	4	15	0
I have likewise paid for sweetmeats sent to Sir E. Hartopp	4	11	0

I am constrained to send your clothes by Buckminster carrier."

Sir John Coke had two stewards—James Mayo at Melbourne Hall, and Edward Reed at the Tottenham house. In January, 1639, Coke wrote to his eldest son: —". . . . My old friend Ed. R. (Reed) being sunk in his estate is now fallen to shifts. An old friend must not be disgraced. Favour his reputation, but take heed of him, and give them at Buckminster warning in a silent way . . . ." Thomas Witherings was the Postmaster who had been chosen by Coke for that position.

On 6th May, 1636, Sir Edward Hartopp wrote to his father-in-law: —

". . . . I am glad to hear of the recovery of your health after the loss of so much blood. Your daughter with her great belly is well."

Sir Edward on 20th August, 1637, wrote to Coke: —

"Thanks for preferment of my old servant, Charnock, a place of more value and convenience than I expected. He is much exposed in his business with false pretences. He is advised by many friends to look to himself—they have been overheard to say that if he got this office they would get his life."

By November of the same year Charnock was dead, and Sir Edward wrote again to Coke to obtain help for his widow and son. By reason of his position Coke was in much demand when his own and his relatives' friends desired to obtain preferment. On 12th April, 1638, Mr. Robert Pullen wrote to him: —

"Having had offer of your noble favours for Sir Edward Hartopp's sake, I move your honour to be recommended to the Lord Keeper in whose gifture is the Vicarage of Trinity in the City of Coventry, where I am not unknown and not unbeloved. I have promised to wait on my good friends at Buckminster."

Coke wrote to his son-in-law in April, 1639: —

"Good son, I was most glad by Mr. Bury to understand from you of my daughter's safe delivery, and pray God with all my heart to bless your little infant, together with your spouse and to continue both your health and increase all your comforts."

On 22nd March, 1641, Sir Edward wrote to Coke giving him worrying news of his daughter and her little girl: —

"I do not forget how much my duty doth oblige me to wait upon you and how often . . . my long absence doth appear a wilful neglect to your Honour. But truly, Sir, I have had such an unlucky disease amongst my horses that it hath made them blind and utterly unuseful for the present, constraining me to keep home . . . My wife humbly commendeth her duty to your Honour: she hath been very lately ill and hath miscarried, but God be praised, she recovereth very fast and groweth strong again. The physicians doth advise her (in respect it did proceed from an internal defect and not from any accident, as also in regard of her little daughter who is far spent with the ricketts) to seek remedy at London this spring, to which I willingly assent, but shall account it a great happiness both to my wife and myself, in respect I cannot go along with her, if my Lady would please to give her leave to wait upon her: not to put her Ladyship to any charge, or further trouble after their arrival at London . . . ."

On 26th February, 1643, Sir Edward wrote again to Coke. He had raised a troop for the cause of the Parliament. "In respect of my Lord Grey's absence having left me in command to give orders, I cannot take the privilege to wait upon you; neither could I formerly with convenience or safety present my duty so frequently by letters, nor dare at this time with so much respect, as is due from me. The occasion of the messenger's long stay was that he might give you a certain account of your daughter's health with her little ones, only the youngest continueth in the same former estate; the rest of your friends are well. Sir, I shall always be diligent to inform you of such passages as may come without prejudice to your hands, but if you please, send not the same man too often, lest Hastings' scouts take notice of him." It is evident that the youngest little girl was still very ill.

Sir Edward wrote once more to his father-in-law on 6th March, 1643: —" I know not how long I shall stay at Leicester, because I have received this morning letters from my Lord General to come with my troop to the army; his Excellency being capable of some neglect towards me, the reasons I dare not write; perchance my Lord Grey is pleased to think that I am too considerable to join with him, and rather desires creatures of his own making. I honour and respect him from my heart, but I am afraid he is transported with particular counsels, that aim at their own ends. Sir, I hope my letters came safe yesterday morning to Melbourne, which will inform you of such news as is stirring. Desire no more from me than what may be conveniently known."

It is probable that when Mary Hartopp came to London she stayed at her husband's house in Church Street and visited her step-mother at Tottenham. Unfortunately, the trip did her little girl no good and on 27th March, 1643, Mrs. Anne Sacheverell wrote from London to Coke: —

" . . . . We heard from my sister Hartopp last week by a gentleman that came from thence, and we had written to you last week of it, but the carrier was gone before our letters could come. My sister Hartopp hath buried her little daughter; but we hear God hath brought her heart to that patient submission to His will in it, that they thought by reason of her very great tender affections to it, that they should have seen her much more impatient to part with it . . . ."

Mrs. Sacheverell was Mary Hartopp's sister who had married her cousin, Henry Sacheverell, in 1638, son and heir of Jacynth Sacheverell, of Morley, near Derby. The following letter is preserved among Coke's papers, dated September, 1643, and endorsed, "Daughters from London": —

" We make bold to present our humble duty to you and to let you know of our all being here . . . (then follows news of Royalist victories) . . . and take leave remaining your most dutiful and obedient daughter, Anne. Daughter Hartopp presents her humble duty and little John his."

This must be one of the first references to Sir John Hartopp, the third Baronet.

After the death of Mary Hartopp's little girl, her sister, Anne, had evidently come to be with her, and perhaps was staying with her at Stoke Newington, though of course they may have been at one of Coke's houses, either at Tottenham or in Drury Lane.

On 9th February, 1654-5, Mary Hartopp wrote to her brother, Thomas: —

" Dame Marie Hartopp to Thomas Coke.

Dear Brother, if this sad occasion has brought you to Buckminster I do not question but you will help what you can with your advice and counsel. I entreat also from you that you and my cousin Bury will consider what is to be done concerning the funeral, that nothing you two judge meet be neglected, as becomes his quality and our duty. Through the Lord's goodness your son is in very good health. If my husband come down, what disturbances may be I know not. Pray consider how anything that belongs to my children may be out of danger, or removed if you and my cousin Bury judge fit."

The funeral referred to was that of Sir Edward Hartopp, the first Baronet, as is made clear in a letter dated 21st February, 1654-5, from James Mayo to Thomas Coke: —

" . . . . I hear old Sir Edward Hartopp is dead . . . ."

In 1656 Mary Hartopp's brother, Thomas, died at Coke's old house at Tottenham. His widow evidently came to stay with her sister-in-law at Stoke Newington, for among the Coke papers at Melbourne Hall is a document dated 21st December, 1656, and endorsed, " Sir Edward Barkham's acquittance for £20 due to Mr. Allen the herald painter " : —

" Received the day and year above written of Mrs. Mary Coke of Newington in the County of Middlesex for the use of Mr. John Allen of London Spotter the sum of £20 videlicet for two dozen and a half buckram escutcheons two great arms six bosses for the horses' foreheads a velvet pall and for his pains and his man's and coach hire coming down with the things and settling them out in their order per me Edward Barkham."

Thomas Coke was buried at Melbourne in December, 1656.

★

In the Buckminster Register there is the following curious entry relating to the first Sir Edward Hartopp: —

" I, William Lloyd, vicar of Buckminster, in the county of Leicester, having power, by virtue of a statute in that case made, to license sick persons within my parish, to eat flesh upon such days as are prohibited by such statute; do, by these presents, license and authorise the right worshipful the Lady Frances Earle, wife to Sir Richard Earle, Bart., the Mrs. Anne White, wife to Thomas White, Esq., being both in the house of Sir Edward Hartopp, their father, at Buckminster, in the county of Leicester, Baronet; and being both sick and weak (the one miscarrying of a child, the other lying in childbed); and also Thomas Pacie, and Margaret Thorpe (servants to the right worshipful Sir Edward Hartopp, Bart.) being both of them sick of agues, to eat flesh during the time of their sickness, for the better and more speedy recovery of their healths. Dated at Buckminster, the 27th day of April, 1631."

Sir Edward died in 1654 and was buried at Buckminster.

The Rev. Arthur M. Dutton, until recently Vicar of Buckminster, is of the opinion that there was a quarrel or difference of opinion, between Sir Edward and the Rev. Samuel Dixon, who then held the living of Buckminster. Sir Edward was one of the Justices of the Peace commissioned by Parliament to celebrate marriages at the Market Cross at Melton Mowbray during the Commonwealth.

Nevertheless, Dixon, a man of strong character and opinions, continued to solemnise marriages in the Church as the registers show. Sir Edward would hardly have let a thing like that pass without objection. Dixon's son and grandson followed him in the living.

Edward Hartopp (1608-1658) as we have seen married Sir John Coke's daughter, Mary, and no doubt was active with his father in superintending the building of the family house at Stoke Newington. He would also have had to pay frequent visits to the country estates in Leicestershire, and was there in 1634 when Charles I visited George, the seventh Earl of Rutland, at Belvoir Castle.* Charles I knighted Edward Hartopp and other sons of the local gentry and the castle, one of the finest in England, must have been a magnificent setting for such a ceremony. Leland wrote of it in his " Itinary " : —

" The castelle of Bellevoire standith in the utter part of that way of Leicestershire, on the very knape of a highe hille, stepe up eche way, partely by nature partely by working of mennes handes as it may evidently be perceived. It is a strange sight to see how many steppes of stones the way goith up from the village to the castel. In the castel be two faire gates, and the dungeon is a faire round towere now turned to pleasure as a place to walk in and to see all the counterye about and raylid about the round and a garden plotte in the middle. There is also a welle of grete depthe in the castel and the spring thereof is very good."

In 1637 Sir Edward's heir, John, was born at Buckminster, and the entry in the parish register reads, " John, son of Sir Edward Hartopp, Bart., and dame Mary, his wife, baptised Oct. 31, 1637." The reference to Sir Edward as being a baronet is wrong, as the first baronet was still alive, and his son only a knight. Two years later a daughter, Mary, was born, later to be the wife of Smith Fleetwood, son of Charles Fleetwood.

When the Civil War broke out the eighth Earl of Rutland sided with Parliament, but owing to the strength of the Royalist forces in the neighbourhood Belvoir Castle was, as often as not, held for the King until finally reduced for Cromwell after the battle of Naseby. On one occasion a skirmish between the garrisons of Belvoir Castle and Burleigh-on-the-Hill actually took place in the village of Buckminster. The steeple of Buckminster Church was used as a watch tower as it commanded a wide view of the surrounding country. Sir Edward supported the Earl of Rutland and was very active on the Parliament side, raising a regiment for Cromwell. He does not seem to have cut much of a figure as a soldier as the contemporary accounts show.

The " Mercurius Aulicus," was the earliest regular English newspaper and was produced weekly by the Royalists at Oxford during the siege of 1643-1645. It contains the following article of intelligence : —

" Colonel Gervase Lucas (governor of Belvoir castle for the king) understanding that the committee of Leicester was gone to Melton Mowbray in that county, to assesse the countrye, and gather up the rents of all such, as are not perfect rebels as themselves, sent intelligence to Sir Richard Byron, governor of Newark, desiring him to assist him with some horse and dragoones, and he made no doubt but to give him a very faire account of the service which Sir Richard very cheerfully assented to (knowing colonel Lucas both vigilant and faithful) and, therefore, furnished him with as many horse and dragoones as made him a body of three hundred in all. With these he marched away on Sunday last in the evening, Nov. 27, and was gotten to Melton Mowbray next morning by breake of day; whither he no sooner came, but presently he entered the town, and surprised the rebels, who were more in number than himself; not a man escaping but one who was cornet to Sir Edward Hartopp, nor any killed save one lieutenant, who was stubborne, and refused to submit himselfe to the conqueror."

Bulstrode Whitelocke records that in 1644 Colonel Charles Fleetwood took two troops of the King's horse near Belvoir Castle. Also that the regiments of Colonel Fleetwood and Colonel Rosseter " beat up the enemy's quarters near Newark, took one hundred and sixty horse, eighty prisoners, Major Heron and other Commanders."

During the skirmishing round Newark and Melton Mowbray the King's garrisons from Belvoir Castle, Newark and Burleigh House must often have ravaged the Hartopp estates. Mrs. Lucy Hutchinson in her " Memoirs of Colonel Hutchinson " records two of Sir Edward's mishaps at Muscam Bridge and Newark in 1644 : —

" At the end of this month, on the fast-day, the national covenant was taken, with a great solemnity both by the soldiers and inhabitants, men and women, of the garrison. This day, unexpectedly, came Sir Edward Hartup, with a thousand horse from Leicester to Derby, to which the governor added between five and six hundred; Sir Edward being appointed to command the party, should have gone with them to take Muscam Bridge, at Newark, before which place Sir John Meldrum was now come, with about seven thousand men, and had laid siege to it. The horse of Newark, as soon the parliament's forces came, made an escape over Muscam Bridge, which Sir Edward Hartup, having more mind to drink than to fight, lingering a day at Nottingham, and then marching to no purpose against it, lost his opportunity of taking; yet God, by a providence, gave it up with 200 men that kept it to the parliament's forces, who, had they then pursued their success, might have carried the town too, but it was not God's time then to deliver the country of that pernicious enemy," and,

" Sir Edward Hartup was sent with the party of horse he before had at Muscam bridge, to pursue those that were gone out of Newark, and fight with them, and hinder their joining with Prince Rupert, who was expected to come to raise the siege; and when Sir Edward came into Leicestershire the whole country rose with him, and the governor of Leicester brought out foot and cannon to assist him. His forlorn hope being of the Nottingham horse, charged the enemy's forlorn hope and routed them, and then fell into their body of foot, which they had drained out of their little garrisons, and routed them also, and if Sir Edward Hartup would have come on with his body, they had all been cut off; but the knight would not stir, but commanded the forlorn hope to retreat, who had slain and taken many prisoners of the enemy, and among them Jammot, who had lately made his escape out of Nottingham Castle. The enemy perceiving Sir Edward would not hurt them, rallied again and joined with Prince Rupert; of which, as soon as Sir Edward had intelligence, he went back to Newark with such shameful haste, that he quitted Melton with all the prisoners the forlorn hope had lately taken. The Leicester forces, discouraged at this carriage, returned to their garrisons and marched no more with him."

Whitelocke in his Memoirs also gives an account of the raising of the siege of Newark and attributes to the misconduct of " Sir E. Hartup " and Colonel Bingley Prince Rupert's coming with his forces entire to the place, and says that a court-martial was directed to decide upon their conduct. There is no record of the decision of the court-martial so perhaps it was never held, nor is there any further reference to any military activities on the part of Sir Edward. He must, however, have been of considerable influence in Leicestershire for when he appeared " the whole county rose with him."

In 1654 the first baronet died and Sir Edward succeeded him. He did not, however, long survive but died in 1658 and was buried at Buckminster on 24th March. He left his wife, and his two children John and Mary, surviving him.

┌─────┐
│ V │
└─────┘

During the seventeenth century Stoke Newington became and remained a celebrated, or in some opinions, a notorious centre of dissent. This was due to two things, the presence of wealthy and prominent nonconformist families such as the Hartopps, Fleetwoods and Abneys, and a long succession of excellent ministers who by their preaching and intellectual prowess were able to build up and hold together large congregations. It is only necessary to name Dr. Thomas Manton, who during the period of Cromwellian supremacy held the living of St. Mary's, Dr. John Owen, a frequent visitor to Fleetwood House, Isaac Watts and Dr. Richard Price. Great houses, such as Fleetwood House and later Abney House, were centres round which the poorer nonconformist brethren were able to gather in sheltered seclusion. Whenever the Government of the day took action against dissenters it was naturally the wealthy and prominent who bore the brunt of the persecution. Heavy fines were levied on both Charles Fleetwood and Sir John Hartopp. As the district was such a refuge for dissenters it is worth trying to find out what they stood for and the reasons for their sudden rise to supremacy in the nation's affairs.

The Roman Catholics had always believed in ruthlessly stamping out heresy, thinking with some justification that if one new sect was allowed to flourish there would soon be many more.

After the Reformation Henry VIII executed Papists and Protestants who denied his supremacy. And during the succeeding reigns of Edward VI and Mary each side in turn had its opportunity to persecute its rival. During the reign of Elizabeth fear of Spain concentrated attention on the Roman Catholics though other dissenters did not entirely escape. It must be remembered that all governments, Roman Catholic and Protestant alike, regarded it as essential to stamp out every kind of heresy.

The Puritans looked forward to the accession of James I with high hopes. He had been educated a Presbyterian, was a professed Calvinist and a sworn Covenanter, but once he was King of England he became a high Episcopalian and a determined Arminian. "No Bishop, no King," he declared, "I will have one doctrine, one discipline, one religion in substance and in ceremony." Arminianism, named after its founder, Arminius, corresponded to what is called "High Church" to-day. The Roman Catholic ritual was accepted but the Pope's authority denied. Already towards the end of James's I reign Laud, later to be Archbishop of Canterbury, was the leading exponent of Arminianism, and was often the victim of bitter attack. Once when present in the congregation he heard Dr. Airey denounce his beliefs from the pulpit, "Might not Christ say ' What art thou? Romish or English? Papist or Protestant? Or what art thou? A mongrel or compound of both?—a Protestant by ordination, a

Papist in point of free will and the like? A Protestant in receiving the Sacrament, a Papist in the doctrine of the Sacrament? What, do you think there are two heavens? If there be, get you to the other and place yourself there; for into this, where I am, you shall never come.' " Sermons in those days could indeed be exciting! Arminianism was feared as the first step towards a return to Roman Catholicism. Memories of Queen Mary's persecutions, the massacre of St. Bartholomew in 1572, the Armada in 1588, and the Gun-Powder Plot of 1605 died hard. The power of Spain, although now on the wane, was still dreaded, and the tremendous influence over James I exercised by Gondomar the Spanish Ambassador did nothing to alleviate anxiety. When Charles I came to the throne he followed the policy of his father and when occasion offered promoted Laud to be Archbishop of Canterbury. His Queen, Henrietta Maria, was a Roman Catholic, which also increased suspicion of his intentions. William Orme, the biographer of Owen, has written: —

"In an evil day Charles I had advanced to the Primacy of England William Laud, a man of undoubted talents and learning, but of high monarchical principles; fond of pomp and ceremony; and, though no friend to the Pope at Rome, having little objection to be Pope in England. His arbitrary conduct in the star chamber, his passion for ceremony in the church, and his love of Arminianism in the pulpit, hastened his own fate and promoted that of his master."

Pym, a man of wide and tolerant views on most subjects, when speaking in Parliament, said: —

"If the Papists obtain a connivance, they will press for a toleration; from thence to an equality; from an equality to a superiority; from a superiority to an extirpation of all contrary religions."

This atmosphere of fear coupled with actual religious persecution was, as always, conducive to the growth of nonconformity, but the rise of these numerous nonconformist sects could only have taken place in a country where the artisan and yeoman classes enjoyed a considerable amount of personal and economic independency, and had made a genuine study of the Bible. If there had been other forms of literature to compete with the Bible there would probably have been no Puritan revolution. Bunyan wrote, "I dreamed and behold I saw a Man clothed with rags, standing in a certain place, with his face from his own house, a Book in his hand and a great burden upon his back. I looked, and saw him open the Book and read therein; and as he read, he wept and trembled; and not being able longer to contain, he broke out with a lamentable cry, saying, 'What shall I do?' "

The typical Puritan of the time was this man described by Bunyan, with his burden of sin seeking redemption with nothing but the Bible to serve as a guide.

After the outbreak of the Civil War, the first of the nonconformist bodies to obtain supremacy were the Presbyterians later to be supplanted by the Independents and various other sects. That the differences between the established church and these two sects was a matter not easily understood even then is apparent from a letter Isaac Watts wrote to his brother giving a series of definitions, some of which are: —" The three chief opinions about religion are, in respect of discipline and order, Episcopacy, Presbytery and Independency.

Episcopacy. These are those called Conformists, or the Church of England. They own that a bishop is an officer appointed by Christ to oversee churches and their pastors . . . all ordination of ministers ought to be by bishops—who have power to impose ceremonies, hence they worship God in a ceremonious way. . . They not only allow but impose forms of prayer . . . though they believe the dissenters worship God aright, yet they have persecuted them almost to death for not conforming.

Presbytery. The true and original notion is that God hath appointed a synod, or class, or assembly of ministers or elders to be superior in power to any particular church or officers thereof, that these synods have power ministerially to determine controversies in faith and doctrine, and that any person in a church may appeal to them for any injury received from any church; the tenets of the Presbyterians are: (1) That a minister ought to be ordained by the laying of the hands of other elders or ministers after examination, fasting and prayer. (2) That a minister may be ordained so as to have power given him to administer ordinances in general, even before he takes the charge of the church upon him. (3) That there is no need of any new ordination when they are called to a particular congregation. (4) That it is the office of a minister to rule in the church, and the people's duty to consent, though generally the minister will not do anything in the church without their consent. (5) If all the church are willing any church act should be done, yet it must not be done without the consent of the minister. This is called the minister's having a negative voice, but is contrary to rigid Independents. (6) Their doctrine is generally Calvinistical, but many of those who are called Presbyterians have of late years inclined more to Mr. Baxter. (7) They preach that good knowledge and a sober conversation are not sufficient evidences of a good state; and yet usually inquire no farther than of the knowledge and conversation of those they admit into their churches; hence it follows they are larger in church discipline than Independents. (8) Most of them own the office of deacons in a church, but generally deny any ruling elders distinct from ministers.

Independents. The tenets of rigid Independents are: (1) That every church hath all the power of governing itself in itself and that everything done in a church must be by the majority of the votes of the brethren. (2) That every church has its minister ordained to itself, and that he cannot administer the ordinancy to any other people, and if he preaches among others it is but as a gifted brother. But the generality of Independents follow rather Dr. Owen's notions; their tenets are such as these: (1) That the power of church government resided in the pastors and elders of every church and that it is the duty of the people to consent; and nevertheless because every act in a church is a church act, they never do anything without the consent of the people, though they receive no new authority by the people consenting. (2) They generally think a minister not to be ordained but to a particular church . . . but he may preach to other churches upon extraordinary occasions. (3) That it is not absolutely necessary that a minister be ordained by the imposition of hands of other ministers. . . (4) They generally hold more to the doctrine of Calvin than Presbyterians do. (5) It is not sufficient ground to be admitted a member, if the person be only examined as to his doctrinal knowledge and sobriety of conversation; but they require . . . some evidence of the work of grace on their souls. . . (6) These relations, which the Independents require are not of the word of scripture, or time or place or sermon, by which they were converted; for very few can tell this; but only they discourse and examine them a little of their convictions of sin, of their being brought to know Christ."

At this time Milton wrote: —

" Methinks I see a noble and puissant nation rousing herself, like a strong man after sleep, and shaking her invincible locks. Methinks I see her, as an eagle, muing her mighty youth, and kindling her undazzled eyes at the full mid-day beam; purging and unscaling her long abused sight at the fountain itself of heavenly radiance; while the whole tribe of timorous and flocking birds, with those also that love the twilight, flutter about, amazed at what she means, and in their envious gabble would prognosticate a year of sects and schisms."

The Presbyterians however were to prove as intolerant as the Roman Catholics, and Milton was not to see his high ideals realised. He came to declare: " New Presbyter is but old priest writ large."

Daniel Cawdry a fiery Presbyterian minister spoke of " reaping with lamentation the cursed fruits of toleration and forbearance in religion; toleration having done more towards the rooting of religion out of the hearts of men in seven years than the enforcing of uniformity did in seventy; a cursed intolerable toleration."

Two more opinions of toleration show only too well the Presbyterian attitude: —

" A toleration would be the putting a sword in a mad man's hand; a cup of poison into the hand of a child; a letting loose of mad-men with fire-brands in their hands; and appointing a city of refuge in men's consciences for the devil to fly to; a laying of a stumbling block before the blind; a proclaiming liberty to the wolves to come into Christ's fold to prey upon the lambs: neither would it be to provide for tender consciences, but to take away all conscience," and,

" A toleration is the grand design of the devil—his masterpiece, and chief engine he works by at this time, to uphold his tottering Kingdom.'

This intolerant attitude was the undoing of the Presbyterians.

Milton wrote, " It is not lawful for any power on earth to compel in matters of religion," and as the Independents professed more liberal sentiments they soon began to increase rapidly in numbers. Richard Baxter, no friend of the Independents, wrote:

" I saw that most of them were zealous, and very many learned, discreet and godly men, and fit to be very serviceable in the church. Also I saw a commendable care to serious holiness and discipline in most of the Independent churches."

Mosheim, one of the most impartial writers on religion, said: —

" The rapid progress of the Independents was no doubt owing to a variety of causes; among which justice obliges us to reckon the learning of their teachers, and the regularity and sanctity of their manners."

The origin of the Independent system was contrary to that of most other sects, making an appeal by reason of its tolerating principles first to the higher social orders, and only when in danger from Presbyterian persecution to the lower. Thus men of the calibre of Charles Fleetwood were early members of Independent churches.

To many the issues of the Civil War seemed simple. The usual rallying cry of " For God and King," was changed to " For God or King." And those who professed to fight for " For God " were to prove the stronger. It would, however, be wrong to assume that Cavalier households were not often just as religious as Puritan. Sir Edmund Verney, Charles's I standard bearer, who was killed fighting for his master at Edghill opposed Laud, and declared, " I have no reverence for Bishops for whom this quarrel subsists." His household was one of great piety. It was true, however, that the war was political and religious and not social. Winstanley, the leader of the small sect called the " Diggers " claimed that the land belonged to the people and had been stolen from them by the squires, and warned the army leaders that the political revolution could only survive if founded on a social revolution. The army leaders sternly suppressed Winstanley's views which the Restoration was to prove to be correct.

The object of those who supported the cause of Parliament was a change of policy and of the men responsible for carrying it out. There was no attack on the constitution of either church or state. Charles I would not have lost his throne and his life if he had consented to govern by regular parliaments, dismissed his high church advisers, and granted a limited religious toleration. The war greatly increased the number of Presbyterians, Independents, Baptists and other sects, but it is unfair to accuse them of being the cause of the war. It was hardly possible for persons in positions of authority to remain neutral. Whether those who supported Parliament were guilty of rebellion is problematical. The monarch, the House of Lords and the House of Commons all form part of the constitution. The constitution was divided against itself with the monarch and the House of Commons making war on each other. It is wrong to charge any man with crime for following his conscience and supporting one side or the other while the constitution was so divided. On the other hand the death of Charles I would clearly seem to be murder, for the law declares that the King can do no wrong and is above punishment. Parliament must consist of the monarch, the peers and the House of Commons, and it was only the last named that acted in the matter, and then only 46 members were present when the King's trial was voted, and of these only 26 gave their assent. Further the House of Commons was never a Court of Law.

The difference between the two sides was largely one of temperament. Dr. Brooke wrote to Laud: " Predestination is the root of Puritanism, and Puritanism the root of all rebellion and disobedient intractableness, and all schism and sauciness in the country, nay in the church itself." Charles I himself said: " The nature of Presbyterian government is to strike or force the crown from the King's head, for their chief maxim is (and I know it to be true) that all Kings must submit to Christ's Kingdom, *of which they are the sole governors.*" This difference in outlook was reflected even in the clothes worn, and it is said that Stoke Newington during the reign of Charles II was sharply divided into two—Puritan and " Church Party." The former maintained their sober attire while the latter imitated the Court and appeared in " short-waisted doublet and petticoat breeches—the lining being lower than breeches being tied above the knees, the breeches ornamented with ribands up to the pocket and half their breadth upon the thigh; the waistband being set about with ribands and the shirt hanging over them." Many of those, however, who helped to establish the Commonwealth changed their views. John Lilburne, a bitter opponent of Charles I, within one year of his death, wrote: " I had rather choose to live seven years under Old King Charles's Government (notwithstanding their beheading him as a tyrant for it) when it was at its worst before this Parliament, than live one year under the Government that now rule." And William Prynne, author of " Histrio—Mastix, the Player's Scourge or Actor's Tragedy," a ferocious attack on the stage, lived to say: " If the King had cut off my head when he only cropped my ears, he had done no more than justice, and had done God and the nation good service."

> VI

Charles Fleetwood (1618—1692) was a younger son of Sir Miles Fleetwood of Aldwincle in Northamptonshire and Cranford in Middlesex, and of Anne, daughter of Nicholas Luke of Woodend, Bedfordshire. The Fleetwood family is a typical one of the time. It had been treated well by the House of Stuart and one might have expected all its representatives to have supported the Royalist cause. That Charles sided with Cromwell was no doubt due to religious rather than civil reasons. Sir Miles Fleetwood was receiver of the Court of Wards, and on his death on 8th March, 1641, his eldest son, Sir William (1603-1674) succeeded both to his father's estates and offices. Sir William sided with the King and consequently in 1644 forfeited the receivership of the Court of Wards which was granted to his brother Charles. Sir William Fleetwood, was also Cupbearer to Charles I and Charles II and Comptroller of Woodstock Park.

★

The genealogy of the Fleetwood family is one that has caused considerable difficulty, but it is to be hoped that it has now been finally drawn up in a correct manner. Both Anthony à Wood and John Aubrey refer to members of the family. In his " Fasti Oxonienses," under the heading " 1632, March 13," Wood writes, " Sir William Fleetwood, Knight, Comptroller of Woodstock Park in Oxfordshire (Brother to the famous General Sir George Fleetwood, a Baron of Sweden) was incorporated Master of Arts as he had stood at Cambridge. John Oxenstierne a noble Sweed, Baron of Kemetso, Lord of Fiholme and Tydoon, being adorned with a scarlet Gown and Hood and presented in convocation by the aforesaid Sir William Fleetwood, was actually created Master of Arts with great observance and solemnity. He was the son of grave John Oxenstierne now Ambassador to the King of England from his father Axel Oxenstierne the grand Chancellor and General director of the Swedish Affairs. Gustavus Horne, another noble Sweed, Lord of Kamhas and Purkala, being adorned with scarlet as the former was, and presented by the said Sir William Fleetwood, was actually created Master of Arts in the same convocation. When the Vice-Chancellor was to admit these two Nobles he openly spake these words to the large Auditory. ' Gradum ambiunt Magistri in artibus duo nobiles juvenes, quorum alterius pater, alterius patruus, pro aris et focis, pro religione, pro libertate, denique totius Germaniae, tanquam duo fulmina belli, in terrorem domus Austriae jamdiu emicuerunt.' They were very nobly treated, while they continued here, had rich gloves presented to them in the name of the University, and Testimonials of their Degree very fairly written and adorned, with the seal of each, put into a silver

Box." Again in the "Athenae Oxonienses" Wood writes, "John Wilmot, Earl of Rochester, was born at Ditchley near Woodstock in April, 1648. . . travelled into France and Italy, and at his return frequented the Court . . . and was at length made one of the Gentlemen of the Bedchamber to His Majesty King Charles II and Comptroller of Woodstock Park in the place of Sir William Fleetwood deceased."

John Aubrey in his "Brief Lives," writing of Sir Henry Lee, elaborates a little, "Sir Henry Lee of Ditchley, Oxon, was a gentleman of a good estate, and a strong and valiant person. He was raunger of Woodstock parke, and (I have heard my old cosen Whitney say) would many times in his younger yeares walke at night in the parke with his keepers. Sir Gerard Fleetwood succeeded him in this place; as his nephew Sir William Fleetwood did him, and him the Earl of Rochester." Elizabeth of Bohemia in one of her letters written during the Cromwellian era refers to George Fleetwood as brother of him that is "Leftenant of Ireland," that is Charles Fleetwood.

Thus, from contemporary evidence it seems certain that there were three brothers, Sir William, George and Charles Fleetwood, nephews of Sir Gerard Fleetwood. Bulstrode Whitelocke, also a contemporary, strengthens the case by writing that in May, 1644, Sir William Fleetwood forfeited the receivership of the Court of Wards to his brother Charles. Sir William would thus seem to have held the offices of Comptroller of Woodstock Park and Receiver of the Court of Wards. V. de Sola Pinto, however, in his recent life of Rochester, says that on the death of Sir William Fleetwood in 1674 the Rangership and Keepership of Woodstock Park were granted to Lord Lovelace, but Rochester, who was anxious to occupy the charming house that went with the Keepership, was successful in getting the appointment of Lord Lovelace set aside and succeeded to both the Rangership and Keepership in 1675. It is strange that both Aubrey and Anthony à Wood, contemporary writers, should have missed this. However, it probably does not affect their general accuracy.

In the calendar of State Papers, Domestic, there are many interesting references to the Fleetwood family and Woodstock Park. On August 30th, 1625, a warrant was issued to Sir Gerard Fleetwood "to pay 12d. a day for looking to the game within the manor of Woodstock and within ten miles about the same." In 1637, one Richard Baynall, requested leave to dig for saltpetre in His Majesty's house at Woodstock, "only in those rooms that have earthen floors, not in boarded, pitched or paved rooms." If he took up any planks he undertook to lay them again at his own expense, and to let Sir Gerard Fleetwood get a mason to direct how near the foundation he could dig. It seems that Sir Gerard Fleetwood* did not continue there many years after 1637, for in 1642 a warrant was issued to Sir William Fleetwood "controller of works and surveyor of woods at Woodstock" to fell 25 trees for the repair of the New Lodge in the High Park.

After the restoration of Charles II a warrant was issued in 1661 to Sir William Fleetwood to preserve the game about Woodstock Park, and in the following year he was paid £616 as " Ranger of Woodstock Park " for a parcel of furze land purchased for enlarging the Park. On December 30th, 1662, he wrote to Mr. Secretary Bennett that he had readily obeyed a warrant to kill a brace of deer and had ordered the two best to be killed that could be found at that season. In 1664 he sent a buck to " Williamson at Lady Anderson's in the Strand," and rejoiced to hear of his recovery. The entries in the Calendar relating to Lord Lovelace, Sir William Fleetwood, and the Earl of Rochester are as follows : —

20th June, 1670.

" Warrant for payment to John, Lord Lovelace—appointed lieutenant of the Manor of Woodstock, in place of the Earl of Clarendon—who is incapable of holding employment, and to whom no more money is to be paid—of £40 a year for the keeper's wages, and £40 for hay for the deer as granted by the King to Philip, Earl of Montgomery, the then lieutenant . . . "

25th September, 1670.

" Warrant for a grant to John, Lord Lovelace, son and heir of John, Lord Lovelace, of the offices of steward, lieutenant and bailiff of Woodstock manor, park, and hundred . . . "

27th September, 1670.

" . . . Lord Lovelace died on the 24th . . . "

11th, October, 1670.

" Grant to John, Lord Lovelace (on the death of his father) of the offices of steward and lieutenant of Woodstock manor, Keeper of the Great Park and ranger of the new forest there . . . "

May, 1671.

" Warrant to pay to John, Lord Lovelace, Lieutenant of the Manor of Woodstock, £40 yearly without account, and £40 yearly for hay for the deer, and £40 to Sir William Fleetwood, balance of £100 spent by him for hay for them in the sickness year."

27th February, 1674.

" Warrant for revocation of a Grant made 2nd November, 1670, to Lord Lovelace of the office of Keeper of Woodstock Park, in so far as concerns the rangership, and for a grant to John, Earl of Rochester, of the said rangership and of the walk and lodge thereto belonging lately held by Sir William Fleetwood, deceased."

2nd May, 1674. ......

" Warrant for revocation of the patent granted 2nd November, 1670, to John, Lord Lovelace, of the Keepership of Woodstock Park, and for a grant to John, Earl of Rochester, of the rangership thereof, and of the Keepership of the walk therein lately belonging to Sir William Fleetwood, with proviso that he shall be subject to the rule of the Keeper, but that the latter shall not have power to make void this grant; also for a grant to the said Earl of Rochester of the Keepership of the said park."

By the year 1632 George Fleetwood had already entered the service of Sweden, and doubtless was well acquainted with members of the Horn and Oxenstjerna familes. It is likely that he asked his brother Sir William, to present John Oxenstjerna and Gustavus Horn in convocation to receive their degrees. There is also a portrait in Sweden of George Fleetwood, inscribed with these words: " Baron George Fleetwood, Governour of Calmar and of the isle of Oeland. In Sweden 1630. Brother of Sir Wm. Fleetwood of Woodstock and of Charles Fleetwood, Lord Deputy of Ireland."

Sir William Fleetwood was established at Aldwincle by 1635, for in that year a certain Lieutenant made a tour of the west of England and kept a journal of his progress which has been published by the Camden Society: —

" A Relation of a short survey of the Western Counties in which is briefly described the Cities, Corporations, Castles, and some other Remarkables in them observed in seven weekes journey Begun at Norwich and thence into the West. On Thursday August 4th 1635, and ending at the same place. By the same Lieutenant that ... made a Journey into the North the yeere before."

The name of the Lieutenant was Hammond, for he says the Town Clerk of Maldon in Essex was his namesake, and Maldon's Town Clerk at that time was Nowell Hammond. In the course of his journey the Lieutenant came down the Nene valley to Oundle: —

" I found the Towne regulated by a Mayor, 2 Bayliffes and 12 Aldermen; to them I left it (i.e. Northampton) and away speed I by that sweet Brook (the Nene) I cross'd before, with a ready and willing guide to Willingbrooke Market (Wellingborough), where I marked a fayre Inn, that was lately graced by the Queen's Highnesse to an Inn of Court during her Majesty's stay there to drinke of that medicinable spring water.

From thence I hasted, and as I rode I had in view a great many goodly spires of churches, fairly built, which brought me with some content to Owndell; by many pleasant, delicate, rich scytuations of Lords, Knights, Ladies and Gentlemen (Moulton, Sir Christopher Hatton's; Drayton, the Earl of Peterborough's and Westmorland's; Frampton, Sir John Washington's; Aldwincle, Sir William Fleetwood's; Sir Barnaby Bryan's; Sir Rowland st. John; the Lady Montague's, Barnwell Castle; Linson, Mr. Elmes's; Stoke, Mr. Polmer's) rendring the time not irksome to weary Travellers in having such pleasing objects ever in view to beguile the same; likewise I pass'd over many fayre, long, and strong, Arch'd, stone Bridges before I came into the Towne aforesaid.

My Lodging heere was at the signe of the Talbot, where I found a good Inne and good usage . . . "

In 1659 Nathaniel Whiting published his " Old Jacob's Altar Newly Repaired " and the biographical parts of the dedication are of great interest to anyone interested in the Fleetwood family. The title page and relevant parts of the Dedication are as follows: —

" Old Jacob's Altar newly repaired; or, the Saints
Triangle of Dangers, Deliverances and Duties, personal
and National, practically improved in many Particulars,
seasonable and experimental. Being the Answer of his own
Heart to God, for eminent Preservations; humbly recommended,
by way of Teaching, unto all, and, as a Special Remembrancer
to the Ransomed of the Lord, to awaken in them a sense of
rich mercy; that they may sing the song of Moses for temporal,
and the Song of the Lamb, for Spiritual Deliverances and to
provoke them to Love and Good Works "

---

by Nataneel Whiting, Mr. of Arts, and Minister of the Gospel
at Aldwinckle.

Gen. 35. 3 Let us arise and go up to Bethel, and I will make
there an altar unto God, who answered me in the day of my
distress, and was with me in the way which I went.
And verse 7. He built there an altar and called the place
El-Bethel.

London
Printed by R. T. for Nathaneel Ekins, and are to be sold at
his shop, at the Signe of the Gunne in S. Paul's Church-yard. 1659.

★

" To the Right Worshipfull
Sr. William Fleetwood Knight
the Right Honourable
Sr. George Fleetwood Baron
of *Swonholme* in *Sweadland*
and Lieutenant General of the King
of *Sweadland's* Army there,
and to his Excellency
Charles, Lord Fleetwood.
Lieutenant General of the whole
Army in *England* and Scotland
and one of his Highness Privy-Council.

Noble and Honoured:

I am taught by the best Teacher, the Holy Ghost, not to forsake mine own friend, and my fathers friend; the Authority of of which advice hath a great influence upon me, being under the direct aspect of it, therefore do I own your antient and obliging favours in this publick Address, under this hope; That good wine will taste never the worse, because presented in a wooden cup, nor Truth lose any of its rellish, because served up in an earthen dish.

If any charge blame upon me, because I have not observed the Rules of Honour in the ordering of your names according to your Titles of Honour and standings in the world, my Reply is this: I pretend not to skill in Heraldry, nor is it my business to dispute Titles; I have therefore, set Eliah in the front, because I may not give away the Honour of Primogeniture from Manasseh, seing he hath not with Esau sold, nor with Reuben, lost the excellency of dignity: He still weares, with Zarah, the scarlet thread upon his hand, though his younger Brethren have broken forth, and gotten the Precedency: Besides, though I owe much to your Honours, I am much yours; yet I am more your Brothers: and my obligations more to him which I must owne; and I am sure, such is your Justice, that you will not entrench upon the right of other men, much less, upon your Elder Brothers: And if your Honours be not offended, why should others?

Again; If any take offence that I preface this Treatise with Three Honourable Names, one of which would have been an honour to a more polite and elaborate Discourse: my Answer is this: When I had designed this Piece unto the Press, I knew none whose Experiences could more fully comment upon the subject treated on than your selves: Your Preservations have been many and signal, at home, abroad, by land, by water: few persons have had such remarkable Deliverances as you have had, and few Families can instance in three Brethren, who can give forth narratives of such notable and numerous Escapes, as you can give: And therefore seeing you have equally shared in the marvellous Protections of a good God, I am bold to make this Application to you All: in which I do humbly Remember you of engaging mercies, that the sence thereof may be awakened in you: that like that Persian Monarch, you may often read over your Diaries, gather up your memorable preservations; own the Lord in them, and by suitable actings improve them to his glory: . . .

I am not ashamed (Right Worshipfull) to tell the world how ancient and how affectionate a Maecenas you have been to me; that I received many encouragements from you when I was a student in the Universitie; how ready I have alwayes found you to lay forth your power and Interest for me: how freely and speedily you placed me at Aldwinckle, and how much I have found the favour of a Patron, and the affections of a friend (I might go higher) for the space of many yeares; which is much, considering what hard measure some good Ministers have found from their Patrons, though good men, in these times of difference, both upon a civil and Religious account; and indeed I think it to be ingenious (whatever others think) and well comporting with the standing of a Minister (whilst the jus praesentandi, by a Law is vested in Honourable hands) as to own God in his providential disposure, so to acknowledge the favour of man, in that Liberty he obtaines to do his Master's work: Sure I am this was a mercy which some godly and gifted Ministers did long want (whilest the Episcopal Monopoly lasted) and long waited for; yea, after all their waiting, could hardly, without snares to their conscience obtain.

If my poor labours have been answered with any success from heaven, (and I trust they have) in my little Congregation; the people have reason (which some of them have done) to bless God that your choice, and, their call had so full a concurrence in one person: But, though they should be silent, I may not, I cannot; I am under such a sense of obligation, that I am pressed in spirit, to make some publick payment of my debt unto you, in a ministerial way (which is a Symony, neither sinfull before God, nor offensive to good men): Therefore, Dear Sir, I beg your acceptance of this poor Present: Give your Minister leave, from the press (wanting opportunity by reason of your non-residency, not his, to speake often unto you from the Pulpit) to minde you of that great deliverance you received from the Lord in the Thames; how often the sentence of Death hath been reversed when you have been under painful and languishing distempers: in what way of Providence God hath loosened you from the noise and vanity of a Court; what Respects you have from men, good and great: what safety you had in the late War; what blessings the Lord hath heaped upon you, in a dear Lady, a numerous and hopeful Progeny: and, in what other wages of mercy the Lord hath appeared graciously unto you; O let all these have a kindly work upon your spirit, to warme your heart more and more towards God, his waies and people: and let them, by way of holy force, fix your heart, Joshua like, with your house to serve the Lord, that Jehovah may still cover you with his feathers, in all future hazards, that you may fill up your dayes in peace, " and may come to the grave in a full age, like as a shock of corne cometh in his season " (Job 5. 27).

My next address is to you, my Lord, your Honour hath seen the work of God, and his wonders in the deep, you have conversed much with people of strange languages; contested with men of fierce and cruel spirits: you have been a man of warre from your youth; expert in all the stages and stratagems of a well-ordered battel, you have long served the Interest of a forraign Prince and state, where you have not onely been preserved but promoted; God hath not onely given you safety, but Honour also; and though you was a stranger in Name, Nation, Language, and something in Religion also, yet God bowed the heart of Prince, Nobles, and others, to give you the respect your worth had merited; and now after Twenty years voluntary Exile, or more, God hath brought you back with Three Sonnes, to your native soil (immediately after the storme of war was blown over it) and that after an honourable rate: all which are mercies worth your owning; and are as silent Monitors from the Lord unto you. Ah, my Lord, be much and often retired; read over the story of Gods Providences towards you, reckon up your Dangers and Deliverances, How often the King of terrours hath faced you with a dreadful look; what bloudy fights God hath safeguarded your life in; and how often you have been brought out of the field; when thousands have been left wounded or dead upon the place; though your Lordship hath the courage of a Roman, not to fear death in the painfulness of it, yet you have the spirit of a Christian, to fear the consequences of an immature death, and therefore have cause to bless God who hath lengthened out your day of grace, and his patience; hath brought you again into your own Nation, where the White Flagge is held forth, and the unsearchable riches of Christ are fully displayed in the powerful plain, and spiritual dispensation of the Gospel . . .

Lastly my applications are to your exellency; your standing is high in Israel, and your name is dear to Gods people: the Lord hath made you great, and the Lord hath made you gracious; without which, all wordly honour is but a shell, a shadow, a meere vanity . . . you set out early for heaven; God dealt with your heart betimes; with good Obadiah you feared the Lord from your Youth; which early buddings of grace and holiness, as they spake the intendments of God to use you in Honourable Employments, so have they rendered you in regard of your large experiences, and long acquaintance with the Lord, his waies and people, more meet to serve the Interest of the Lord and his people, in that high trust you are called unto: I shall not report what persons of great Honour and Integretie have spoken concerning your Pietie and Praierfulness: Inventories are not taken untill men be dead: he that is a Jew inwardly hath his praise from God, and therefore expects it not from man; but shall humbly entreat your Excellency, to consider how you went out a young Gentleman, and a raw Soldier into the late warrs, in which your eyes beheld much of God, and your spirit tasted much of his mercy, how he protected your Person, and prospered your warfare; every bullet flew with his Commission, and every weapon was guided by his appointment; so that you walked in the midst of fire and smoak, as the Jewish worthies did in the furnace, and have had no hurt, at least, neither to limb nor life; nay, the smel of a bloudy warr hath hardly passed upon you: O the power of an Almighty God! O the safety of Gods Noahs in his Ark of Providence, when it sails upon seas of bloud! . . . though your excellency be not upon the Throne yet you are near unto it; you stand in a publick capacity, both Civil and Military, and are eminent in both; and so, have great opportunities of doing good: I hope you lose none. I am sure you have improved many: God hath led you to the second Chariot, much in Joseph's way; be still a Joseph to the house of your brethren; let the Israel of God be dear unto you; be a covering cherub over them, and an Advocate for them; they are a considerable number in the Land, yea, the most considerable in the census of Heaven . . . The Lord make your excellency eminently instrumental to repair Zions breaches, and bless you out of Zion, with peace and joy in your own spirit, and when " you shall have served out your own generation according to his will, receive you up into heavenly Jerusalem, amongst the spirts of just men made perfect." (Hebrews 12, 22 and 23).

I shall shut up this Address (Dear and Honoured) with this one Request, that you will accept the humble tender of real Repects " in this small bundle of goats hair "; was it better I know no persons in the world, that can lay a fuller challenge unto it, then you can; nor to whom I should more readily offer it than unto your selves: If in the perusal of this Treatise, you shall finde one spark to encrease your warmth of spirit for heaven and holiness, own the Lord in it and let me be but a poor sheard, in which the coal is brought from the hearth: If any passage in it takes your soules aside, and gives them a review of your Dangers and Deliverances, offering any hint to direct or incite you to those Duties, which the Lord calls for from his ransomed ones, I have my end; my Expectations terminate in Gods Glory, and your spiritual good and growth. The Lord make you progressive in Greatness, but more in Grace, that Religion, in the life, and spirit, and power, may be cherished in your hearts, and houses, that your practices may be Ecclesia, Aula, Schola, as was the family of George Prince of Anhalt, or like Cyrus his Court, where, if a man chose blind-fold he could not miss of a good man; or like the Family of your Noble Parents, where many were Proselited to the Faith, and some now alive, do own that Providence, as happy, which planted them under their roof; That your Children may keep up sincere Profession in your name and race and that " the Lord, who hath delivered you out of the mouth of the lion, would deliver you out of every evil work, and would preserve you unto his heavenly Kingdome, that you may be presented faultless before the presence of his glory, with exceeding joy," is the hearty Prayer of

Your Worships, Honours, and Excellencies
humble and devoted Servant, in the Lord's
work, and for his honour,
Nath. Whiting."

Whiting was of Queen's College, Cambridge, having been entered on 1st July, 1628. He matriculated as Pensioner on 30th March, 1629, and proceeded B.A. 1631, and M.A. in 1635. He had a good knowledge of Greek, Latin, Hebrew, and Italian, and in his earlier days was something of a poet. In 1633 he contributed Latin and Greek verses, decidedly Royalist in tone, to a Cambridge miscellany celebrating the birth of the Duke of York. His muse was somewhat harsh and discordant, being written, in the words of George

Saintsbury, " in a singular jargon almost as much out of the common
way as the wildest freaks of Benlowes." The following curious lines
are a specimen: —

"The Author to his Book.

Go gall-less infant of my teeming quill,
Not yet bedewed in Syracusa's rill,
And like a forward plover gadd'st abroad
Ere shell-free or before full age has strowed
  On they smooth back a coat of feathers
  To arm thee 'gainst the force of weathers
  Doom'd to the censure of all ages,
  Ere mail'd against the youngest rages.
    Perchance some nobles will thee view
    Smile on thee, at thee, like thee new
    But when white age has wrinkled thee
    Will slight thy measures, laugh at me.
      At first view called pretty,
      And perchance styled witty,
      By some ladies, until thou
      Wearest furrows on they brow.
        Some plumed gallants may
        Unclasp thy leaves and say
        Th'art mirthful but ere long
        Give place unto a song.
          Some courteous scholar,
          Purged from all choler,
          May like, but at last,
          Say thou spoil'st his taste
            First lawyers will
            Commend thy skill,
            Last, throw thy wit
            With Trinit's writ.
              Chamber - she's
              On their knee
              will thee praise,
              and thy bays.
                At first,
                till thirst
                of new
                death you,
                then all
                men shall
                  Flee
                  thee
                  Bee
                  me. . ."

He was evidently one more example of a type that favoured the cause of Parliament for religious reasons. Sir William Fleetwood presented him to the living of All Saints, Aldwincle, the date of his institution being 20th March, 1652. But as soon as 4th May in the same year he signed the accounts as " Minister," thus showing where his sympathies lay. Christopher Hollis in his " Life of Dryden," another Aldwincle worthy, says, " Gilbert Pickering had a son, Henry Pickering, who became a clergyman. His churchmanship was such as to gain him favour under the Commonwealth and he held the living of Aldwincle, All Saints, up to his death in 1657. John Dryden's mother was his daughter . . . [and] Dryden was born at his grandfather's vicarage on August 9th, 1631." The year given for Henry Pickering's death—1657—must be wrong if Whiting had been presented to the living in 1652. Indeed, the Dictionary of National Biography states that Henry Pickering died in 1637, aged 75. Whiting wrote some lines " to the right honourable, right worthy, and truly ennobled hero, John Lord Lovelace, Baron of Hurley, N.W. S.P.O." (Salutem plurimam optat). Lord Lovelace and his son, also John, are mentioned elsewhere as successors to Sir William Fleetwood at Woodstock Park. After the restoration he was deprived of his living and moved to Cranford, near Kettering, and collected a congregation there. He had been master of the free school at Aldwincle, and dying childless was a benefactor of that school.

In the parish registers at Aldwincle several entries relate to the Fleetwood family: —

" Charles Fleetwood born 1657 (Dec:)
His mother, Elizabeth, died in childbirth;
Sir William Fleetwood was buried 1673;
Miles Fleetwood son of Miles M.P. died 1688;
Chas. Wm. son of Miles Fleetwood died as
Rector of All Saints
in 1725 aged 66."

The first two entries would appear to refer to the deaths of Elizabeth Harvey, wife of Sir William Fleetwood, and of Sir William Fleetwood himself. But Nathaniel Whiting writing in 1659 rather suggests that Sir William's wife was then still alive. The Dictionary of National Biography gives the date of Sir William's death as 1674, but this may be due to a wrong assumption based on the entry in the Calendar of State Papers for 27th February, 1674, quoted above. There may have been a lapse of three months or so before steps were taken to fill Sir William's position at Woodstock, or the difference may be simply due to the custom during the Civil War period of beginning the year on 25th March.

There are other interesting references in the Calendar of State Papers to the Fleetwood family's association with the Court of Wards. Sir William Fleetwood, father of Sir Miles, and grandfather of the three brothers to whom Nathaniel Whiting dedicated his book, held the office of Receiver General of the Court of Wards and Liveries. On 6th September, 1604, a grant of this office in reversion after Sir

William Fleetwood, was made to Sir Miles. On 28th July, 1609, Sir William Fleetwood is referred to as " late Receiver General of the Court of Wards." It is probable that he had retired, for a letter dated 18th December, 1612, exists from " Sir William Fleetwood to Dudley Carleton " saying that King James' eldest son, Prince Henry, had died from pestilential fever and not from poison, and begging a pound of quick silver from the mines of Istria for a friend, as it could not be had without a special licence. On 2nd April, 1614, he asked for three or four pounds of pure mercury from the mines of Istria. On 22nd March, 1610, Sir Miles received a definite grant of the Receivership of the Court of Wards, and thereafter the Calendar contains frequent references to his activities. On 9th October, 1627, Mr. Secretary Conway wrote to him that the King was content with his work, and had agreed to dispense with his attendance for the time he desired, being interested in the preservation of his health.

Sir Miles Fleetwood died in 1641, and his eldest son, Sir William, succeeded him as Receiver of the Court of Wards. He did not hold the office long, for in May, 1644, Bulstrode Whitelocke says that he had forfeited the office, having sided with Charles I, and that Parliament had rewarded his youngest brother, Charles, with a grant of the office and Mr. Miles Corbet* with that of Clerk of the Wards. In 1646, Whitelocke records in his " Memorials," " A committee made to consider of the losses of the Lord Say, Sir Rowland Wandesford, Colonel Fleetwood, and other officers of the Court of Wards by the taking away that Court, and how they may have a satisfaction." The Court of Wards and Liveries was finally abolished in the twelfth year of the reign of Charles II by Act of Parliament.

Mark Noble, however, writing about a hundred years after Anthony à Wood, in his " Memoirs of the Protectorate House of Cromwell " gives the following family tree of the Fleetwood family: —

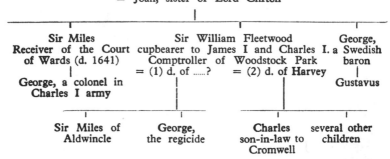

Sir William Fleetwood of Cranford Receiver of the Court of Wards = Joan, sister of Lord Clifton

Sir Miles Receiver of the Court of Wards (d. 1641) — George, a colonel in Charles I army

Sir William Fleetwood cupbearer to James I and Charles I. Comptroller of Woodstock Park = (1) d. of ......? = (2) d. of Harvey

George, a Swedish baron — Gustavus

Sir Miles of Aldwincle — George, the regicide — Charles son-in-law to Cromwell — several other children

* Sylas Neville (1741-1840), a wretch who was wont to eat calf's head every year on the anniversary of the murder of Charles I, wrote in his fascinating diary: " Among other memories drank to that of Miles Corbet, Recorder of Yarmouth and Member for the town in the Great Parliament, and one of Charles Stuart's judges . . . "

Anthony à Wood's works had been published and would have been easily available to Mark Noble, as would Nathaniel Whiting's "Old Jacob's Altar newly Repaired," but those of Aubrey were still in manuscript. The "Bibliotheca Topographica Britannica" published within a few years of Mark Noble's book gives roughly the same, but a more detailed, pedigree of the Fleetwoods: —

Sir William Fleetwood of Cranford, Receiver of the Court of Wards
= Jane d. of William Clifton, sister of Lord Clifton

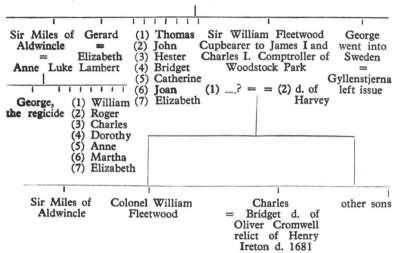

The year given as that in which Bridget Cromwell-Ireton-Fleetwood died has been proved to be nearly twenty years after the event. It will also be noted that in both family trees George Fleetwood of Sweden is shown as the uncle of Charles Fleetwood.

The Sir William Fleetwood shown in both family trees as having been married twice is clearly the son of Sir Miles Fleetwood and brother of George and Charles. Nathaniel Whiting who had been presented to his living by him would surely have known the details of the family. Further, in the Calendar of State Papers there are two interesting references to his marriages. In 1624 King James wrote to Thomas Barley of Elmingham in Essex to favour Sir William Fleetwood as a suitor for his daughter. The King favoured him for his own and his father's services. Sir William was born in 1603 and therefore of a suitable age to be married. As the King wished the marriage to take place we can perhaps assume that it did, and that Sir William's first wife was a daughter of Thomas Barley.* In 1638 a pension of £250 was granted to Elizabeth Harvey, wife of Sir William Fleetwood, for life if she should survive her husband. This completes a blank in both family trees and enables the Christian name of Sir William's second wife to be filled in as "Elizabeth."

At this time there were probably three persons of the name Sir

*See Addenda, 6.

William Fleetwood alive. Firstly, Sir Miles Fleetwood's father, Sir William Fleetwood, who had relinquished the Receivership of the Court of Wards in favour of his son. A letter from Sir Thomas Edmondes to William Trumbull dated 20th September, 1609, may explain his reason for so doing. " Sir William Fleetwood, receiver of the Court of Wards, is bankrupt in the sum of 18 (sic) and is reported not to have any state to satisfy the same." It is possible, however, that he had died before 1624. Secondly, Sir Miles Fleetwood's eldest son, Sir William, and thirdly, Sir William Fleetwood of Missenden. His father, William Fleetwood (1535(?)-1594), had married Mariana, daughter of John Barley of Kingsey in Buckinghamshire, so his son may well have been contemplating marriage with a daughter of the Barley family with whom he would be well acquainted.

In the first volume of the Camden Miscellany was printed a letter from George Fleetwood to his father, describing the battle of Lützen and the death of Gustavus Adolphus. Modern historians, such as Miss C. V. Wedgewood in her " The Thirty Years' War," base their account of the battle on this letter. Sir Philip de Malpas Grey Egerton, Bart., who edited and introduced the letter wrote: " The author, George Fleetwood, was son of Sir William Fleetwood of Cranford in Middlesex, Knight, Receiver of the Court of Wards, and brother of Sir William Fleetwood, Cupbearer to James I and Charles I and Comptroller of Woodstock Park. He went into Sweden, was a famous general there, and was created a Baron. He had a son named Gustavus who inherited his Swedish honours. His uncle, Sir George Fleetwood, married Catharine Denny, niece to Arthur, Lord Grey of Wilton, author of the Grey Manuscript. It is possible that this family connection may account for the circumstance of the two manuscripts being found together."

It will be seen that this neither follows Mark Noble, nor the contemporary writers already quoted. In 1889 the volume of the Dictionary of National Biography dealing with the Fleetwoods was printed. C. H. Firth, one of the soundest of historians contributed an article on Charles Fleetwood, and C. H. Derby, one on George Fleetwood. Both writers evidently went back to contemporary sources for they do not follow the statements of Mark Noble and Egerton. Finally in 1897, a revised edition of Waylen's " House of Cromwell " was published. James Waylen was for a time secretary to Thomas Carlyle, and had the advantage of helping him prepare his celebrated work on Cromwell. Waylen wrote: " Charles Fleetwood was the third son of Sir Miles Fleetwood of Aldwinkle, Northamptonshire. In the Civil War the family became, like many others, divided, for while Sir William Fleetwood of Aldwinkle suffered for the King, his brother Charles was in the opposite ranks, becoming Oliver Cromwell's son-in-law and Commander-in-Chief of the Forces in England." Later Waylen makes a curious statement: " He (i.e. Charles Fleetwood) passed from the activities of a camp to the social obscurity of a meek Dissenter in the suburban region of Stoke Newington. Meanwhile his royalist *father,* Sir William, resumed his ancient position at Court in the capacity of cup-bearer to the restored monarch." He must have meant to write " brother " for " father." The papers of the Lord Chamberlain's department preserved in the Public Record Office show Sir William Fleetwood as cupbearer in 1641, and again in 1660, when a complete list of the household of Charles II, just restored to the throne, was drawn up. Sir Miles Fleetwood is also said to have been cupbearer to James I and Charles I. This office has been refered to as " potman to majesty " but it was an old and honoured traditional position much coveted by gentlemen of the Court.

★

George Fleetwood*, son of Sir Miles Fleetwood, was born in 1605. His mother, Anne, was a daughter of Nicholas Luke of Woodend, Bedfordshire. He was baptised at Cople, Bedfordshire, on 30th June in that year. When grown up he soon decided to be a soldier, and in 1629 raised a troop of horse and went to Germany to join the army of Gustavus Adolphus of Sweden, the greatest general of the age. He was given the rank of lieutenant-colonel. In the following year he returned to England and raised a regiment of foot which he also took to Germany. Several entries in the Calendar of State Papers, Domestic, for the year 1631 refer to him. He is described as being " in His Majesty's service in Denmark." His father, Sir Miles Fleetwood, wrote to the Committee of the Council of War that at his son's leaving England to serve the King of Sweden he directed a servant of Sir Miles to receive two sums unpaid him in the Denmark service—£50 for raising his Company, and £89 for conduct money but no part of the same had been received. Later it is said that at his coming home from Denmark a sum of £900 was due to him. Sir Thomas Roe wrote to Sir John Hepburn, one of the Colonels of His Majesty of Sweden that he had procured a warrant for Colonel Fleetwood to raise 1,200 men for the service of the King of Sweden and that Fleetwood had chosen their friend Pottly for his lieutenant-colonel. It will be seen that service with the King of Sweden was proving remarkably attractive to foreigners favouring the Protestant cause. Many English and Scottish soldiers later returned to their own country and considerably influenced the tactics of the Civil War.

Gustavus Adolphus had become King of Sweden in 1611. He was one of the ablest monarchs of all time. Sir Thomas Roe said of him, " he thinks the ship cannot sink that carries him," and again, " the King hath the singular grace to content his followers without money, because he is ' commiles ' with every man, and gives besides excellent words and good usage as much as he hath." He had early realised the danger to his country from the outbreak of the Thirty Years' War. In 1627 he said, " as one wave follows another in the sea, so the papal deluge is approaching our shores." He finally decided in 1630 to enter the war. He fully realised the seriousness of the step he was taking and his farewell speech to the Riksdag shows it clearly: —

*See Addenda, 3.

"And as it generally happens that the pitcher is carried for water so long that it breaks at last, so will it in the end go with me. After having sacrificed my blood on several occasions and in manifold dangers for the welfare of the kingdom of Sweden—so far by the gracious care of God without serious bodily harm—yet in the end I must also give my life. I therefore commend all Swedish subjects and Estates, present as well as absent, to God, the All-Highest, both to soul, life and material welfare hoping that after this wretched and troublesome life we may, by the mercy of God, meet each other in the heavenly life which the Lord has prepared for us with joy everlasting . . .

I commend the members of the Council more especially to God's care, wishing with all my heart that with you sound advice may never be lacking, so that you may perform your public duties to the glory of God, and that His Holy Word and Doctrine may abide unadulterated with you and your children's children; further that peace and concord may be verdant and flourish among you, and that all ill-will, discord and revolt may be far away, and that you will never be found wanting in wise counsel for the safety and peace of our Fatherland; and that in the end among your descendants may grow up men who, by their strength and uprightness, will uphold the Kingdom and the government . . .

My wish for the common man and peasantry is that their meadows may be green, and their fields give a hundredfold, so that their barns may be filled, and that they will all grow and increase in prosperity so that they may cheerfully and without murmur perform their duties and exercise their rights."

The King's great Chancellor, Axel Oxenstjerna—"that axle on which the world turns"—referred to his decision as an "inspiration of genius." Oxenstjerna and Richelieu were the two greatest statesmen of the age. The Swedish Chancellor said, "the French manner of negotiating is very strange and depends much on finesse." But his own method, described by Richelieu as, "un peu gothique et beaucoup finoise," was equally effective. The King's and his Chancellor's characters were well contrasted. The King remarked: "If my ardour did not thaw your chilliness you would long ago have been frozen to ice," to which Oxenstjerna replied: "If my coldness had not moderated your heat, your Majesty would long ago have been consumed by fire."

Gustavus Adolphus sailed from Alvsnabben and landed at Rügen on 24th June, 1630. He is said to have stumbled on disembarking—a bad omen—but to have concealed it by falling to his knees in prayer. The Swedish ambassador to the Netherlands, Cammerarius, remarked, "the King of Sweden has not crossed the Rubicon but the wide sea."

Such were the two men of genius under whom George Fleetwood was to serve. For he was to prove much more than a soldier, and twenty years later was to be actively employed in diplomatic missions. On 3rd June, 1632, he became a Swedish Knight. At first the Swedish campaign went well, culminating in the great, but tragic victory of Lützen in 1632. George Fleetwod was present and wrote to his father describing the battle and the death of the Swedish King: —

" . . . the Kinge lodged that nighte (5th-6th November) in the playne feildes, about an English myle from Litzen, where the enimies randavou was. The six of November the King at break of the day marched his army . . . himself leading the righte winge, the Duke Bernerd Weamer the lefte, and Kniphowsen general maior had the command of the forte. The enimies army was ordered like ours . . . and had the advantage of Lypsicke highwaye, on either side of which a grafte, and close by the towne stood 4 wyndmills, which is fortefyed by nature very stronge; . . . the King about 8 of the clock, first shott his looseninge and soe advanced towards the enimie . . . upon which they retyred again behinde the dike, where they had cast upp a kind of a brestworke . . . And the battle joyned about tenn of the clock. it being then a faire day, but there fell soe great a miste that we cold not see one another, which, if it had not bene, I beleeve wee had quickly made an ende of that daies work (but all must be as God will have it). At our first falling on they likewise sett the towne of Litzen on fire, which did us much inconvenience, the wynde bloeing the smoke just upon us. The King at the first charging to the graft, was shott through the arme and his horses neck; upon which they would fayne have perswaded him to have retyred, which he refused, rideing to the heade of the right winge of horse, incourageing them, saying nothing ailed him, and with that, commandeing them all to follow him, he leaped over the graft and charged the enimie; but there followed him but fower regiments, which were encountered with soe many of the enimie that they were forced to retyre. And there the King fell, being shott through the head and through the bodye. There fell just by him one Truckes his chamber younker, whoe was brought off alyve, but since deade: he reported that when our horse retyred there came an officer of the enimies, whoe asked him whoe the Kinge was, which he refused to tell; he shott him through the bodye, and with that went to the Kinge demanding of himself what he was, to which he replyed he was the Kinge of Swethen; upon which he thought to have carryed off the bodye, but seeing our horse comeing againe to charge, he stroak the Kinge through the body with a broade sworde twyce, and then rann away, for then Herticke Bernerd himself charged with the horse, beat the enimie back, and brought the corps off, which had receaved in all tenn woundes. The report of the Kinges death comeing amongst the soldyers (quite contrarie to expectation), yet made them fight the braver, as seemeing to resolve to revenge his death or dye. And soe the victorious Prince dyed with a victorye for he was killed at the first charge of the horse between eleaven and twelve and the battaile lasted till fyve; but I beleeve it had not soe longe contynued had it bene cleare weather, for the miste was so greate that when wee had beaten them wee cold not see to follow the victorie. . .

Thus, feareing to bee too troublesome, presenting my humble duty
to you and my mother, and my love to all my frendes, I rest,
Your dutifyl sonne till death,
George Ffleetewood."

Victory was due to the presence of mind of Duke Bernhard of
Weimar who took charge of the Swedish forces. Richelieu described
him as " an excellent commander, but so much for himself that no
one could make sure of him." He, however, continued to fight for the
Protestant cause until, in 1639, " untimely and premature death, for
such was the decision of God, commanded the hastening foot to stay
in the very midst of its victorious race and marked out the limit to
his further ambition." Duke Bernard was of an aloof, religious
character, in great contrast to many commanders of the period.
His last words were said to have been, " Into thy hands, Lord Jesus,
I commend my spirit."

Gualdo Priorato, an Italian who fought against Gustavus Adolphus,
described the effect of his death: " The news of the King's death
was rapidly spread abroad, and the event called forth different
comments in various places—To many this message seemed a mockery,
a delusion, a dream, for in their imagination they could not comprehend that the King had fallen. Only a short time ago he had been
crowned with victories and triumphs. He seemed to have subdued
fortune, and not only to have won her favour. . . In France, in
England, in the Netherlands, everybody was stricken dumb by the
hand of fate. Kings and princes in those countries admitted that a
noble King had passed away . . . the Catholics, even, who were
his enemies, dared not lift their heads in rejoicing. . . No prince
was ever so beloved as he was. . . No general was obeyed with greater
affection and readiness. . . "

Gustavus Horn and Oxenstjerna, described in the King's lifetime,
" as his two arms," now took charge of the respective spheres of war
and diplomacy. Queen Christina, the new Swedish monarch, was but
a child, and as Oxenstjerna wrote, " I have a weight round my neck
under which a brave man may well stagger. But I assure you that
as far as it is in my power, and as behoves a true patriot of my
position, I shall endeavour to serve the interests of my country."

In 1634 Duke Bernhard and Gustavus Horn suffered a severe defeat
at Nördlingen, Horn being taken prisoner. Oxenstjerna is said to have
been unable to sleep on only two nights in his life—after hearing of
the death of Gustavus Adolphus and of the defeat of Nördlingen.
The superb succession of Swedish captains, however, remained
unbroken. Johan Baner now took command. Several of his letters
to Oxenstjerna throw interesting sidelights on the course of the terrible
Thirty Years' War: " I had not thought to find the Kingdom of
Bohemia so wasted' and spoiled, for between Prague and Vienna all
is razed to the ground and hardly a living soul to be seen in the
land." Discipline seems, for a time, to have broken down: " Quarter-
master Ramm has stayed behind in Mecklenburg without my consent,

and I do not know what has become of him." "I could do no more than promise to pay them again and again in Her Majesty's name . . . with the most plausible excuses I could think of." And, "There would be no serious gaps in their numbers if only the stragglers, plunderers, and robbers, whose irresponsibility there is no means of checking would come back to their colours."

The Swedish council of regency was therefore understandably anxious to recall their forces from Germany, but Oxenstjerna saw that the miserable condition of the Palatinate would for some years to come render it incapable of supporting itself, and sent his son, young Axel Oxenstjerna into England to ascertain decisively what help was to be expected from that quarter. It was whispered he was to propose a marriage between Christina and the eldest Prince Palatine in return for military aid from Charles I. Young Axel Oxenstjerna passed through The Hague and was received by Elizabeth of Bohemia. Charles I was unable to promise aid in money or men but offered Axel Oxenstjerna a present of gilt plate which he declined, as he would not receive benefit from an embassy which had been of no use to those who sent him. Charles I was already in difficulties with his Parliament, and finding it hard to raise money. In 1636 Oxenstjerna sent George Fleetwood on another mission to England. In the following year Elizabeth of Bohemia wrote to Sir Thomas Roe that Sir George Fleetwood had returned from Sweden and showed her the Chancellor's answer to the King, which is either to give assistance of men or money, and they will continue the war, or else the King should send a little army into Germany, and he would deliver all the places between the Rhine and the Weser into his hands. She wished the King would accept the last offer but she feared it to be too good to be done. On 3rd May in the same year Laud wrote to Elizabeth of Bohemia that on 6th April he had received a letter from Colonel Fleetwood concerning his employment and the state of that great business concerning which he could as yet say little until he had heard again from France.

Thomas Verney writing from Stockholm in 1637 says: —

"Colonel ffleetwood hath had within this month, or such a matter, four of his companies cutt by the enimy, only his officers saved, which doe lye heavy upon his hand; therefore I believe he will not be able to do me any cortesy where he is now."

In his next letter he writes: —

". . . . I have taken up two and fifty pound starling, to cleare my lodging, and the rest which is left to bring mee to Collonell ffleetwood, if the enimy will permitt mee; I must pass through three of the enemies countreys, through Denmark, through Pomerland, and through great part of Poland."

As Fleetwood had more officers than men he was unable to give Verney a commission.

The war dragged on, with the Swedes more than holding their own. Queen Christina evidently feared that her supply of great captains would fail as she wrote: "Baner is dangerously ill and in all human probability will not recover. Nobody troubles about this here. They think they can find someone to take his place, but men such as he are not shaken out of one's sleeve. Things will go ill if Baner dies..." However, Lennart Torstensson took over the command. He has been described as, "the equal of Baner in genius, his superior in energy, mastering by the greatness of his soul a body wasted by captivity and disease." Peace was eventually concluded at Westphalia in 1648. Oxenstjerna sent his son to the conference, making his celebrated remark, "Do you not know, my son, with what little wisdom the world is governed." George Fleetwood had continued to play his part. He was commandant of Greifswald and Colberg in 1641. In the previous year he had married Brita Gyllenstjerna of the family of Christina Gyllenstjerna, who had, in 1520, defended Stockholm against the Danes.

In 1653 Cromwell sent Bulstrode Whitelocke on a special mission to Sweden. Whitelocke kept a fascinating Journal of his "Ambassy," and records many meetings with Sir George Fleetwood: —

13*th February,* 1654.

"Sir George Fleetwood, an english gentleman, visited and performed many civilities and kindnesses to Whitelocke; he came into this countrey many years past, with some of his countreymen, to serve the King Gustavus Adolphus, from whom he had great favour, and was made a collonel, and afterwards governor of a town, and a generall major; he marryed an heir in this countrey, by whom he had severall children, and a fayre estate, and was now settled heer, and well beloved att court, and in the army, and in the countrey, as if he had been a native of it. He is a gentleman of a good family, and of much honour and integrity, and of perticular friendlyness and did very good offices for Whitelocke, and also informed him of many materiall and usefull matters: he also had the newes of the queen's design to quit the crown, and was one of the first without doors that acquainted Whitelocke with that newes."

19*th February.*

"This Lord's Day, Sir George Fleetwood, Colonel Hamilton, Mr. Butler, and Mr. Cooper, English and Scotts men, came in the morning to Whitelocke's house to heare the sermon there."

Whitelocke evidently had some disagreement with Sir William Ballendin, a gentleman of the Court, and considered that, when entering the Queen's apartments, a curtain had been deliberately allowed to fall back into his face. On 22nd February, 1653, Whitelocke noted in his Journal, "Sir George Fletewood informed Whitelocke, that he had spoken with Ballendin about the affront which he putt uppon Whitelocke, and told him plainly of it; and that Ballendin, with many asservations, denyed that ever he had the least intention to offer any incivility to Whitelocke or any of his company, butt was ready to doe them all service; that the reason why he did not speake to Whitelocke to goe in to the queen was, bicause he saw him buisy with one of his secretaries in the window, and therefore would not interrupt him; but spake to one of his sons; and that the hanging fell down by accident, and prayed Whitelocke to pardon it.

Fletewood told Whitelocke also, that, being with the Chancellor, he spake of it, and much condemned Ballendin, and said that Whitelocke might undoe him if he should complain of it to the queen; butt he thought it more honourable for Whitelocke to passe it over, and forgive this foolish action, which the Chancellor prayed him to doe; and being, Ballendin denyed any intention of doing Whitelocke an affront, and desired his pardon, he thought it best to take it for a satisfaction, and told Sir George Fletewood that it being the advice of his father the Chancellor and of his son Grave Eric, and of him, to any of whom he could not deny a farre greater matter, he did freely passe by this carryage of Ballendin, and did forget it; which being told Ballendin, he seemed very glad of it by healthing to the ambassador."

14th May.

" This Lord's day Sir George Fletewood did Whitelocke the favour to beare him company at his house, and told him, that the queen and her lords were pleased with his deportment att his last audience, and with his speech then made which they commended. He and others also acquainted Whitelocke that the Queen tooke great pleasure att his carryage att the solemnity of the nuptialls att Court, and that he would daunce with them; and both the queen and her courtiers said, that the english ambassador knew how to lay aside the gravity of an ambassador when he pleased, and could play the courtier with as good a grace as any one that ever they saw with much to the like effect."

17th May.

" The resident of Holland came to visit Whitelocke neer dinner time, which gave him occasion to invite his stay; and he and Sir George Fletewood, Mr. Bloome, colonell Hambleton, Monsieur Lillycroon, and two Dutch gentlemen did Whitelocke the favour to be att his table."

Whitelocke began his return journey to England on 20th May, 1654.

" Whitelocke tooke coach between seven and eight a'clock in the morning, Sir George Fletewood, Potley, Ingelo, and Andrewes in his coach with him, the rest on horseback."

The journey from Upsala to Stockholm lasted until nearly six in the evening. Whitelocke spent several days in sightseeing. On 26th May he wrote in his Journal: —" After Whitelocke had walked a tour in the northern mallum, that is the north suburbs of this citty, Sir George Fletewood came to him; with whom he had much conversation in the latter time of his being in Sweden, both at Ubsale and in this town, who showed much kindness and respect to Whitelocke: he informed Whitelocke, that by letters from Ubsale he understood that the ricksdagh had given leave to the queen to goe to Colmar, which signifyed that she could not goe without their leave, and that she would find much difference between commanding as a queen, and obeying as a subject; and that, by the law of this Kingdome, no queen can depart out of it, without leave of the ricksdagh, on forfeiture of all her estate.

A ship called the Swart Hundt was, by the queen's command, appointed and fitted to carry Whitelocke's copper and other goods, from hence to England. By advice of friends, Whitelocke, under his hand and seale, desired Sir George Fletewood to consigne the copper to Whitelocke's brother-in-law, Mr. Willson."

On the following day "Whitelocke visited Sir Geo. Fletewood att his lodging in Stockholme; and finding, with him, vice admirall Thysen, and Peterson, both Hollanders, and in the service of the crown, Whitelocke brought them all home with him to dinner, and advised with them about his voyage."

On 28th May, "The Lord's day, Whitelocke according to his custome, had a good sermon in his lodging preached by one of his chaplains in the morning, and another good sermon preached there in the afternoon by Mr. Biger, a Scotts minister, and chaplain to Sir George Fletewood, then with him." On the following day Whitelocke "could not persuade Sir George Fletewood to stay longer with him: he thought it necessary for him to goe to Ubsale, to be present at the King's coronation; and att his request Whitelock sent by him to Marshall Wrangel a letter."

On 25th June Whitelocke was at Hamburgh, delayed by bad weather. "About six a'clocke att night, Mr. Smith son to alderman Smith of London, and two other young merchants of the english company at Hambourgh, came on board to Whitelocke, and brought letters to him from the resident Bradshawe, with those the resident received by this weekes post from London; wherein was little newes and no letters came to Whitelocke, bicause (as he supposed) his friends believed him to be upon the sea. Whitelocke wrote letters of thankes to the resident, and inclosed in them letters of complement to the ricks chancellor, and to his son Grave Eric of Sweden, and to Sir George Fletewood, and others, his friends, and intreated the resident to send them into Sweden."

Whitelocke's letter from Hamburgh brought the following reply from Fleetwood: —

"Right Honorable,

Youers dated the 25th of June is safely come to hande. I am hartily glade to heare of your excellencie's . . . and well contented journie soe farre, but especially youer prosperus arivall at Graves-ende, which I am informed . . . resident's letter, and hope ere long to have it from your lordship's penne. Ouer Kinge hath bin very inquisitive after your excellencie, and seemed to be very well contented, that youer honer was safely come on in England, which I informed him yesterday. Concerninge ouer late queene's resignation and coronation, I dare not particularise, supposinge ere this, it is in print in all languages. Ouer noble Kinge (who gaineth the affection daily of all men by his affable carriage) is involved in new troubles, before he is once setled; a warre fomented by the Bremers, and begune without . . . unknowne to his majestie or the privie counsell heare (as they all pretende). I suppose it will not be soone ended, being confident the Bremers would not have begun, had they not been backed by greate ons; but . . . they are like to be loosers. Ouer whole worke heare in sending out forces hence, divers from Colmer and Gottenburge allready gon; those from this porte to go aborde to-morrow; earle Gustofe Stenebocke to commande them under Koningsmarke. They say, in all, 8000 shall be sent out. God send them good successe.

Before ouer late queen's resignation, the Portugal embassador was commanded to departe, not acknolinge his principall; but our Kinge did underhande excuse it, and since with all civilitie salved it what possible as I heare.

Thus I suppose, we have two tastes of ower Spaniard his designes, and feare to many will follow.

Count Ericke is to set saile from hence in fewe dayes to Keele, and thence to the duke of Holsten's courte to fetch ower new queene (the duke's second dauter unmarried). Ower Kinge regulates his jornie according hee seeth the winde serve, intending to meete at Colmer, where the nuptials are solemnised. They repaire heather, where this winter a parlament shall stande. Then the queene is to bee crouned and all affaires of the kingdome settled.

Count Slissenbacke is sodainely departinge hence ambassador to all the princes in Germanie, to demonstrate the Bremers unrite proceedings, and to protest against any mischance can happen to the empire by this means.

The riks-chancellor was lately very sicke, but now (God bee praised) reasonable well recovered. The Kinge courts him much. Thus much for publique. Count Gabriel Oxensterne, aboute two dayes since, desired me to write to your excellencie, that now the hotte weather was past, hee would sende over the lord protector's rine-deare; they are now six or seven alive, and these very fresh and lustie; that he questioned not there liveinge now. He desireth youer lordshipee would sende over one skillful in ketching hawkes, and you shall have as manie as you please; but withall importuned mee, to put youer excellencie in minde of English horses and doges hee pretendeth promised.

Thus fearing to bee to troublesome, this is onely to beg youer excellencie accounte of mee as I shall alwaies shew myselfe, to power.

your faithfull servant,

George Fleetwood.

Stockholme, 22, July, 1654.

The fifteenth of this present kame ould felt-marshal Lesly heather, and departeth hence in few dayes; his business, as hee pretendeth, to give ouer queene thanks for hir gratius assisting him in his business by the lord protector, which compliment he hath loged of to ouer Kinge."

Queen Christina during the time of Whitelocke's embassy was considering abdicating in favour of her cousin Charles. She had not taken to the routine duties of a monarch's life, and desired leisure for an artistic and intellectual life. One of her last acts as Queen must have been to create George Fleetwood a Baron on 1st June, 1654. On 6th June she finally abdicated and left Sweden for ever. Hers was a fascinating character. One of her opinions—a strange one for a woman—was: —

" Some people are silly enough to be slaves and martyrs to clothes and fashions and are unhappy if they do not spend their lives between the mirror and the comb. Tidiness is only for the idle."

On her way to France she passed through the Netherlands, and Elizabeth of Bohemia saw her at a play: —

" I saw the Queen of Sweden at the play; she is extravagant in her fashion and apparel, but she has a good well-favoured face, and a mild countenance."

In the same year we find Elizabeth of Bohemia writing to Mr. Secretary Nicholas (he had been Charles I's secretary) on 15th September: —

"... This day the assemblie of Hollande begins. Their agent in Sweden writt to the States Generall that Sir George Fleetwood, brother to him that is Leftenant of Ireland, tolde him that he knew Cromwell had saide he would keepe the peace with the States no longer than he thought it good for his interests, and would break with the first occasion that he can for the good of his deseins. Those of Hollande are verie angrie at the agent for writing this . . . ."

Back in England, Whitelocke on 6th July made his report to Cromwell and his Council in the course of which he said: —" I had good assistance from my countreymen, generall major Fleetwood, a true friend to England, my lord Douglas, collonell Hamilton and others." In his "Memorials" Whitelocke records his speech in detail: —

" This day I gave an account to the protector and his council of my embassy in Sweden and spake to this effect: —

. . . and of my countrymen, I had the assistance of major-general Fleetwood, a faithful servant to England."

And again: —

"I was not without friends of my own nation ... General Douglas, a Scotch gentleman was very civil to me: so was a true English gentleman, major-general Sir George Fleetwood, a person of great interest and respect in those parts, and with all that know him: he testified extraordinary respect and affection to you and to your servant, and was very courteous and helpful to me ... the magistrates and people of Stockholm were very respectful to your servants, and general Wrangel, and major-general Fleetwood, with here Lagerfelds, and others, accompanied me forty English miles to their chief city. There they freely showed me not only the stately castle, town, haven and ships, but their works, magazines, arsenals, workhouses for arms and shipping, which were very strong and considerable."

In 1655 the new King of Sweden, Charles X, sent Fleetwood as an envoy extraordinary to Cromwell in response to Whitelocke's embassy. Fleetwood brought his eldest son, Gustavus Miles, with him to pursue his civil and military education in this country. He remained here until Charles II had returned and was enrolled in his life-guard. George Fleetwood became a Swedish lieutenant-general in 1656 and returned to Sweden in 1660.

In 1655 Cromwell was thinking of sending Whitelocke on a further embassy to Sweden, and the latter was not at all anxious to brave the discomforts of such a journey a second time. In his "Memorials," Whitelocke wrote: —" The lord deputy Fleetwood and Colonel Sydenham told me that his highness and the council had appointed them to acquaint me with a business of very great importance . . . to send an extraordinary embassy to the King of Swedland about a business . . . most conducing to the good of the protestant cause, which was, the uniting of that interest and preventing the differences that were likely to fall between that King and the United Provinces and the Elector of Brandenburgh; for which ends they had thoughts of me and Sir Christopher Palk to go to the King as ambassadors . . . I thought I had enough of danger and trouble in my former embassy . . . (so) I alleged . . . that the King of Sweden's ambassador here might probably conclude upon the business intended, without sending one from hence to him . . . and I proceeded in the treaty with the Swedish ambassador at his house . .. The Swedish ambassador kept a solemnity . . . for the birth of the young prince of Sweden. All the glass of the windows of his house, which were very large were taken off, and instead thereof painted papers were fitted to the places with the arms of Sweden in it, and inscriptions in great letters testifying the rejoicing for the birth of the young prince: in the inside of the papers in the rooms were set close to them a very great number of lighted candles glittering through the painted papers . . . the company at supper were the Dutch ambassador, the Portugal and Brandenburgh residents, mynheer Coyet resident for Sweden, the earls of Bedford and Devon, the lords St. John, Ossery, Bruce, Ogleby . . . the Count of Holac, a German, the lord George Fleetwood, and a great many knights and gentlemen . . . . " The negotiations for the treaty continued and "in case the treaty here with the Swedish ambassador came to a good conclusion, the Lord George Fleetwood had commissions to levy for the King of Sweden two thousand men more than the four thousand already granted, and designed to form those two thousand into two regiments and to be colonel of both those regiments himself."

" May, 1656. This day (3rd May) the protector gave the honour of Knighthood to mynheer Coyett, the King of Sweden's resident here, who was now Sir Peter Coyett, and gave him a fair jewel with his highness's picture and a rich gold chain; it cost about £400. The

Lord general Fleetwood told me that I had some enemies at Court who were willing to keep me from being of the Council . . . ."

It was evidently not long after that George Fleetwood was once more on active service, for on 18th July, 1656, the Dutch ambassadors to Prussia, Slingerlandt, Dorp and Huybert, wrote to their government from Marienburgh " . . . a few days since arrived in the Pillaw 1600 Scots, and the lord Fleetwood is said to follow with a considerable number."

There does not seem to be much evidence linking George Fleetwood with his brother Charles. The following entry, however, appears in the " Calendar of State Papers, Domestic " : —

" 28th October, 1656. Fiennes and the Lord-Deputy (i.e. Charles Fleetwood) to consider what was today propounded by his Highness concerning Sweden, and of sending someone to speak with Lord Geo. Fleetwood and others, and report their opinion of the whole matter to his Highness and Council."

On 22nd August, 1657, Thurloe delivered certain secret instructions to Major-general Jepthson, in which George Fleetwood's negotiations are referred to : —

" 1. Haveing discoursed with the Kinge of Sweden upon the matter of your other instructions, you shall let his majestie knowe, that the lord ambassador Bond, during his residence here, and the lord George Fleetwood since, have in his majestie's name very much pressed us to ayd and assist him in his warrs by money, ships, and men . . . .

2. You shall further informe his majestie, that wee allways had a deepe sence of the condition of his affaires and although wee were not, nor are in a condition to contribute money (our late warrs . . . haveinge in a great measure exhausted this nation) yet wee were not unwilling to consider our own affaires, in order to such assistance as wee were able to afford him, and might consist with the treaties wee have with other states . . . but not finding them impowered to treate with us upon the termes of that assistance . . . We were not able to come to any resolutions thereupon . . . .

6. If his majestie shall upon this or any other occasion take notice of what was writt to him hence by the lord George Fleetwood, touchinge the puttinge of the dukedome of Bremen into our hands, you shall endeavour to understand what his majestie's inclinations are thereunto, and acquaint him, that some discourses of that kinde had been upon occasion of the ayde and assistance, which was desired from us by the sayd Lord Fleetwood upon this ground, that it was not fitt for us to expose our ships and the lives of our men in a forreine war without some place of strength and securitie to have recourse unto . . . ."

George Fleetwood was in London at the time of the Protector's death, for on 18th November, 1658, he wrote from Covent Garden : —

" Geo. Fleetwood and H. von Tischendorf, Swedish Commissioners, to Sir Oliver Fleming, master of the ceremonies.

The enclosed shows us what place we are to expect at the

funeral, and our belief is confirmed because the mourning sent us was the same given to the agent of Dantzic and every town.

We too much respect his memory who showed us so much civility to dispute places, but our relation to our master, as public ministers, requires better places. Our master treats Sir Philip Meadows after a higher rate. We request either to be placed next the ambassadors, or to be dispensed from attendance. We depend on your friendship and discretion."

On 23rd May, 1659, George Fleetwood and Henry Fresendorff presented the following memorial to the English council of state: —

" May it please your lordships, understanding that divers captains who are in his majesty of Sweden's actual service as likewise some native Swedes, who are sent from his majesty's fleet, are stopped in several ports of England, whereof one captain Swart hath been detained above a month without the least intimation of the reasons thereof given unto us, his majesty's ministers residing here; we are forced to give your lordships this present trouble, and humbly crave your redress, in regard it is the constant practice amongst all princes and free states in amity, to have a free access to each others havens; and in the late wars betwixt this commonwealth and Holland, the subjects of England used the same freedom in the haven of Gottenburgh, whither when any prizes were brought, they were suffered either to sell them there, or to take them out of port, notwithstanding the opposition made by the Holland ministers there, and long since practised by the Hollanders against the subjects of this commonwealth, bringing in English vessels into their havens with Spanish commissions and selling them there as good prizes. We humbly desire your lordships will take these premises into your serious consideration and suffer the said captains, now so long detained with those prizes they have lawfully taken, to be set at liberty; and if not permitted to sell them here, yet at least to depart unmolested out of your havens, and transport them to his majesty's dominions. Which favour his majesty, upon the like occasion, will be ready to acknowledge . . . .

The lord George Fleetwood representeth as followeth: —That captain Cornelius Peterson Swart, commander of a private man of war which now lies at Rye, having taken two prizes and brought them up to Dover, upon some complaint made against him, he was sent for up by Mr. Secretary; and there being upon examination, no just cause found to detain him, he was dismissed, it appearing he is a native Swede, and that he came from Gottenburgh with a commission from the King of Sweden.

That he made application to Dr. Walker for advice, how to proceed against the said two prizes; who told him, that in regard of the late change there was nothing at present to be done . . . ."

George Fleetwood made similar representations regarding Captains Cornelius Claeson, Hamilton, and Arrington. This trouble was caused by the trade treaty concluded with Holland and the consequent desire of the English government for better relations with that country,

Sweden and Holland still remaining on bad terms.

The following entry in the " Calendar of State Papers, Domestic " may relate to this question of captured enemy ships: —

" 18th June, 1659. Order in Parliament, on a letter from Carolus Gustavus King of Sweden, given at his Castle of Cronenburgh, 31 May 1659, that Council give audience to his envoys, viz., Lord George Fleetwood, lieut-general of the King's infantry, and John Frederick Freizendorf, councillor of the said King in Prussia, receive their propositions, treat with them and report."

In 1665 George Fleetwood became a member of the Swedish council of war, but only survived two more years, dying on 11th June, 1667. He was buried at Nyköping. He enjoyed a great reputation for energy, prudence and honesty in the country of his adoption and thoroughly deserved the honours with which he had been rewarded. He left four sons and two daughters and the genealogy of his family is contained in " Attartaflor, or Swedish Tables of Nobility," Stockholm, published in 1859.

Charles Fleetwood seems to have been much younger than his brothers, and, as a younger son, had only an annuity of £60 charged upon his eldest brother's estate. In 1638 he was admitted a member of Gray's Inn. He soon showed that his sympathies lay with the cause of Parliament, for four years later he, and other young gentlemen of the Inns of Court, entered the Earl of Essex's lifeguard as simple troopers. Essex was in command of the Parliament's army and in September, 1642, sent Fleetwood to the Earl of Dorset with a letter containing proposals of peace with the King. He was sent back without a reply. By the time of the first battle of Newbury at which he was wounded, he had risen to the rank of Captain, and in 1644 he was commanding a regiment in the Earl of Manchester's army. Already he was attracting attention for his extreme religious views. " Look at Colonel Fleetwood's regiment, what a cluster of preaching officers and troopers there is." It is worth examining how Cromwell's army was built up and the reasons for its ultimate victory. Fleetwood can be regarded as a fine example of the best type of officer it produced.

★

When the war broke out the King had an enormous superiority. Most of the gentry fought for him and were far better soldiers than the type of men joining the Earl of Essex's army. This superiority was particularly noticeable among the cavalry. Prince Rupert, son of Elizabeth of Bohemia, was not only a professional soldier but one of the supreme leaders of horsemen of all time, and had based his methods on a study of those of the great Gustavus Adolphus. The headlong charge at the gallop of cavalry so often depicted and described in prints and books is quite false. The riders advanced in line at the trot, receiving the enemy's fire but holding their own until they broke in among the opposing ranks. Prince Rupert certainly increased the pace of the charge. Unfortunately, as well as having the professional soldier's good qualities, he had also the bad, and was a great source of worry to Charles I on account of his ruthless methods and the licence given to his men to plunder. His soldiers were described in a contemporary pamphlet, " These are those cursed Ishmaels which do not only dishonour and abuse God his Annoynted by their oaths and blasphemies, and would if it were possible pull God out of heaven for they make it, a common saying amongst them, We will drinke and be drunke, whore, and be damned, and will not be beholding to God to save us; And that they had rather be in hell with their comrades than in heaven with the Roundheads: and they have such new invented oaths, implications and healths, so full of wickednesse and blasphemy, that the like were never heard of before amongst either Turkes or Pagans, for it is usuall amongst them to say: The Divell that made us damme us, and damme me, and ram me into the mouth of a Canon, and shoote me nine miles into hell."

Both Charles I and Cromwell realised very clearly that victory might well go to the side whose army had the greatest respect for the civilian population, and because of this atrocities were few, and such events as the siege of Colchester stand out with great vividness. In after years Cromwell recalled a conversation with John Hampden, " Our troops" 'said I,' "are most of them old decayed serving-men and tapsters and such like kind of fellows; and their troops are gentlemen's sons, younger sons and persons of quality; do you think that the spirits of such base and mean fellows will ever be able to encounter gentlemen, that have honour and courage and resolution in them? You must get men of spirit, of a spirit that is likely to go on as far as gentlemen will go: or else you will be beaten still." Cromwell was to raise such an army. " I raised such an army as had the fear of God before them, as made some conscience of what they did; and from that day forward, I must say to you, they were never beaten; and whenever they were engaged against the enemy, they beat them continually." Only truly religious men were to be enrolled, such as would be above fighting for pay only. Cromwell said, " A few honest men are better than numbers ... for being well armed within by the satisfaction of their own consciences, and without by good iron arms, they would as one man charge firmly and fight desperately." The term " Ironsides " was first applied to Cromwell himself and only later to the soldiers of the New Model Army. Royalist pamphleteers made amusing play with the religious side of the opposing army, and particularly picked on Fleetwood, who was said to be " indebted neither to his skill in the military line, or to the depth of his capacity, for his grandeur: his influence in the camp was owing intirely to his gift of praying; which in an army composed of religious fanatics, must make the possessor of such a powerful accomplishment, however else ridiculous, of no small consequence: it is almost incredible

58

to what excesses his devotion carried him: praying, he thought, the best means of opposing an enemy: it was better, he said, than trusting to 'carnal weapons,' or 'exerting the arm of the flesh.' " He was even taunted with cowardice. The writers sitting at home in safety might have their amusement, but the fighters cannot have found the hero of Worcester at the head of a regiment of the new Model Army a laughing matter. His record in the field speaks for itself. When Bulstrode Whitelocke, Keeper of the Great Seal of England, and Cromwell's Ambassador to Queen Christina was in Sweden the following curious conversation between him and the Queen took place:—

"Queen—I have been told that many officers of your army do themselves pray and preach to their soldiers. Is that true? Whitelocke—Yes, Madam, it is very true. When their enemies are swearing, or debauching, or pillaging, the officers and soldiers of the parliament's army use to be encouraging and exhorting one another out of the Word of God, and praying together to the Lord of Hosts for his blessing to be with them, who hath showed his approbation of this military preaching, by the successes he hath given them. Q.—That's well. Do you use to do so too? W.—Yes; upon some occasions, in my own family; and think it as proper for me, being the master of it, to admonish and speak to my people when there is cause, as to be beholden to another to do it for me, which sometimes bring the chaplain into more credit than his lord. Q.—Doth your generals and other great officers do so? W.—Yes, Madam, very often, and very well. Nevertheless, they maintain chaplains and ministers in their houses and regiments; and such as are godly and worthy ministers, have as much respect, and as good provision in England, as in any place of Christendom. Yet, 'tis the opinion of many good men with us, that a long cassake, with a silk girdle and a great beard, do not make a learned or a good preacher; without gifts of the Spirit of God, and labouring in his vineyard: and whosoever studies the Holy Scriptures, and is enabled to do good to the souls of others, and endeavours the same, is nowhere forbidden by that word, nor is it blameable. The officers and soldiers of the parliament's army held it not unlawful, when they carried their lives in their hands, and were going to adventure them in the high places of the field, to encourage one another out of His word, who commands over all; and this had more weight and impression with it, than any other word could have; and was never denied to be made use of but by the popish prelates, who, by no means, would admit lay people (as they call them) to gather, from thence, that instruction and comfort which can nowhere else be found. Q.—Methinks you preach very well, and have now made a good sermon. I assure you I like it very well. W.— Madam, I shall account it a great happiness if any of my words may please you."

★

In 1645 Charles Fleetwood's regiment was summoned south from Lincolnshire to join Fairfax's army at Windsor. The next campaign brought him into direct conflict with his brother, Sir William, at Woodstock. Whitelocke wrote: " Colonel Fleetwood fell upon the King's quarters near Woodstock, took fifty horse and divers prisoners," and, " Eight troopers of Colonel Fleetwood's charged twenty of the Oxford horse who had been out to fetch money, took fourteen horse and men and £146 in money: his regiment and Colonel Rainsborough's straitened Oxford."

In April, 1646, commissioners from Oxford, including Sir William Fleetwood, agreed on articles for the surrender of Woodstock House to the parliament with their arms, and provisions. Among the commissioners for the parliament was Colonel Charles Fleetwood. The two brothers were thus negotiating from opposite sides of the table. The House of Commons soon after ordered Sir William Fleetwood to be sent prisoner to Warwick Castle. He seems to have been released after the surrender of Woodstock House, but later gave himself up to Colonel Rainsborough.

The war was now over for Sir William Fleetwood. In 1649 Whitelocke noted: " Upon a recommendation of the general ordered that Sir William Fleetwood (and others) shall have the benefit of the articles of Oxford."

In the following year Aubrey, always curious regarding matters of the supernatural, was collecting information about the " just devil of Woodstock," which inspired Sir Walter Scott to write ," Woodstock: or the Cavalier. A Tale of the year 1651." When the Commissioners of the Parliament had been sitting at Woodstock they had been much alarmed by certain mysterious noises and incidents. John Lydall wrote to Aubrey on 11th March: " Concerning that which happened at Woodstock, I was told by Mr. Hawes (who now lives with Sir William Fleetwood in the park) that the Committee which sat in the Mannour were pelted out of their chambers by stones thrown in at the windows; (but from what hands the stones came they could not see); that their candles were continuously put out, as fast as they lighted them; and that one with his sword drawn to defend a candle, was with his own scabbard in the meantime well cudgelled; and others were forced to remove, some of them to Sir William Fleetwood's house, and the rest to some other places." Lydall's letter suggests that Sir William had been allowed to return to Woodstock to live quietly in retirement.*

In 1660 a pamphlet called " The Just Devil of Woodstock" was published, in which occurs the following sentence: ". . . . besides many more, who each night heard the noise; as Sir Gerrard Fleetwood and his lady, with his family . . . ." This is one more instance of the many confusing references to the Fleetwood family. Lydall is probably right in referring to Sir William Fleetwood.

Charles Fleetwood continued to distinguish himself and commanded a regiment of horse at Naseby, and played a prominent part in the defeat of Sir Jacob Astley at Stow-in-the-Wold. In 1646 he was

*See Addenda, 6 and 22.

returned as member of parliament for Marlborough. Apparently he took no active part in the second civil war and was in no way concerned with the trial and execution of Charles I. In 1649 he was appointed Governor of the Isle of Wight, and in the following year accompanied Cromwell to Scotland as lieutenant-general of the horse, and helped to win the battle of Dunbar. He was now elected a member of the third council of state and recalled to London and placed in command of all the forces in England. It was thus that he was responsible for raising the army to oppose the advance of Charles II into England. He met Cromwell at Warwick on 24th August, crossed the Severn to Upton, and from there on 3rd September began the battle of Worcester. He forced his way over the Teme and drove Charles II's army into Worcester. The House of Commons passed a vote of thanks and re-elected him to the Council of State. It was only a few weeks after Worcester that Fleetwood lost his wife, Frances, a daughter of Thomas Smith of Winston in Norfolk. She was buried at St. Anne's, Blackfriars, on 24th November, 1651.

Sir John Bramston in his Autobiography, published by the Camden Society, gives an account of how Fleetwood became possessed of the Feltwell estate.

John Bramston " my father " . . . was married " in the yeare of our Lord 1606 to Bridget Moundeford, one of the daughters of Thomas Moundeford, doctor of phisick, a learned and eminent man in that profession as any in that tyme; he was one of the younger sonns of Sir Edmund Moundeford, of Feltwell in Norfolke, a name and familie antient and honourable, but now totally extinct, Sir Edmund Moundeford, Knight of the Sheire in the Parliament begun 3rd November, 1648 beinge the last male, who dyinge without issue, (though he had two wives, one a Gaudie, the other a Heveningham) he gave the estate in the greatest part to his sister of the whole blood, who had no issue by Simon Smyth, to whom she was longe married; she gave the seat Feltwell and the land thereto belonginge, to a daughter of her husband's brother, whome she married to Charles Fleetwood, the rebell, Lieutenant-Generall to Cromwell, whoe now injoyeth it, and is noe way allied in blood to the familie; the other sisters, beinge of the halfe blood, inherited noethinge but what was allotted to them for portions by their father, who before had sold (as I thinck) the mansion-house of his name, which I did see converted to an inn or alehouse . . . "

It was to Feltwell that Fleetwood retired for a time on the restoration of Charles II. The following pedigree explains the relationship:—

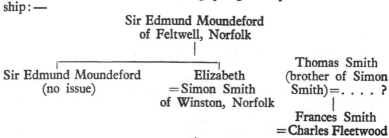

Sir Edmund Moundeford
of Feltwell, Norfolk

Sir Edmund Moundeford (no issue)   Elizabeth = Simon Smith of Winston, Norfolk   Thomas Smith (brother of Simon Smith) = ... ?

Frances Smith = Charles Fleetwood

★

Of Cromwell's children it was said that "those who wore breeches deserved petticoats better; but if those in petticoats had been in breeches, they would have held faster." Cromwell was devoted to his daughters and Elizabeth, the second, who married John Claypole, was his favourite child, but Bridget, the eldest daughter, married successively his two favourite officers, Henry Ireton and Charles Fleetwood. She was born in 1624, and married Ireton in 1642. He was the ablest of all Cromwell's officers, and a staunch republican. On 25th October, 1646, Cromwell wrote his daughter a very human letter : —

"Dear Daughter,
I write not to thy husband, partly to avoid trouble, for one line of mine begets many of his, which I doubt makes him sit up too late; partly because I am myself indisposed (i.e. having other matters in mind) at this time, having some other considerations . . . Dear Heart press on; let not Husband, let not anything cool thy affections after Christ. I hope he (i.e. her husband) will be an occasion to inflame them. That which is best worthy of love in thy husband is that of the image of Christ he bears. Look on, that, and love it best, and all the rest for that. I pray for thee and him; do so for me.
I am,
Thy dear Father,
Oliver Cromwell."

Bridget seems to have been rather addicted to "enthusiasm" and after she had gone to Ireland with her husband a Mr. Thomas Patient wrote to Cromwell : —"I have been at headquarters ever since a little before my lady Ireton came over. I do by good experience find, as far as I can discern, the power of God's grace in her soul; a woman acquainted with temptations and breathing after Christ." Two days after the burial of Fleetwood's wife Ireton died. He had overworked and neglected his health, and when illness came his powers of resistance were too low to overcome it.

★

The marriage of Bridget Ireton to Fleetwood was attributed to her desire to regain the prominent position she had lost on her first husband's death. That this interpretation of her character is false is shown by contemporary records, her charming portrait and by the account in Mrs. Lucy Hutchinson's "Memoirs of Her Husband, Colonel Hutchinson," of the meeting between her and Fleetwood : —
"There went a story that as my Lady Ireton was walking in St. James's park, the Lady Lambert, as proud as her husband, came by where she was, and as the present princess always hath presidency of the relict of the dead prince, so she put my Lady Ireton below; who, notwithstanding her piety and humility, was a little grieved at the affront. Colonel Fleetwood being then present, in mourn-

ing for his wife, who died at the same time her lord did, took occasion to introduce himself, and was immediately accepted by the lady and her father, who designed thus to restore his daughter to the honour she had fallen from."

This shows a romantic and sympathetic side of Fleetwood's character which was not often revealed. Cromwell no doubt encouraged the marriage for personal as well as political reasons. Soon afterwards he wrote to Fleetwood: —

"Dear Charles,

I thank you for your loving letter. The same hopes and desires upon your planting into my family, were much the same in me that you express in yours towards me. . . Salute your dear wife from me. Bid her beware of a bondage spirit. Fear is the natural issue of such a spirit; the antidote is love. The voice of Fear is: If I had avoided that, how well it had been with me! I know this hath been her vain reasoning: ' poor Biddy!' . . . Pray for me. I commit you to the Lord; and rest, your loving father,

Oliver Cromwell."

Fleetwood was now appointed Commander-in-Chief in Ireland, where he remained from September, 1652, until September, 1655. We find Dorothy Osborne writing to Sir William Temple on 15th May, 1653: —

". . . when your father goes into Ireland lay your commands upon some of his servants to get you an Irish greyhound. I have one that was the General's; but 'tis a bitch, and those are always much less than the dogs. I got it in the time of my favour there, and it was all they had. Henry Cromwell undertook to write to his brother Fleetwood for another for me; but I have lost my hopes there. . . "

Dorothy Osborne might have married Henry Cromwell but remained true to Sir William Temple. In the same year Cromwell wrote to Fleetwood on the occasion of the birth of a child: —

"Dear Charles,

. . . my love to thy dear wife—whom indeed I entirely love, both naturally, and upon the best account; and my blessing, if it be worth anything, upon thy little Babe. . .

Your truly loving father,
Oliver Cromwell."

(This letter was published in the Annual Register for 1761 " copyed from the original in the hands of Mrs. Cook (grand-daughter to Lieutenant-General Fleetwood) of Stoke Newington, Middlesex, November 5th, 1759, by A. Gifford.")

The three years which Fleetwood spent in Ireland were among the most active and difficult of his career. He had not only to step into the shoes of Ireton, the most forceful of all Cromwell's subordinates, but also to attempt to restore order in a country largely Catholic and Royalist, among a people notoriously hard to rule. This period of his life is the best documented, for a long series of his letters is preserved in John Thurloe's, " Collection of State Papers." On 14th

February, 1653, he wrote to Thurloe from Dublin on the general situation in Ireland: —

" Sir,

We have much groundes of suspition, that the Irish have some designe to make some disturbance. Their great want is of armes and ammunition: they have hopes of supplies from beyond seas. There are three Brest men of warre, which lie upon the Westerne coast, and through the negligence of the states shippes are like to continue. They give out, that they expect a fleete to come into those portes. We have some intelligence, which gives us much ground of suspition, that the intelligence, which my lord protector formerly gave me, might be a reall designe. I am sending more forces to strengthen those portes, and I doubte not, if there be occasion, but that we shall find the same presence of the Lord, which hitherunto we have had. The state is much abused, through the carelessness of those men of warre, which attend this coast: they loose much time in harbours, under pretence of victuallinge.

Your very affectionate friend
and servant,
Charles Fleetwood."

It is evident that Fleetwood had not forgotten his early legal training in Gray's Inn, for he is often concerned with the establishment of a proper judicial system: —

" Sir,

Since my last to you, the high courte of justice did again sitte, but have adjourned for three weeks or a month without doeing anything. The occasion of their sitting was upon tryal of the Lord Muskerrie; but by reason of the late acte sett out by my lord protector, which hath declared what shall be treason, they conceive themselves not in a condition to proceede to the tryall of any person, untill that acte shall be explained, because murther by the lawes of this land is treason; and by our proceedings heere upon the acte of settlement, and the lawes of this land, all accessories and abettors are proceeded against as principalls, even before the principalls be attainted: but by reason of this late act, they can only be tryed as felons.

This inclosed paper from the attorney-general will more particularly informe you concerninge this business; besides there are other things, as burneing of houses, corne, etc., alsoe by the laws of this land are treason, which were made soe by reason of the barbarisme of this people, soe apte to such crymes; but indeede this of murder has been so high a wickedness, and almost unheard of cruelties have been exercised by these natives, that I am sure it was farre from my lord protector's intentions, or any others concerned in makinge that lawe, that I most earnestlie presse you will send us a full and speedie explanation thereof.

I have one thing more to adde, that the coyne heere is exceedingly debased and corrupted and this countrie will be ruined, if not timely prevented. I must therefore entreate your special assistance in procuring us a minte here, according to the letter to my lord protector from the commissioners heere. Excuse this trouble from your very affectionate friend and servant,

Charles Fleetwood.

Dublin, 16 Feb., 1653.

I desire you will send mee word how my lord St. John does, and whether he actes with you or not. Sir, it is said the Venetian embassador shalle have liberty to transporte men from Ireland. If my lord of Muskerry his innocency appears, and he be acquitted, he will be the fittest person to command them, of any other, and of most advantage to the publicke.

Charles Fleetwood."

For my most honoured friend John Thurloe esq.

Secretary to the lord protector, att the Cockpit.

For the special service of the state. Haste, haste, haste."

In a further letter he again referred to the esablishment of proper law courts : —

" Sir,

I kindly thanke you for your continued correspondencye, which I shall desire still the favour of. As for our judicatures heere, it is in a very unsettled condition. Wee very much want good instruments for such a work; and I feare our povertye will not afford us libertie to allow that encouragement to persons of worth to come over to us; but indeed that affaire of the administration of justice is in such a posture, that the people are in a very sad and oppressed condition, through delays and want of justice. We heere are of opinion that there is no necessity at present of more courts of justice, than one in the nature of common pleas, and another for adjudication of titles. The commissioners have thought of making Sir Gerrard Lowther, Sir James Barry, justice Donellan, the attorney general, and the recorder of this towne, to be judges. If wee have a common pleas, we must have a seale, which at present we have none, I hope my brother Cromwell hath given you a full account of all affaires here. There is little of newes since his departure; only Mortogh O'Brien with 1200 men are transported beyond sea, and more are ready to goe after him. I much desire to heare how the Lord deales with us as to the business of Holland; but in that we have so far pursued peace, if they reject it, 'twill be a great witness against them. If my lord protector intends that design which he writt unto me about, wee shal be able to furnish him with the men; but the difficulty wil be to transport the horse. If the design goes on, I desire to have timely notice. I am,

Your very affectionate friend and servant,

Charles Fleetwood.

I desire to heare how my lord
chief justice doth.

8th April, 1654."

Although established on the other side of the Irish Channel Fleet-wood did not cease to take an interest in what was happening at home and abroad, though Cromwell and Thurloe were apt to forget him in the pressure of nearer events. It was evidently difficult on occasions for Fleetwood to procure enough money to carry on an efficient government.

"Sir,

I have sent you heere inclosed some letters which came to my view uppon the occasion of an unexpected providence, and hath here a very deepe resentment among some good men, as indeed I thinke there is just cause, if what is alleged therein be true. Though I am satisfied that my lord protector's heart abhors, that any disturbance should be given to any good people whatsoever; yet indeed I look uppon it as a duty uppon you, to beare the utmost witness against these peace breakers; for certainly the enemies of our spiritual as well as civill peace, doe much boast and hope for an advantage against good men; and the sooner that spiritt be crushed, the more shall we discharge our duty to the Lord, and those that feare him. There is some sadness on good people here because of such reporte. I know it will much trouble our dear lord protector, that any under his government should thus insult. There are some precious good people in Wales, though very few: the generality of people in those parts, I fear, are little better than the Irish; they have invenomed hearts against the wayes of God, and we very well know, were the forwardest and greatest promoters of the King's interest in the time of war, and therefor ought to be particularly to be looked after. I doe earnestly desire you will make inquiry into this business, and to take care, that sober good men may be put into the magistracy there, and that you would get a troop of horse or two to quarter in North Wales and the like in South Wales, to suppress the cavaleering spirit. . .

Your very affectionate frinde and servant,

Charles Fleetwood.

Phenix, 28th April, 1654."

On 17th May, 1654, Fleetwood wrote from Cork that he thought the peace with the Dutch a great advantage to the Protestant cause: —

"I am very glad our act for navigation is preserved and certainly that act privately made with the states of Holland is very honest and honourable."

On 2nd June, he wrote a warning letter: —

"We have ground to believe, that the Irish have some desperate thing in design to execute speedily and to believe that the late bloody intentions to my lord's own person was part of this designe; and that the contrivers in England, both cavaliere and Irish are engaged in one business. I therefore begge you will suffer no Irishman, under what pretence so ever, to come neare my lord's person, though he comes with my own licence."

The situation in Ireland was evidently none too easy, for on 28th June, Fleetwood wrote: —

". . . I must tell you if wee have not a speedy supply of moneys sent, we shall be in a great necessity. . . I hope the vaine reports of men will not be credited to the losse of mens lives and perishing for want. It is not heere as in England or Scotland that they can live upon the country, when they have no money; but most of our forces lye in wasted country, and oftnesses must have supplies sent them."

On 8th August, he wrote to the Protector himself: —

"May it please your Highnes, I have only a most faithfull heart to your highnes to pleade with your highnes, why I shoulde be so left alone, as a person allmost forgotten since this last charge. But wer it myselfe only concerned, I hope I should be contented with anything; but indeade your affayres here have and doe very much suffer through want of a settlement. . . I know your highnes burdens. I showld rather choose to beare more than add to yours; which make me thus abrupt, who am

>Your Highnes most obedyent
>and most dutyfull sonne
>>Charles Fleetwood.

My deare wife's most humble duty to your highness and my lady. Her time now drawes neare. The remembrances of hir condicion before the lord I doubt not."

Again on 27th September, he wrote to Thurloe from Dublin: —

"I must once more earnestly desire you will let me know whether 'tis intended we shall have 32,000 per mensem continued to us; without which I must tell you plainly, I doe not see how we shall be able to pay the forces."

At the end of 1654, and the beginning of 1655, Fleetwood was able to assist Cromwell in Scotland by dispatching troops to him there. Evidently he felt out of things and thought Cromwell should have kept him better informed as to what was afoot. He sent these letters to Thurloe: —

"Sir,

I doe very much wonder to receive the good newes from Scotland which you sent, and yet a positive command from his highnes to send presently a regiment of horse to Scotland, which at this time of yeare is very difficult; but it shall be obeyed. Shipps must be pressed from Chester side to Knockfergus. Indeade I think it somewhat strange, I showld no more understand in any thing more than what is communicable to every one. I suppose ther may in thes dayes be more privat resolves, which out of curiosity I should not much care for, but so long as providence continues me in this condicion, I thinke it might be for his highnes service, I should know more than I doe, I thankfully acknowledge your correspondencyes. . . The army heare is still through mercy in a very good condicion and firme to my lord protector. . .
15th December, 1654."

"Sir,

I have writt so largly to my lord protector that I have not time to adde much. I have according to his highnes commands

order'd about 3000 to be at waterside the 8 inst. and will I presume, be at Liverpoole about the 14 of this month, unlesse contrary order come. . . I intend the commissary general shall command them. He hath a desire to it: the Lord prevent any occasion for to use them. It woulde be a sadde houre, especially if good men should so divide; but I trust the lord will give a healing spirit, and prevent such sadde effects of division. I feare not the old enimy, but to see saint against saint is sadde, and hath bine for thes last 2 yeares strangely encreasing, and few sensible hearts thereof. . .
3rd January, 1655."

Fleetwood was always in favour of rule by parliament and religious toleration, and these letters to Thurloe give his views: —
" Sir,
I should rejoyce, if the Lord please so, to heare, that there was a probabilitie of a good understanding betwixt my lord protector and parliament; which if not, I know my lord wil be forced to put for the something to a publicque view, uppon which will depend great part of our future quiett and peace; and therefore as comprehensive as possible you can uppon those two essentials, which hath bine hitherunto the great incouragements to those, who have continued faithfull to the publicque interest, will certainly be of very necessary and great concernment; I meane that, which concernes our civill and religious liberties, that of tender consciences and successive parliaments, without perpetuities. I know this business is to great for me to venture on, and it is the Lord alone, that must direct you to a right ordering of this affaire. . . "
" I am very glad to hear his highness hath declined the legislative power, which by the instrument of government in my opinion he could not exercise after this last parliament's meetinge; and therefore those things, which wee heare are attempted to be done in England concerninge Ireland, will be prevented, through want of that power. . . "

The chief duty that Fleetwood had to carry out in Ireland was to superintend the transplantation of condemned Irish landholders to Connaught and the settlement of disbanded soldiers on their confiscated estates. He himself fully believed in the policy he was carrying out, but many did not. Vincent Gookin published a book against transplantation which irritated Fleetwood, and made him eager to take steps to punish him: —
" There is a very strange scandalous book, intitled ' Arguments against Transplantation ' that is now come forth, which doth verie falsely and unworthily asperse those, that did and now doe serve the state heere. The person who is said to write this, will, I doubt, as much deceave your expectation in England, as he hath bine disingenuous to us heere, who have bine ready on all occasions to show respect to him; but those who know him better than I doe, have before this tyme bespoken what manner of spirit he was of, which I in too much charitie did hope had bine otherwise. . . "

In another letter to Thurloe he set out some of the difficulties he had experienced in carrying out his policy: —

"You may please to remember that I gave you my feares and thoughts, that the worke of transplatation might receive some obstructions from England, through misrepresentations, and that you may not be deceaved into a prejudice against the worke by what reports may come from hence, by reason of some late orders. I shall give you a brief account thereof, that upon our journey we found officers objecting in several places, that some of our own orders had obstructed the work of transplantation . . . the words of the order were so penned, as gave them libertie to keep Irish proprietors on there estates, which words were disowned by most of the councell, not to be within there intentions to grant; and we finding those orders to be pretended hinderers of the work, wee did recall them; the orders themselves alsoe giving us a libertie therein, they being but till further order. This is a true state of the case; and though I should be willing to incourage and gratifye these persons wherein I may, yet to obstruct so good and necessary a work for my particular interest, it would be against our trust. I clearly see that we must encounter with more and more difficulties, when the adventurers and soldiers are in possession, Irish tenants being easier to get, and of more present profitt than English. . . "

One of the most pleasant traits of Fleetwood's character was his willingness to put in a word for an old comrade-in-arms who had fallen out with authority. He thus interceded for Colonel Alured, Colonel Rich, and Adjutant-General Allen, and only proceeded against Ludlow with the utmost reluctance.

In 1655, Cromwell recalled Fleetwood to England and appointed his own son, Henry, in his place. The reason for this change may have been Fleetwood's support of the anabaptists and other extremer sects at the expense of the Catholics and Presbyterians. He wrote to Thurloe on 7th August: —

"I have now received his highnes positive commands to returne into England, and can now undertake my jorney with much comfort, trusting the Lord hath given mee a call thereunto; and upon that account I have satisfaction, though I expect in no place or condition to be without my trialls. . . I shall endeavour to put things into as good a condition as I can before my returne and make the work easie to my brother as maybe, who though he may have sometimes some melancholy thoughts yet I hope he will find it much better than he may at present expect; and I am confident will find the army as obedient and faithfull to his higher service, as can be expected from men. . . if the Lord pleases I intend to sett forward from hence about the beginning of September: sooner I would, by reason of my wife's condition, but that I fear affairs heere will not permitt it. . . "

At least two months before Fleetwood's letter of 7th August there had been talk of his recall. Carlyle wrote: —"Lord Deputy Fleet-

wood is by some thought to be of too lax a temper for his place . . .
(i.e. towards the Anabaptists and extremer sects). Rumour has even
risen that Henry Cromwell is now sent to supersede him (June, 1655)
which however the Protector expressly contradicts. . . . Some fifteen
months hence Henry is appointed Lord Deputy; Fleetwood in some
handsome way recalled . . . " (i.e. from his position in Ireland as
commander-in-chief of the forces). Nevertheless on 22nd June, 1655,
Cromwell had written him a very friendly letter: —

" Dear Charles,
I write not often: at once I desire thee to know I most dearly
love thee. . . . It's reported that you are to be sent for and Harry
to be Deputy, which truly never entered into my heart. . . . Dear
Charles, my dear love to thee; and to my dear Biddy, who is a
joy to my heart, for what I hear of the Lord in her. Bid her be
cheerful, and rejoice in the Lord once and again: if she knows the
Covenant, she cannot but do so . . . if you have a mind to come
over with your dear wife etc., take the best opportunity for the
good of the Public and your own convenience. The Lord bless
you all. . . .
I rest, your loving father,
Oliver P."

Henry Cromwell was apparently not as well liked by the Anabaptists
as Fleetwood, for on 21st April, 1665, the Protector wrote to his son,
" I think the Anabaptists are to blame in not being pleased with you.
That's their fault. . . . "

Sir Charles Coote wrote to Henry Cromwell on 21st November,
1655: —

" Your excellencie was pleased to lett me know that your lordshipp was informed that there is a petition carryed up and downe
. . . to obtaine subscriptions. which reflects upon my lord
Fleetwood . . . I assure your lordshipp that I heard nothing of
any such matter. . . "

On 2nd December, however, Colonel Hewson, Henry Prittie and
Richard Laurence presented a petition of a very different kind to the
Protector requesting him to send Fleetwood once more to Ireland as
commander, and referring to him in the most flattering terms: —

" May it please your Highness, we came over with you into
Ireland, being well satisfied in your pious conduct . . . and when
your highness was called back into our native country we enjoyed,
by your favour, our dear and precious lord deputy Ireton,
who by his graciousness dispelled wickedness and by his
wisdom so guided the reins of this government that our hearts
were much comforted and hands strengthened in the service of the
publick. But to our great grief, our God for our sins took him
from us . . . the Lord was pleased to move your highness's heart
to send us for our chief commander, our present precious lord
deputy Fleetwood, which was a refreshment to all the godly in
this nation; and his sweet healing peaceable spirit hath not only
drawn over the hearts of some, scrupling in some points con-

cerning the government, so that the most fearing the Lord are convinced there is no other means visible, whereby the interests of God's people can be secured but in your highness's hands . . . (We) humbly implore your highness's favour, that our precious lord deputy may still be continued in his conduct over us, under whom we have enjoyed so much satisfaction, and by whom justice hath been impartially administered to the whole nation . . . and that the chief government of this nation under your highness may rest in the hands of our present lord deputy; and that as soon as publick affairs will permit, he may return to his charge over us. . . ."

Fleetwood had been appointed lord deputy in 1655, and held this post, after his return to England, until replaced by Henry Cromwell in 1657. It is another pleasing aspect of his nature that he was a loyal supporter of his superiors and did not resent others being promoted even at his own expense.

Cromwell seems to have been angered by the petitions and cross-petitions organised by the supporters of Fleetwood and Henry Cromwell, and decided to leave the former as Lord Deputy and the latter as Commander-in-Chief of the forces in Ireland for the time being. Neither Fleetwood nor Henry Cromwell had anything to do with getting up the petitions. Henry Cromwell, however, had noticed the weak spot in Fleetwood's policy, for he had written to Thurloe, " I have taken the freedom to be very plain with my brother (i.e., Fleetwood) . . . I doe think he is a little too deeply ingaged in a partial affection to the persons of the Anabaptists to answer your end: though I doe believe it rather to proceed from tenderness than love to their principles . . . " Soon after sending Fleetwood to Ireland the Protector had written to him, " The Lord give you abundance of wisdom and faith and patience. Take heed also of your natural inclination to compliance." Fleetwood sincerely wished to be fair and hold the balance evenly between the various sects, but was too tolerant towards those noisiest in complaining of intolerance with the result that one sect was on occasion too much favoured. After Fleetwood had left for England Henry Cromwell experienced the same doubts as had the former. Money was short, and it was often difficult to pay the army. He felt that Fleetwood and others in England were neglecting him, and consequently became suspicious, and misunderstandings arose between them. Fleetwood, perhaps, was busy with matters nearer at hand which seemed more important than far-away problems in Ireland.

On 24th November, 1657, he wrote to Henry Cromwell: —

" Deare Brother,

I have not heard anything from Ireland this 2 or 3 weekes, and we have little of anything of importance to impart to you . . . I doubt not but Mr. Secretary will inform you of the fresh intelligence we receive of new designes from our old enemy, in order to our disturbances, who have layd their buyness with that confidence that they think nothing can disapoynt them: but our comfort is that they consider not that the Lord is above them . . . I think you will do well to be the more carefull; for no question but the designe is generall, and will concern all parts to be in readynes; . . . We have newes, which I canot be confydent of, that the Sweeds have entered Sealand; which if true, is of great importance. . . "

On 15th December, 1657, Fleetwood wrote again to Henry Cromwell. There had evidently been a disagreement regarding a reduction in the size of the army maintained in Ireland: —

"I perceive you are pleased to have a very ill resentment of what past heare, in order to the buisnes of reducement; wherein had I bine guilty I should readily confesse it; but if upon a mistake you misaprehend me, I hope you will excuse me if I say, I am not deservedly blamed in this action; and so great a desire have I of being deare in your opinion as to all things, in which I may be concerned relating to yourselfe, that I shall presume to give the trouble of an account concerning that affayre.

The counsell considering, how much the charg exceeded their revenue, did referre the consideration how to lessen the present charge, by reducing what we could with safety the forces in the three nations . . . and as for what you mention concerning the arrears, it's very well known, that I did argue that case even to anger; and all that could be answered was, the necessityes we are in for want of money . . . Ther was a clause in your letter, which I would not willingly understand, that you had not bine well dealt with. Indede if you mean myselfe, give me leave to say, I never did deale unworthily with any person, much lesse with yourselfe; and really whilst you listen to reports, or take actions in the worst sence, I shall still have cause to bewaile my former unhappyness in being misunderstood by you . . . "

Henry Cromwell replied: —

"Dear Brother,

. . . besides, I hope I should be able to rectify the misunderstanding (if any remain) which others have been working between us, which indeed I look upon as a great mercy . . . "

On his return to England Fleetwood at once took a leading place at Court, and was appointed one of the major-generals having charge of Norfolk, Suffolk, Essex, Oxford, Cambridge, Huntingdon and Buckingham. He strongly opposed the suggestion that Cromwell should take the title of King, though in every other respect he was in complete agreement with the Protector. In foreign affairs he believed Cromwell to have been " particularly raised up to be a shelter to poor persecuted Protestants in foreign parts." Cromwell's own wife was opposed to him taking the title of King, and went as far as to advise her husband to secure the return of Charles II, pointing out the certain ruin of his family in the event of a restoration. She received a very realistic and typical reply: "You are a fool. Charles Stuart can never forgive me his father's death, nor the injustice he has suffered from me, and if he can, he is unworthy of the crown." Mrs. Hutchinson, however, said that, " Oliver's wife and children were setting up for principality, which suited no better with any of them than scarlet on the ape. Only to speak the truth of Oliver himself, he had much natural greatness and well became the place he had usurped. His daughter Fleetwood was humbled, and not exalted with these things; but the rest were insolent fools."

It would seem from a statement of Bishop Burnet that Fleetwood had a decisive influence in causing Cromwell to give up the idea of taking the title of King. " Before the day in which he refused the offer of the Kingship that was made to him by the Parliament, he had kept himself on such a reserve that no man knew what answer he would give. It was thought more likely he would accept it: but that which determined him to the contrary was, that, when he went down in the morning to walk in St. James's Park, Fleetwood and Desborough were waiting for him: the one had married his daughter, and the other his sister. With these he entered into much discourse on the subject, and argued for it: he said, it was a tempting of God to expose so many worthy men to death and poverty when there was a certain way to secure them. The others insisted still on the oaths they had taken. He said, these oaths were against the power and tyranny of Kings, but not against the four letters that made the word King. In conclusion, they, believing from his discourse that he intended to accept of it, told him, they saw great confusions would follow on it: and as they could not serve him to set up the idol they had put down, and had sworn to keep down, so they would not engage in anything against him, but would retire and look on. So they offered him their commissions, since they were resolved not to serve a King: he desired they would stay till they heard his answer. It was believed, that he, seeing two persons so near him ready to abandon him, concluded that many others would follow their example; and therefore thought it was too bold a venture. So he refused it, but accepted of the continuance of his protectorship . . ." According to Ludlow, Cromwell met Desborough alone in the Park, and on another occasion took Fleetwood with him to dine with Desborough and " began to droll with them about monarchy and speaking slightly of it said it was but a feather in a man's cap, and therefore wondered that men would not please the children and permit them to enjoy their rattle. But he received such an answer from them as was not at all suitable to his expectations or desires."

On 23rd February, 1658, Fleetwood again wrote to Henry Cromwell, referring to the Protector's poor state of health: —

" Union in the armyes, and to speake one thing, is very desirable at this time. I presume Mr. Secretary hath given you an account of the grounds his highnes went upon in dissolving the parliament; since which time, through his highnes indisposition of health, little hath bine done in publicke affayres; . . . this providence of his highnes illness hath much retarded our result. We have had intelligence of the caviliers design to transport men from Flanders . . . We have many enemyes; they compasse about lik bees . . . "

The Protector's health did not improve and on 31st August,

Fleetwood wrote one more to Henry Cromwell: —

"The Lord's hand hath bine very sorely upon us in the continuance of his highnes under a very great distemper, called an ague, but mostly his heate gave us the sadde apprehension of danger he was under; . . . but the Lord is pleased to give some little reviving this evening. After few slumbering sleepes his pulse better, his water good all this day, till now at night ther hath bine very great feares, what the wombe of to-morrow might have brought forth . . . "

On the following day Dr. Thomas Clarges wrote to Henry Cromwell that Fleetwood had ordered the army to observe a fast for his father. It was of no avail and on 7th September Fleetwood wrote: —

"Deare Brother,

the sadde condition, wherein the Lord is pleased to lay us under by this late grevious stroake, is, I doubt not, com to your hands before this, though the particulers thereof, is referred to this bearer's relation, who deserves respect from us. Oh! that the Lord would give us hearts to search and try our wayes, and turn to him, who hath thus sorely smitten us! Great displeasur is broken forth. We have cause to lay our mouths in the dust and to say, We have sinned; that we have great cause to bewaile; else there would not have beine such a sore rebuke . . . the Lord keeps the army in a quiet condition, and have expressed a readyness to what is don, by their attendance and affection in what was required or expected from them, though I think with the saddest hearts reflecting upon what they lost, as ever army did, who have not lost a generall and protector only, but a dear and tender father to them and all the Lord's people; . . . he hath left us a blessed example for us to walke by, his heart was full of love to the interest of the Lord's people, yea above all other concernments; and made everything else bow down unto it . . . "

It is thought that Cromwell some time before his death nominated Fleetwood as his successor and left a letter to this effect. Thurloe writing to Henry Cromwell says: " . . . it is certain that he had and sealed it up in form of a letter and directed it to me . . . but kept the paper himself and that after he fell sick at Hampton Court, he sent Mr. John Barrington for it, telling him it lay upon the study table at Whitehall, but it was not found there, nor elsewhere though it had been narrowly looked for." Some think that one of the Protector's daughters, knowing its contents, destroyed it.

Fleetwood played a leading part in the elevation of Richard Cromwell to the lord protectorship, presented the army's loyal address and wrote to Henry Cromwell expressing joy at his brother's peaceable accession. Richard Cromwell appointed him lieutentant-general of all the army, and commander-in-chief under himself. Friction arose, however, between the army and parliament, and on 22nd April, 1659, Fleetwood forced the Protector to dissolve Parliament by a military demonstration. Fleetwood wished to remain on good terms with Richard Cromwell, and intended no disloyalty to him. The minor officers favoured the revival of the Long Parliament and the setting up of a republic and this caused dissension among the officers, and resulted in Fleetwood and his supporters losing influence as they were "looked upon as self-seekers in that they are for a protector now they have got a protector of wax whom they can mould as they please, and lay aside when they can agree upon a successor." There is, however, no doubt that Fleetwood was a loyal supporter of Richard Cromwell and had no intention of deposing him. The Long Parliament was recalled, and Lambert was re-admitted to the army, which did much to weaken still further Fleetwood's position. On the surface he appeared more powerful than ever, and was appointed a member of the committee of safety on 7th May, one of the council of state on 13th May, and commander-in-chief of the army on 9th June, " . . . giving and granting to the said Charles Fleetwood full power and authoritie to conduct and lead the said armies and forces, and every part thereof against all enemies, rebells, traytors, and other like offenders against this commonwealth . . . " These powers however were only to last " during the continuance of parliament, or till parliament should take further order." The situation which had arisen since the death of Cromwell revealed only too well that there was no one capable of acting with his vigour and determination. It was obvious that the Royalists were daily increasing their activities, but still the disputes between the army and parliament continued. Fleetwood, an able military commander and administrator, seems to have been no politician. Indeed with the exceptions of Julius Caesar, Napoleon and Cromwell himself, few have excelled equally on the field and in the council chamber. Cromwell might have said as Napoleon did: " In general there are very few real statesmen. I certainly possess the most capable ministers in all Europe, but it would soon be seen how far they fall short of their reputation if I no longer put the wheel in motion."

After the suppression of Sir George Booth's rising a letter of intelligence from The Hague, dated 5th March, 1660, said: " The Lord Lambert had lately done so well, dissipating the insurrection of Booth; others likewise; but what doth doing well signify, unless a man persevere? Men know how to overcome others but not themselves. Everybody laughs at the lord Fleetwood and Disbrowe. In short we laugh at all. Those gentlemen seem to have been drunk with their fortune, ' dulci fortuna ebrii.' Wise and prudent men know, that it is a mere folly, yea madness, to be at difference, and that the greatest states of the world crumble to dust through civil dissensions; yet there is hardly one, that will yield a little to preserve the whole." This reveals the ardent hopes with which the supporters of Charles II were now inspired.

After the death of Cromwell it had been evident to the Royalists that of all his supporters Fleetwood was the most to be dreaded, for he was a man of principle. Thus when he was seen to be in difficulties, with the foundations of republicanism cracking beneath his feet, and many of his colleagues openly advocating the restoration of the monarchy, they made him the chief victim of their jubilant lampoons and pamphlets, expressing their hatred, fear, and hopes in such phrases as , " Fleetwood has now nothing to do but to seek the Lord, for his army will no more be found." " Fleetwood has fallen like an ass under the burden." " Fleetwood's whining should not excuse his treasons." And, " Fleetwood sits peaking in his chamber at Wallingford House, as if it were moulting time with him and all birds of his feather."

Lambert petitioned that Fleetwood should be made permanent commander, and most of the other officers supported him. Parliament, however, cashiered nine leading officers, and declared Fleetwood's commission to be void. The command was now vested in seven commissioners, of whom Fleetwood was one. His wife told Ludlow, " that her husband had been always unwilling to do anything in opposition to the parliament, that he was utterly ignorant of the contrivance of the officers at Derby to petition the parliament in so insolent a manner, and had not any part in their proceedings upon it afterwards." On 12th October, Lambert violently expelled the parliament and went north to meet General Monck leaving Fleetwood to maintain order in London. The latter attempted to justify the conduct of the army: " I dare say our design is God's glory. We have gone in untrodden paths, but God hath led us into ways which, if we know our own hearts, we have no base or unworthy designs in. We have no design to rule over others." Royalist agents now began to approach Fleetwood, and in particular his brother, Sir William, and Bulstrode Whitelocke urged him to declare for a free parliament, and to negotiate with Charles II. Fleetwood missed his opportunity of doing this through loyalty to Lambert, and Charles II was restored without his aid.

It was General Monck who most accurately interpreted the feeling of the times. He saw that what most people wanted was a free parliament, and that this would, beyond doubt, mean the restoration of Charles II to the throne of his father. He accordingly advanced into England from Scotland with his well disciplined army and set up his headquarters at Coldstream on the Tweed. Later it was from his men that the Coldstream Guards, the Grenadiers and Household Cavalry were formed. Fleetwood said: " God has forsaken me and therefore I will meddle no more with the business of this world." He was also alleged to have said that, " God had spit in his face and would not hear him," which set the Royalist poets, now confident of a restoration, in high glee producing such doggerel verses as : —

> " Then suddenly Fleetwood fell from his grace,
> And now cries, Heaven has spit in his face,
> Tho' he smelt it came from another place."

Fleetwood now passes out of the limelight into retirement. He had behaved honestly and sincerely, and accurately stated his own case when he wrote to Henry Cromwell, " you know my state and condition, I cannot make an advantage of my public employments, as many have, or other suppose I doe." Clarendon summed up his character: —

"The character which we have always received of the man is not such as makes him equal to any notable design or to be much relied on tomorrow for what in truth he resolved to do yesterday. However, as his wit is not so great as some of the rest, so his wickedness is much less apparent, and therefore industry and dexterity must be used to dispose and confirm him in his good inclinations and let him take his own time for the manifestation of it."

Samuel Pepys noted in his diary on 31st January, 1660: —

"Called in at Harper's with Mr. Pulsford, servant to Mr. Waterhouse, who tells me that whereas my lord Fleetwood should have answered to the Parliament to-day, he wrote a letter and desired a little more time, he being a great way out of town. And how that he is quite ashamed of himself, and confesses how he had deserved this, for his baseness to his brother. And that he is like to pay part of the money, paid out of the Exchequer during the Committee of Safety, out of his own purse again, which I am glad of."

Monck succeeded in restoring Charles II and personally greeted him on the beach at Dover with every sign of loyalty and affection. The Rev. Thomas Jackson in his lecture on Stoke Newington depicts Fleetwood in his house in Church Street "trembling over the progress made at Breda for bringing home King Charles II, . . . and weeping over the loss of the sceptre offered him so often by the pretorian guards." As Fleetwood did not come to live in Church Street until three years after the return of Charles II, we can dismiss the story of his trembling and weeping as nothing more than an ardent Royalist's wishful thinking. He had taken no part in the trial of Charles I and as both Monck and Lord Lichfield spoke for him, his only punishment was to be declared "perpetually incapacitated from all offices of trust." He lost his wife Bridget in June, 1662, and she was buried at St. Anne's, Blackfriars, on 1st July. Eighteen months later he married at the same Church on 14th January, 1664, Dame Mary Hartopp, widow of Sir Edward Hartopp, the second baronet, and daughter of Sir John Coke. The entries relating to this marriage read: —

(1) "Charles Fleetwood, Esq., of Feltwell, in the Co. of Norfolk, widower, aged about fifty, to marry Dame Mary Hartopp of Newington, Middlesex, widow, aged about forty. They are to marry at St. Anne, Blackfriars: St. Mary Colechurch, London, or Newington aforesaid."

(2) "1664. Jan. 14. Charles Fleetwood, Esq. and Madame Mary Hartof."

Other entries in the registers of St. Anne's relating to Fleetwood are: —

"1646, Dec. 2nd. A still born child of Colonel Charles

Fleetwood and Frances his wife.
 1651, Nov. 24th. Lieutenant-Generall Fleetwoods wife.
 1662, July 1. Col. ffleetwood second wife."

$$\boxed{\text{VII}}$$

On 15th March, 1658, Arthur Annesley wrote to Henry Cromwell: —

" . . . Dr. Owens hath gathered a church in the Independent way and the Lord Fleetwood, Lord Desborough, Lord Sidenham, Berry, Goffe and divers others were admitted members since my last, which hath divers constructions put upon it and is not that I can heare very well liked at Whitehall."

John Owen (1616-1683) was born at Stadham. He made rapid progress at a private school and was only twelve when admitted a student of Queen's College, Oxford. On 11th June, 1632, he became B.A., and on 27th April, 1635, when only nineteen, M.A. He continued at the University, but when, in 1637, Laud drew up, as Chancellor of Oxford University, a new body of statutes, Owen was unable to submit and left the University. He acted as chaplain to Lord Lovelace, presumably the father of John, Lord Lovelace, who succeeded Sir William Fleetwood at Woodstock Park. When the Civil War broke out he sided with Parliament. Lord Lovelace accordingly dismissed him, and his uncle, a rich man without children who had made him his heir, disinherited him. He then came to London and went through a period of considerable spiritual conflict. One Sunday he went to Aldermanbury Church to hear the celebrated preacher, Edmund Calamy. Some unexpected circumstance prevented Calamy from preaching and an unknown minister from the country took for his text, "Why are ye fearful? O ye of little faith." Owen left the church with the darkness of his mind removed and his doubts resolved. In 1642 he published his "Display of Arminianism" in which he said, "Never were so many prodigious errors introduced into a church, with so high a hand, and with so little opposition, since Christians were known in the world. The chief cause I take to be that which Eneas Sylvius gave, why more maintained the Pope to be above the Council, than the Council above the Pope. Because Popes gave archbishopricks, and bishopricks, but the Councils sued in 'forma pauperis'; and therefore could scarce get an advocate to plead their cause." As a result of this publication he was presented to the living of Fordham in Essex, where he met and married his first wife. The sequestered incumbent, Richard Pully, died soon afterwards, whereupon the patron presented another to the living and dispossessed Owen. It is interesting to note that the parliamentary presentations did not deprive the patron of a living permanently of his rights, but only during the life of the ejected minister. The Earl of Warwick now presented Owen to the living of Coggeshall about five miles from Fordham. Until coming to Coggeshall he had inclined towards Presbyterianism, but now became an Independent and formed his church on Congregational principles.

During the siege of Colchester he acted as chaplain to Lord Fairfax. In January, 1649, Owen was called to preach before Parliament on the day after the execution of Charles I. Cromwell heard him for the first time and was so impressed that he insisted on Owen accompanying him to Ireland, and later to Scotland. In 1652 he preached Ireton's funeral sermon.

In September, 1652, Owen became Vice-Chancellor of Oxford University; Cromwell having been chosen Chancellor in the preceding year. Anthony à Wood gives an interesting, if hostile, account of Owen's manners and conduct. " He endeavoured to put down habits, formalities and all ceremony, notwithstanding he had before taken an oath to observe the statutes and maintain the privileges of the University. While he did undergo the said office, he, instead of being a grave example to the University, scorned all formality, under-valued his office, by going in quirpo, like a young scholar, with powdered hair, snake-bone band-strings or band-strings with very large tassels, lawn band, a large set of ribbands pointed at his knees, and Spanish leather boots, with large lawn tops, and his hat mostly cocked."

When Parliament and the army were at cross purposes in 1659, Fleetwood and Desborough invited Owen and Dr. Manton, late Rector of Stoke Newington, to their consultations at Wallingford House. Owen offered an opening prayer, and Manton coming late heard a loud voice from within saying, " He must down, and he shall down." Manton knew the voice to be Owen's and for some reason understood him to be urging the deposition of Richard Cromwell and therefore did not go in. Fleetwood, as we have seen, loyally supported Richard as Protector. After the Restoration, Clarendon received Owen with respect and advised him to occupy himself with writing against the Roman Catholics and not to disturb the peace by keeping conventicles. Nevertheless, nonconformists suf-fered considerable persecution, and Owen must have enjoyed few emoluments from his religious work. His books no doubt brought him in a small income, and in 1668 his relative, Martyn Owen, a rich London brewer, died leaving him a handsome legacy. In 1671 he was invited to become the President of Harvard but declined the honour. Supporters of the established church continued to attack him. He was denounced by the Rev. George Vernon as "the Ahithophel of Oliver Cromwell—a blasphemer and perjured person, and a libeller of authority after the restoration of Charles II, a praiser of God for shedding the blood of Christian Kings." In 1672 Charles II issued a declaration of indulgence suspending the penal laws against nonconformists. Many scrupled about availing them-selves of this privilege on the ground that the King by dispensing with the laws of Parliament in ecclesiastical matters had assumed an illegal power.

In 1673 Mr. Joseph Caryl, pastor of a congregation which met in Leadenhall Street, died and his church was amalgamated with Owen's. This is the origin of the famous church in Mark Lane.

Fleetwood, Sir John Hartopp, Lady Hartopp, Desborough, Lady Abney, and in due course Mrs. Bendysh, were all members, and later Isaac Watts was to be its minister. Lady, or rather Mrs. Abney, for her husband had not then been knighted, was a daughter of Joseph Caryl. In 1700 Sir Thomas Abney married again, his second wife being the daughter of John Gunston. She, too, became a member of the church. Caryl had first preached at his own house in Bury Street after being deprived of the living of St. Magnus. He left behind him one hundred and thirty-six communicants; Owen brought with him thirty-five, so the united church consisted of one hundred and seventy-one members. Owen's successors were David Clarkson, Isaac Loeffs, and Isaac Chauncey. It was during Loeffs' pastorate that the congregation moved to Mark Lane.

Owen married for the second time in 1677. His wife was Michel, widow of Thomas D'Oyley. She brought him considerable property. After his death she remained a member of the Mark Lane church under Clarkson, Loeffs, Chauncey and Watts, the last of whom preached her funeral sermon in 1703. Owen's health was now declining and he was often for long spells unable to carry out his duties. In the last year of his life there was a contemptible but unsuccessful attempt to involve him in the Rye House plot to murder the King and the Duke of York. Not long before he had gone to live at Kensington and from there he moved to a house of his own at Ealing. He died there on the 24th August, 1683, and was buried in Bunhill Fields. Almost his last act had been to dictate a letter to Charles Fleetwood, with whom he had been on terms of close friendship for over thirty years. It is not improbable that Fleetwood met his third wife, Lady Mary Hartopp, among the congregation at Owen's first Independent church in London.

Anthony à Wood says, " Owen's personage was proper and comely, and he had a very graceful behaviour in the pulpit; an eloquent elocution; a winning and insinuating deportment; and could, by the persuasion of his oratory, in conjunction with some other outward advantages, move and wind the affections of his admiring auditory almost as he pleased. He was well skilled in the tongues, Rabbinical learning and Jewish rites and customs."

In 1657 Owen was drawn into one of the numerous arguments on the meaning of the word, " Schism," and produced, " Of Schism, the true nature of it discovered and considered, with reference to the present differences in religion." Hales wrote: —

" Schism has long been one of those theological scare-crows, with which they, who wish to uphold a party in religion, use to frighten such, as making any inquiry, are ready to relinquish or oppose it, if it appear either erroneous or suspicious."

And as Vincent Alsop wittily said: —

" Schism is an ecclesiastical culverine, which being overcharged, and ill managed, recoils and hurts the canoneer. He that undertakes to play this great gun had need to be very careful, and spunge it well, lest it fire at home."

Owen argued that the separation of an individual from any church on the ground of conscience is not the sin of schism, an interpretation which, if generally accepted, would abolish one of the most fruitful causes of theological argument.

Needless to say rival sects from whom the Independents had attracted converts did not agree, and Mr. Daniel Cawdry, the Presbyterian, wrote a pamphlet, " Independency, a Great Schism," the very first sentence of which is, " The crime of Schism is so heinous in itself, and so dangerous and noxious to the cause of God; that no invectives against the evils of it can well be too great or high," which is what every church or party claiming for itself an exclusive monopoly of the truth always has and doubtless always will maintain.

Owen and Fleetwood had been close friends for over thirty years, and Owen must often have been a guest at his friend's house. The following entries in the Stoke Newington parish registers probably refer to two of Owen's children, all of whom predeceased him: —

" 1664. Judeth, the daughter of Mr. John Owen was buryed the 29th of May.

1665. Mathw, the daughter of Mr. . . . Owing, was Buryed the 9th of April in ye year 1665."

In 1721 a complete collection of Owen's sermons was published and Sir John Hartopp, the third Baronet, contributed many manuscripts. It is probable that he had inherited them from Fleetwood whose friendship with Owen had been much closer than his own.

When in 1664 Fleetwood moved into his wife's house in Church Street he brought with him his two children by his first wife, Smith Fleetwood and Elizabeth Fleetwood; two children, possibly more by his second wife, Cromwell Fleetwood and Mary Fleetwood, and his second wife's three daughters by her first marriage, Jane, Bridget and Elizabeth Ireton. There were also his third wife's two children by her first marriage, John and Mary Hartopp. Sir John Hartopp, the third baronet, was the eldest of these children, having been born in 1637, his sister Mary in 1639, Smith Fleetwood in 1644, and Cromwell Fleetwood in 1653. The great house must have been a lively place with so many young people living in it.

One of Fleetwood's children by his second wife, Anne, had died very young and been buried in Westminster Abbey. One of the first things the Royalists did after the restoration was to see that the bodies of all prominent supporters of Cromwell were exhumed and removed from the Abbey, and among these was that of Anne. Cromwell's own body, with that of Ireton, was taken up and conveyed to the Red Lion Inn in Holborn. The bodies were then drawn on sledges to the gallows, taken out of their coffins, hanged up till sun set, then beheaded, and the trunks thrown into a hole beneath the gallows. The heads were set upon poles at Westminster Hall. These indignities were inflicted on the anniversary of the death of Charles I. The Royalists must have looked upon the poet who, years before had celebrated Cromwell's fall from the box of his coach, as something of a prophet: —

> " Every day and hour hath shew'd us his power,
> But now he hath shew'd us his art.
> His first reproach was his fall from a coach,
> His next will be from a cart."

Indignities of this kind were not of course inflicted on Anne Fleetwood's body. On the whole the Royalists behaved with considerable restraint after the restoration, and, apart from the Regicides, few suffered.

It was not long before romance blossomed among the young people in Fleetwood House, and the families of Fleetwood and Hartopp were united by a double marriage. Sir John Hartopp married Elizabeth Fleetwood in 1666, and Smith Fleetwood married Sir John's sister, Mary.

Fleetwood himself now led a very retired life, his main interests being centred on religious matters. He was a member of the congregation of Dr. Owen's Church and a very close friend of his, and no doubt frequently entertained him as a guest. Several of Owen's

written very near the end of Owen's life. The following letter which
refers to the illness of Owen's own wife is the earliest: —

"I received yours, and am glad to hear of your welfare; there
is more than ordinary mercy in every day's preservation. My
wife, I bless God, is much revived, so that I do not despair of her
recovery; but for myself, I have been under the power of various
distempers for fourteen days past, and do yet so continue. God is
hastening his instruction concerning the approach of that season,
wherein I must lay down this tabernacle. I think my mind has
been too much intent upon some things, which I looked on as
services for the Church, but God will have us know, that he has
no need of me nor them, and is therefore calling me off from
them. Help me with your prayers, that I may through the riches
of his grace in Christ, be in some measure ready for my account.
The truth is, we cannot see the latter rain in its season, as we have
seen the former, and a latter spring thereon: death, that will turn in
the streams of glory upon our poor withering souls, is the best
relief. I begin to fear that we shall die in this wilderness; yet
ought we to labour and pray continually, that the heavens would
drop down from above, and the skies pour down righteousness,
that the earth may open and bring forth salvation, and that
righteousness may spring up together. If ever I return to you in
this world, I beseech you to contend yet more earnestly, than ever
I have done with God, with my own heart, with the Church, to
labour after spiritual revivals. Our affectionate service to your
Lady, and to all your family that are of the household of God. I
am, &c."

The next letter was written in 1682 as the "Mr. C" referred to
can be identified as David Clarkson, chosen as co-pastor with Owen
in July, 1682. He was a fellow of Clare Hall, Cambridge, tutor to
Archbishop Tillotson and author of several learned works.

"The bearer has stayed long enough with us, to save you the
trouble of reading an account of me in my own scribbling; a
longer stay I could not prevail with him for, though his company
was a great refreshment to me. Both you and your whole family,
in all their occasions and circumstances, are daily in my thoughts;
and when I am able to pray, I make mention of you all without
ceasing. I find you and I are much in complaining: for my part I
must say, and is there not a cause? so much deadness, so much
unspirituality, so much weakness in faith, coldness in love, instability in holy meditations, as I find in myself, is cause sufficient
of complaints; but is there not cause also of thanksgiving and
joy in the Lord? Are there not reasons for them? When I begin
to think of them I am overwhelmed; they are great, they are
glorious, they are inexpressible. Shall I now invite you to this
great duty of rejoicing more in the Lord? Pray for me that I may
do so; for the near approach of my dissolution calls for it earnestly:
my heart has done with this world, even in the best and most
desirable of its refreshments: if the joy of the Lord be not now

strength unto it, it will fail. But I must have done. Unless God be pleased to affect some person or persons, with a deep sense of our declining condition, of the temptations and dangers of the day, filling them with compassion for the souls of men, making them fervent in spirit in their work, it will go but ill with us. It may be these thoughts spring from causeless fears; it may be none amongst us has an evil a barren heart but myself; but bear with me in this my folly; I cannot lay down these thoughts until I die; nor do I mention them at present, as though I should not esteem it a great mercy to have so able a supply as Mr. C but I am groaning after deliverance; and being near the centre, do hope I feel the drawing of the love of Christ with more earnestness than formerly: but my naughty heart is backward in these compliances. My affectionate service to Sir John Hartopp and his lady, and to the rest of your family when God shall return them unto you. I am, &c.

J. Owen."

Owen's final letter to Fleetwood is dated 22nd August, 1683, two days before his death: —

"Although I am not able to write one word myself, yet I am very desirous to speak one word more to you in this world, and do it by the hand of my wife. The continuance of your entire kindness, knowing what it is accompanied withal, is not only greatly valued by me, but will be a refreshment to me, as it is even in my dying hour. I am going to him whom my soul has loved, or rather, who has loved me with an everlasting love; which is the whole ground of all my consolation. The passage is very irksome and wearisome, through strong pains of various sorts, which are all issued in an intermitting fever. All things were provided to carry me to London to-day, according to the advice of my physician, but while the great Pilot is in it, the loss of a poor under-rower will be inconsiderable. Live and pray, and hope and wait patiently, and do not despond; the promise stands invincible, that he will never leave us nor forsake us. I am greatly afflicted at the distemper of your dear lady. The good Lord stand by her, and support and deliver her. My affectionate respects to her and the rest of your relations, who are so dear to me in the Lord. Remember your dying friend with all fervency. I rest upon in that you do so, and am yours entirely.

J. Owen."

Fleetwood, in the following year, lost his wife, who died on 17th December, 1684, and was buried in Bunhill Fields. It must indeed have been a sad time for him. Within eighteen months his best friend and his wife had both died. Further trouble was soon to fall upon him as a result of the opinions of his son-in-law, Sir John Hartopp, now a member of Parliament, who attracted attention to himself by his advocacy of the Exclusion Bill aimed at preventing the Duke of York (openly a Roman Catholic) succeeding to the throne.

Soon after James II became King " the informers broke in upon Sir John Hartopp and Mr. Fleetwood and others at Stoke Newington to levy distresses for conventicles," and fines of £7,000 were imposed. The Middlesex Sessions records for July, 1686, state that, " Paul Warren (Wallyn), John Webb, Stoke Newington headboroughs, and John Saywell, constable, were ordered to attend the Court on Friday and bring with them the warrants under which they have distrained on the goods of Sir John Hartopp, Charles Fleetwood, Smith Fleetwood, John Gould (or Gold), Thomas Spencer, and William Coward under the Act for the suppression of Seditious Conventicles."

During the period 1662-1689 the Hearth Tax was imposed on all houses except the smallest cottages. The rate was two shillings on each hearth. " Lady Hartop " was assessed on twenty-five hearths, easily the greatest number in Stoke Newington, indicating that Fleetwood House was the biggest house in the district.

In 1679 Fleetwood's son, Cromwell Fleetwood, had married Elizabeth Nevill, and on 21st February, 1677-8, his daughter, Mary, had married, at Stoke Newington, Mr. Nathaniel Carter of Great Yarmouth, a merchant aged about forty. At one time writers considered that Mary Fleetwood was the daughter of Ireton and had changed her name because of her mother's remarriage to Fleetwood. This, however, is not so. She was the daughter of Fleetwood by his second wife, Bridget (Cromwell-Ireton-Fleetwood). The entry in the Stoke Newington registers is correct: —

" 1677-8 Mr. Nathaniel Carter of Yearmouth, and Miss Mary ffleetwood, were married by licence the 21st of ffeb. 1677."

On her monument in the Church of St. Nicholas, Yarmouth, her name is given as " Mary Fleetwood."

Another entry in the Stoke Newington registers caused great difficulty until cleared up by Colonel Chester in " Notes and Queries ": —

" 1681. Bridgett ffleetwood was buried ye 5th of September in Wollen, according to an Act of Parliament in yt Case provided, as was attested within ye time limited before Justice Cheyney: Church."

Robinson in his " History of Stoke Newington " quoted from Strype's edition of Stow's " Survey " the inscription on a monument in Bunhill Fields: —

" Charles Fleetwood, Esq., and Dame Mary Hartopp his wife. He departed 4th October, 1692, aged 74: she December 17, 1684," and added, " this was the Lord General, but must be a mistake in styling Dame Mary Hartopp his wife; she may very probably have been his son-in-law's mother."

As we have seen, Bridgett Cromwell-Ireton-Fleetwood had been already dead eighteen years before the entry was made in the Stoke Newington registers. It seems likely that the Bridget Fleetwood referred to was a daughter of Smith Fleetwood and Mary Hartopp, but her identity has never been definitely established.

Fleetwood died in 1692 and was buried in Bunhill Fields. His will, of which the following is an abstract, was proved in November of the same year: —

"I, Charles ffleetwood, of Stoke Newington, in the County of Middlesex, Esqr, being, through the mercie of the Lord, in health and memory, do make, etc. First I commend my Soule and Spirit into the hands of my gracious God and father, through our Lord Jesus Christ, by the Holy Spirit enabling me to lay hold upon the imputed Righteousness of Christ for my Justification, and in the vertue of that righteousness doe I hope to stand at the greate day of the Lord. My body to be buried in the same grave, or as near as may be to my last dear wife. Debts, wages, etc., to be paid within one year of death. To my daughter, the Lady Elizabeth Hartopp, £100, as a last expression of my thankfulness for her constant deare love and duty shee hath alwayes manifested unto me. I give unto deare daughter Carter £100. To my cousin Mary Waterson £20, over and above the £20 my last dear wife owed her by bond, which I now direct my executor to pay. To Ann Pace £10 for myself, and £10 more which my last wife gave her. (Two devises left blank follow.) I give to the poor distressed people of God £200, such as my executor, with two of my trustees hereafter named (Sir John Hartopp to be one) shall think fit objects of charity; £10 to be paid to the poor of that Society with whom I have had Christian Comm'ion in the gospel; as also £6 to my ancient friend James Berry, Esqr, and £3 to Mr. Howard, Minister of the Gospel at Cambridge, and Mr. Pelloe, Minister of the Gospel at Sudbury; and £2 to any others that I shall name in a paper behind me. I give and devise to Sir John Hartopp, Bart., Samuel Desborrow, Doctor of Physic; Capt. John Nicholas, and Nathaniel Gould, merchant, their heirs and assigns, all my Manor or Lordship of Burrough, alias Burrugh Castle, co. Suffolk, in trust to pay legacies, etc., and afterwards to convey same to my son and heir, Smith Fleetwood, and his heirs for ever. To each of my said trustees £5 for mourning. And whereas there is a debt due to me from my son Bendish, my will is that my executor shall not demand the said debt until God shall in his providence make a comfortable provision for his wife and children. My son Smith Fleetwood to be sole executor.

Signed January 10th, 1689, in the presence of Edward Terry, Mary Waterson, and John Wealshdale."

In it he mentions "his last dear wife," and directs that he be buried "in the same grave or as near as may be to her." In 1869 when the cemetery was re-opened as a public garden Fleetwood's monument was found seven feet below the surface of the ground and restored at the expense of the corporation.

*

Meantime Sir John Hartopp and his wife had been living and bringing up a family alongside Fleetwood's in the other half of the house. Sir John unlike his father and grandfather seems to have spent most of his time in Stoke Newington rather than on his Leicestershire estates at Freeby and Buckminster. He was one of the most eminent lay nonconformists of the time and at a very early age had joined the Independents. That he was absolutely sincere in his views is shown by his staunch adherence to his religion through the reigns of Charles II and James II, although heavily fined and put to much other inconvenience. On the 17th April, 1682, he was " chosen one of the Churchwardens and overseers for the Poore for the ensuing year." It was probably known that he would not accept the offices but he seems to have escaped payment of the usual fine unlike Defoe when chosen Churchwarden some years later. The entry in the vestry minutes continues: " which said offices he cannot attend by reason of his oft absence from his dwelling and other affairs, and having desired that Mr. Edward Carpenter one of the Churchwardens for the last year might execute and serve the said offices which is accepted of. Therefore the said Edward Carpenter is chosen one of the Churchwardens and overseers for the poor for the ensuing year and the said Sir John Hartopp excused therefrom."

In 1671 Sir John was High Sheriff for Leicestershire and in 1681, and on two other occasions, was chosen representative for his native County in Parliament.

Numerous children had been born to Sir John and his wife, but as was so often the case in those days many of them died very young. Charles died in 1672, Anne in 1674, Edward in 1679, John in 1679 and Helen in 1691. A second John was born in 1682, and lived to be the fourth and last Hartopp baronet. Dr. Owen wrote the following letter to Lady Hartopp on the occasion of the death of one of the children: —

" Dear Madam,

Every work of God is good; the Holy One in the midst of us will do no iniquity; and all things shall work together for good unto them that love him, even those things which at present are not joyous, but grievous; only his time is to be waited for, and his way submitted unto, that we seem not to be displeased in our hearts, that he is Lord over us. Your dear infant is in the eternal enjoyment of the fruits of all our prayers; for the covenant of God is ordered in all things, and sure: we shall go to her, she shall not return to us. Happy she was in this above us, that she had so speedy an issue of sin and misery, being born only to exercise your faith and patience, and to glorify God's grace in her eternal blessedness. My trouble would be great, on the account of my absence at this time from you both, but that this also is the Lord's doing; and I know my own uselessness wherever I am. But this will I beg of God for you both: that you may not faint in this day of trial; that you may have a clear view of those spiritual and temporal mercies wherewith you are yet entrusted, all undeserved; that sorrow of the world may not so overtake your hearts, as to disenable to any duties, to grieve the Spirit, to prejudice your lives, for it tends to death. God in Christ will be better to you than ten children, and will so preserve your remnant, and so add to them, as shall be for his glory and your comfort; only consider, that sorrow in this case is no duty, it is an effect of sin, whose cure by grace we should endeavour. My heart is with you, my prayers shall be for you, and am, &c.

J. Owen."

Owen also wrote to Sir John at a time when Lady Hartopp seems to have been very ill : —

"My duty, my obligations, and my inclinations, do all concur in the esteem I have for you both; and I do make mention of you daily in my poor supplications, and that with particular respect to the present condition of your lady. That God who hath revealed himself unto us, as the God who heareth prayer, will yet glorify his name, and be a present help unto her in the time of trouble. In the meantime, let her, and you, and me, strive to love Christ more, to abide more with him, and to be less in ourselves. He is our best friend. I pray God with all my heart, that I may be weary of every thing else but converse and communion with him; yea of the best of my mercies, so far as at any time they may be hindrances thereof. My wife presents her humble service unto your lady and yourself, as doth also, Sir,

J. Owen."

The first of Owen's letter, that to Lady Hartopp, was printed in the appendix to Asty's " Memoirs of Dr. Owen, 1721," a work which Sir John assisted Mr. Asty in writing, and no doubt he supplied a copy of this letter together with copies of Owen's letters to Fleetwood.

In 1696 Sir John decided that it was time he obtained a resident tutor for his son and heir, and invited Isaac Watts to come and live at Fleetwood House. It is possible that he had heard of Watts from a member of the Mark Lane church, or from the Rev. Thomas Rowe, head of the Academy at Newington Green

IX

Isaacs Watts was born at Southampton on the 17th of July, 1674. He was a sickly child which is perhaps not surprising as his father was in and out of Southampton Gaol at this time for his nonconformist views, and his mother, of an excitable and worrying disposition, was consequently in a poor state of health. Being debarred from the usual rough boyish sports young Isaac was early attracted to learning, and whenever a few pence were given him he would say to his mother " A book, a book! Buy me a book!" When he was six years old he was sent to Southampton Grammar School, then kept by the Rev. John Pinhorne. In 1683 his father was again imprisoned. A note in his son's handwriting says: " My father persecuted, and imprisoned for Nonconformity, six months; after that forced to leave his family and live privately in London for two years." The accession of James II, described by Thomas Bradbury as " a monster with the fumes of popery in his head and the spirit of it in his heart," greatly alarmed nonconformists and caused the elder Watts to lie low for a further period. Great importance was of course attached in the Watts' household to family prayers, and it is recorded that Isaac's early propensity for making rhymes once earned him a severe reprimand from his father. While prayers were being said he was heard to titter, and when asked why he replied: " Because I saw a mouse running up that bell-rope by the fireplace, and the thought came into my mind,

' There was a mouse for want of stairs,
Ran up a rope to say his prayers.' "

Watts left school in 1690, and it was decided that he should go to the Nonconformist Academy at Newington Green, then kept by the Rev. Thomas Rowe, who was also minister of the church that met at Girdler's Hall in Basinghall Street. Watts became very attached to Rowe and in later years wrote:

" I love they gentle influence Rowe,
Thy gentle influence, like the sun,
Only dissolves the frozen snow,
Then bids our thoughts like rivers flow,
And choose the channels where they run."

In 1694 Watts left the Academy and returned to Southampton where he remained during the next two and a half years.

In the autumn of 1696 Watts received the invitation from Sir John Hartopp to return to Stoke Newington and live at Fleetwood House as tutor to his family, and in particular to his son and heir, John. He accepted the offer and wrote in his diary, " Came to

Sir John Hartopp's, to be a tutor to his son, at Newington ... Oct. 15, 1696." No doubt he also performed the duties of Chaplain. Watts regarded teaching as both a pleasure and a noble occupation for he wrote to a schoolmaster: "Youth, my dear friend, is the time to acquire knowledge; and as you have the important charge laid upon you of instructing some of the rising generation, let me beg, as you wish well to your precious and immortal soul, that you will leave nothing undone to make your pupils love the beauties of religion. Teach them that religion has nothing in it of a gloomy nature; for how can that be gloomy which leads to everlasting pleasures?" And again, "How lovely is it to see a teacher waiting upon those that are slow of understanding, and taking due time and pains to make the learner conceive what he means without upbraiding him with his weakness."

It always pleased Watts to assist his pupils by writing books and verses for them. In 1700 he wrote: —

"The Disdain
To John Hartopp, Esq.

I.

HARTOPP, I love the Soul that dares
　　Tread the Temptations of his Years
　　Beneath his youthful Feet:
FLEETWOOD and all thy heavenly Line
Look thro' the Stars, and smile divine
　　Upon an Heir so great.
Young HARTOPP knows this noble Theme
That the wild Scenes of busy Life,
The Noise, th' Amusements, and the Strife
Are but the Visions of the Night,
Gay Phantoms of delusive Light,
　　Or a vexatious Dream.

II.

Flesh is the vilest and the least
　　Ingredient of our Frame:
We're born to live above the Beast,
　　Or quit the manly Name.
Pleasures of Sense we leave for Boys;
Be shining Dust the Miser's Food;
Let Fancy feed on Fame and Noise,
Souls must pursue diviner Joys,
　　And seize th' Immortal Good."

It was also at this time that he wrote his "Logic: or the Right use of Reason in the Enquiry after truth," not published until 1724, and parts of the "Improvement of the Mind," published in 1741.

Both of these works were for the guidance of John Hartopp. He also wrote and inscribed the following poem to his pupil, being an imitation of an ode by Casimire: —

"To Sir John Hartopp

Live, my dear Hartopp, live to Day,
Nor let the Sun look down and say,
    Inglorious here he lies,
Shake off your Ease, and send your Name
    To Immortality and Fame,
    By ev'ry Hour that flies.

Youth's a soft Scene, but trust her not:
Her airy Minutes, swift as Thought,
    Slide off the slipp'ry Sphere;
Moons with their Months make hasty Rounds,
The Sun has pass'd his vernal Bounds,
    And whirls about the Year.

Let Folly dress in green and red,
And gird her Waste with flowing Gold
Knit blushing Roses round her Head,
Alas! the gaudy Colours fade,
    The garment waxes old.
Hartopp, mark the withering Rose,
And the pale Gold how dim it shows!

Bright and lasting Bliss below
    Is all Romance and Dream:
Only the Joys celestial flow
    In an eternal Stream.
The Pleasures that the smiling Day
With large Right Hand bestows,
Falsely her Left conveys away,
And shuffles in our Woes.
So have I seen a Mother play,
And cheat her silly Child,
She gave and took a Toy away,
The Infant cry'd and smil'd.

Airy Chance, and Iron Fate
    Hurry and vex our mortal State,
And all the Race of Ills create;
    Now fiery Joy, now sullen Grief,
Commands the Reins of human Life,
    The Wheels impetuous roll;
The harnest Hours and Minutes strive,
    And Days with stretching Pinions drive—
down fiercely on the Goal.

> Not half so fast the Gally flies
>   O'er the Venetian Sea,
> When Sails, and Oars, and lab'ring Skies
>   Contend to make her Way.
> Swift Wings for all the flying Hours
>   The God of Time prepares,
> The rest lie still yet in their Nest
>   And grow for future Years."

It was on his birthday in 1698 that Watts preached his first sermon, and in the following month returned to Southampton where he preached several times. Sir John Hartopp in this year suggested that Watts should be invited to become assistant preacher at the Mark Lane chapel. The suggestion was adopted and Watts took up his duties in February, 1699. He usually preached in the morning and Dr. Chauncey in the afternoon.

Dr. Chauncey was a poor preacher and this famous chapel, situated in the street of "corn and wine," had been declining since the days of Dr. Owen. Watts on the other hand was a brilliant orator, but owing to ill-health was not an active visitor in the homes of his congregation. He wrote a poem called "Happy Solitude," inscribed to his friend, Thomas Gunston, which seems to refer to complaints and to vindicate his retired life: —

"To Thomas Gunston, Esq.

> The noisy World Complains of me
> That I should shun their Sight, and flee
>   Visits, and Crowds, and Company.
> Gunston, the Lark dwells in her Nest
>   Till she ascend the Skies;
> .... And in my Closet I could rest
> Till to the Heavens I rise.
>
> Yet they will urge, ' This private Life
> Can never make you blest,
> And twenty Doors are still at strife
>   T'engage you for a Guest.'
> Friend, should the Towers of Windsor or Whitehall
>   Spread open their inviting Gates
>   To make my Entertainment Gay;
> I would obey the Royal Call,
> But short should be my Stay,
>   Since a diviner Service waits
> To employ my Hours at home, and better fill the Day."

While at Fleetwood House Watts had become acquainted with Sir Thomas Abney and his wife, Sarah, daughter of the Rev. Joseph Caryl, who were then living at Highgate Hill. In 1700 Sir Thomas married Mary Gunston, daughter of Mr. John Gunston, after losing his first wife in 1698. To Thomas Gunston, Lady Abney's brother, Watts became much attached and frequently visited the Gunston's home adjoining Fleetwood House, an old mansion standing in very fine grounds. Watts and Gunston used to walk under a row of " reverend elms " or sit at ease in " the wilderness " as they called the shrubbery, or stand on " the mound " overlooking an ornamental lake and an heronry. Thomas Gunston was said to have been engaged to Mary Hartopp and in 1700 he pulled down the old house and began to build a new red-brick mansion with a turret and surmounted with a gilded ball, " the golden sphere " of Watts' poem on Gunston. In 1695 Thomas Gunston had been elected to parish honours, but declined on account of weak health and on the ground that he was deeply engaged in preparations for building his new home—Abney House. One of the front upstairs rooms was known as the Painted Room, its walls being ornamented with illustrations of Ovid's " Metamorphoses." The picture over the fireplace showed Actaeon being turned into a stag with a lake in the foreground. While the artist was absent Watts painted in a swan to the former's great amazement. The two friends often ascended to the turret and there on a bench they

" alone would sit
Free and secure of all intruding feet."

The interior of the house was still unfinished when Gunston was taken ill and died. Watts recorded the event in his diary: " 1700. Nov. 11. Mr. Thos. Gunston dyed," and composed a long funeral poem presented to Lady Abney.

" Oft have I laid the awful Calvin by,
And the sweet Cowley, with impatient eye,
To see those walls, pay the sad visit there,
And drop the tribute of an hourly tear.

Still I behold some melancholy scene,
With many a pensive thought, and many a sigh between.
Two days ago we took the evening air,
I and my Grief . . . .

The unhappy house looks desolate and mourns,
And every door groans doleful as it turns;
The pillars languish . . . while vast emptiness
And hollow silence reign through all the place.

O sacred seat,
Sacred to friendship! O divine retreat.
Here did I hope my happy hours to employ
And fed beforehand on the promised joy.

> When weary of the noisy town, my friend,
> From mental cares retiring, should ascend,
> And lead me thither . . . .
> In the lonesome vault,
> Mindless of Watts and friendship, cold he lies
> Deaf and unthinking clay."

The funeral was on November 22nd, and poor Gunston was borne away to his last rest in the vaults of St. Mary's amid a torrential downpour and every sable embellishment of grief that human ingenuity could devise.

Little can Watts have thought that years later in 1736 he was to return to Abney House as the guest of Lady Abney, to whom the property passed on her brother's death, and that he would spend there not only " happy hours " but happy years.

★

At this time another friend was David Polhill, to whom he was probably introduced by Sir John Hartopp. Polhill was born in 1675. He was the son of Thomas Polhill and Elizabeth Ireton, the daughter of Fleetwood's second wife, Bridget, by her first marriage to Henry Ireton. Polhill sent Watts a satirical poem, " Advice to a Painter," written against William III, and Watts sent him a poem in reply with this letter: —

" To David Polhill, Esq.   1698.

Sir,

When you put this satire into my hand, you gave me the occasion of employing my pen to answer so detestable a writing; which might be done much more effectually by your known zeal for the interest of his majesty, your counsels and your courage, employed in the defence of your king and country: and since you provoked me to write, you will accept of these efforts of my loyalty to the best of kings, addressed to one of the most zealous of his subjects, by

Sir,

Your most obedient servant,

I. Watts."

The House of Commons now tried to thwart the King's plans against France, and Mr. Polhill with four other gentlemen on behalf of the freeholders of Kent, presented a petition to Parliament asking that the King be voted the necessary supplies for carrying on the war. For their pains they were arrested by the sergeant-at-arms and confined in the Gate-house prison. Watts, a great admirer of William III, wrote this poem in December, 1702: —

"To David Polhill, Esq.

An Epistle.

Let useless souls to woods retreat,
Polhill should leave a country seat
When Virtue bids him dare be great.

Nor Kent, nor Sussex should have charms,
While Liberty, with loud alarms,
Calls you to councels and to arms.

Louis, by fawning slaves ador'd,
Bids you receive a baseborn lord;
Awake your cares!   Awake your sword!

Factions amongst the Britons rise,
And warring tongues, and wild Surmise,
And burning Zeal without her eyes.

A vote decides the blind debate;
Resolv'd, 'Tis of diviner weight
To save the steeple than the state!

The bold machine is form'd and join'd,
To stretch the conscience, and to bind
The native freedom of the mind.

Your grandsires' shades, with jealous eye,
Frown down to see their offspring lie
Careless, and let their country die.

If Trevia* fear to let you stand
Against the Gaul with spear in hand,
At least petition for the land."

★

Daniel Defoe, who lived for many years within sight of Fleetwood
House, was also actively concerned in the affair of the Kentish
Petition.   On 14th May, 1701, " guarded with about sixteen gentlemen of quality " he entered the House of Commons and presented
the Speaker with a paper known as " Legion's Memorial to the
House of Commons."   He did not stay for an answer, which was
just as well for it would have needed more than sixteen gentlemen
to protect him if Members of the House had known the Memorial
contained such passages as: —
" And though there is no stated proceeding to bring you to your
duty, yet the great law of reason says, and all nations allow that

*Polhill's wife of the family of Lord Trevor.

whatever power is above law, it is burdensome and tyrannical; and may be reduced by extra-judicial methods. You are not above the People's resentments! . . . For Englishmen are no more to be slaves to Parliament than to a King. Our name is Legion and we are many."

The five gentlemen of Kent were freed, were given a banquet at the Mercer's Hall, and were cheered by crowds their whole way home. Some weeks later Defoe wrote another pamphlet, " The History of the Kentish Petition."

★

Watts' duties at Mark Lane were now taking up more and more of his time, and in 1702 this entry appears in his diary: " This year by slow degrees removed from Newington to Mr. Thos. Hollis's in the Minories." Mr. Hollis was the father of the Thomas Hollis who was such a generous benefactor of Harvard College.

★

Sir John Hartopp was the owner of a house in Church Street, Epsom, and Watts occasionally preached in the Independent chapel which adjoined it. He also accompanied the family to their country house at Freeby, near Melton Mowbray, and conducted the services in the ancient stone meeting house there. In 1905 two stained glass windows were installed in the meeting house, one on each side of the pulpit from which Watts had preached. In that to the left Watts is shown in a preaching gown looking upon a cross. The gown is purple, the shoes brown, the book red, the Cross yellow and the leaves dark green. In that to the right Mistress Mary Hartopp is shown with a spinning wheel. Her bodice is dull blue, with sleeves and panniers of light buff, the dress a deep rich brown and the side hangings bright green. The spinning-wheel is grey, the spaces between the spokes brown and the distaff crimson. The words on the scrolls are: —

" Dr. Isaac Watts in this Building Preached the Cross of Christ," and

" He was Tutor at that time to Mistress Mary Hartopp of Freeby."

The fronts of the scrolls are white and the backs bright crimson.

Presumably the Mary Hartopp depicted in the window is the girl to whom Thomas Gunston was said to have been engaged, and who died in 1749. The Parish Registers record another Mary Hartopp as having married John Allen in 1696. There is, however, no other mention of her. Sir John Hartopp had two sons called John and two daughters called Anne, but this duplication of names only occurred because the first John and the first Anne died very young. Who this Mary Hartopp was is a small mystery which perhaps will never now be cleared up.

$$\boxed{X}$$

Charles Fleetwood's son by his first marriage, Smith Fleetwood, married Mary Hartopp in 1666, and judging from the entries in the Parish Registers he continued to live with his father, or very frequently visited him, until the latter's death in 1692. The entries relating to his family are: —

"1675.   Charles Fleetwood, the sone of Mr. Smith Fleetwood was Buried the 14th May.

1676.   Mr. Charles ffleetwood, the sone of Esqr. ffleetwood was buried the 14th of May.

1680-1.   Mary, the wife of Esqr. ffleetwood ye younger, of this parish was buried ye 21st January in Wollen: Church.

1681.   Bridgett ffleetwood was buried ye 5th of September in Wollen.

1683-4.   A still borne child of Mr. Smith ffleetwood was buried in Wollen ye 31st of January. Anne Fleetwood, the wife of Mr. Smith Fleetwood was buried the 29th of February in Wollen.

1708-9.   Smith Fleetwood, Esq. of the Parish of Armingland, in the county of Norfolk, was byried ye 4th of february. Certified by Erasmus Earle, Esq. J.P. for Norfolk.

1728.   Elizabeth Fleetwood Buried in a velvett coffin in the Church, June 30th.

1731.   Ellen ffleetwood buried in a velvet coffin, July 23rd.

1744.   April 18. Caroline Fleetwood in wollen.

1749.   April 14th. Frances Fleetwood.

1761.   Nov 7. Jane Fleetwood."

The author of " the Bibliotheca Topographica Britannica " writes of Smith Fleetwood and Mary Hartopp: " They had issue two sons and six daughters; Charles Fleetwood of Armingland Hall and Winston, Esq. who died unmarried and was succeeded in his estates by his brother Smith Fleetwood, of Wood Dalling, Esq., at which place he was buried Oct. 28, 1726, aged 52. He married Elizabeth, daughter of Mr. Athill (who was afterwards married to John Gibson, Esq.) by whom he had issue Elizabeth, sole daughter and heiress, married to Fountain Elwin, of Thurning, gent. and buried at Dalling, Dec. 2, 1732, in the 22nd year of her age. She had issue only one child, Fleetwood Elwin, who died young, and was buried at Thurning as his father also was in 1735. Upon her death the estates became the joint property of the survivors of the six sisters of her father the last Smith Fleetwood, who were, 1. Mary, married to the Rev. Abraham Coveney of Oulton in Norfolk, died without issue in 1720, and is buried at Dalling, 2. Frances. 3. Elizabeth. 4. Carolina. 5. Anne, married to William Gosney, died at Boston without issue. 6. Jane. This lady and her sister Frances, the two last descendants

of the male line of the family, resided in a house that they rented of
the lady of the manor, being parcel of the demesne." Miss Jane
Fleetwood left a legacy to the poor of the parish. In another place
the author refers to the entries in the Parish Registers with the
following comments: —

"1676. Mr. Charles Fleetwood, the sone of Esqr. Fleetwood.
This is supposed to be a younger son of the General,
but there is no positive proof of this.

1683-4. Anne Fleetwood, the wife of Mr. Smith Fleetwood.
This was probably the mother of the still-born child of
Mr. Smith Fleetwood in the preceeding entry, and is
supposed to have been a second wife, but there is no
positive proof of this.

1731. Ellen Fleetwood. With regard to her, I have not the
least gleam of information."*

It will have been seen that there are several mysteries here. Neither
the work referred to, nor the Dictionary of National Biography nor
Mark Noble, make any mention of Smith Fleetwood marrying a
second time, but if the entry relating to the death of Mary Hartopp
is correct he was only 36 or 37 at the time of her death and quite
likely to remarry. The entry relating to Bridget Fleetwood can
perhaps be accounted for on the assumption that she was a child
of Smith Fleetwood and his first wife, Mary Hartopp. Another
explanation might be that she was a child of Charles Fleetwood and
his second wife. This is quite likely, as it was usual to call a daughter
after her mother, and there are contemporary references which
suggest that there were more than three children of this marriage—
Cromwell, Anne and Mary. It would seem almost certain that the
two entries relating to Charles Fleetwood are to children of Smith
Fleetwood, who died in infancy, though it is curious that two Charles
Fleetwoods should have died in successive years on the 14th May.
Perhaps the entry was made twice in error. This might be possible
if the entries were allowed to accumulate and were not made correctly
as events happened. A better explanation perhaps is that Smith
Fleetwood was determined that his eldest son should bear the christian
name of his own distinguished father, and therefore repeated the
name Charles until, at the third attempt, a male child survived to
bear the name.

It must be accepted as certain that Smith Fleetwood married three
times. His second wife was called Anne, and died in 1684, and
his third wife, Ellen, survived him many years. There are references
in her will to "her son" Charles, and "daughters" Elizabeth,
Frances, Jane and Carolina. These were actually her step-children,
being the children of her husband and his first wife, Mary Hartopp.
Mr. John Asty is mentioned in her will, and also in the will of
Elizabeth Fleetwood.

John Asty was the son of Robert Asty of Norwich, being born in
about the year 1672. Little is known of his early years, but in his
funeral sermon by John Guyse he is said to have made "thankful

acknowledgments for his privilege in descending from godly parents, and for the advantages received from a religious education." In 1713 he was ordained as pastor to a congregation meeting at Rope-makers' Alley, Moorfields, where he continued until his death in 1730. He had a doctrinal dispute with Martin Tomkins, a non-conformist minister living at Stoke Newington, and was a great admirer of Dr. John Owen. Mr. Asty preached Elizabeth Fleet-wood's funeral sermon at Stoke Newington on 23rd June, 1728, and a sentence in the dedication suggests that he had for a time, prior to 1713, been resident in Fleetwood House. In the sermon he refers to her in the following terms: —

"I could justly say a great many excellent Things of this our dear Friend, whom God has taken away from us, a Person greatly beloved, and deservedly respected by them that knew her. It was not agreeable to her to have any Thing said in her Praise; but I judge it useful and necessary to give some Account of her, that may set forth the Riches, and Glory of Divine Grace, so eminently displayed in her, and at the same Time to commend Religion, in her bright Example, to others, for their Choice and Imitation.

Not to mention her rare Endowments of Nature, or the Quality of her honourable Birth and Education, I shall only observe briefly that she was by Grace; and none more ready to ascribe all to Grace than she was.

It was very evident, she was a sincere, humble Christian, who hated all Guile, and had the lowest Thoughts of herself. She had experienc'd a great and thorough Work in her Conversion, as appear'd in the Progress of her Sanctification, and in her close Walking with God. She had been led by the convincing Spirit into a great Sense of indwelling Sin, which laid a deep Foundation of Humility in her; and the same Holy Spirit had also given her a spiritual Knowledge, and lively Apprehension of the Excellency and Glory of Christ, his Person, and mediatorial Character, and he was exceeding precious to her Soul. She could say with much Satisfaction, Surely in Jehovah have I Righteousness and Strength.

I am not able to describe in Words what I saw and knew of her serious Frame, and holy Walk. She lived much in the View of God, and of the heavenly World. She had a good Judgment, and improved Knowledge of the pure Doctrines of the glorious Gospel. She had a zealous Regard for those Truths of the greatest Importance in our Religion, the Doctrine of the ever blessed Trinity, Election, free Justification by the imputed Righteousness of Christ, Union with him &c. She had a great Sense and Relish of these Doctrines of Grace, and tasted the Joy and Comfort of them in her own Soul.

How unable was she to bear, either the growing Errors, or the spreading Impiety of the Day!

She was a great Lover of Christ, and did shew it in her Value for all that bore his Image: A true Christian Charity and Modera-

tion happily attemper'd and govern'd her Zeal for the Honour of
Christ.

She was eminent for Holiness of Conversation, very tenderly,
and strictly Conscientious. She greatly loved the Habitation of
God's House; and it was an observable Excellence in her, that
she was very devout in Worship: Her Seriousness in that Employment was uncommon. She had such a great sense of God, that
she thought the important Concerns of Religion deserved the
utmost Intention of the Mind. She employ'd much of her Time
in private Exercises of Devotion, wherein she found so much
Pleasure and Advantage. She had no idle Hours, but what she
knew how to fill up to the best Purposes.

She was very affectionate and tender Relative, and faithful
Friend, very desirous of promoting their Welfare both spiritual
and temporal. Indeed, she was of so kind and compassionate a
Disposition, that she sympathized with all about her, and made
their Troubles very much her own. In a word, her Life was
spent in close Communion with God, and she has now changed
her Place (as one said) but not her Company, being admitted into
the immediate Presence, and full Vision of God, Father, Son, and
Holy Ghost.

God has taken her away, but he has taken her to himself, as it
was said of Enoch, Gen.v.20.

It is her unspeakable Gain, but her Removal is a great Loss to
the Family, and to the Church, to which she belong'd; and I
know it is sensibly felt, and tenderly lamented."

The Dedication reads as follows: —
" TO
Mrs. Frances, Mrs. Carolina,
and Mrs. Jane Fleetwood;
and to the other near Re-
latives of that worthy Family.

Honoured Friends,

It is the peculiar Advantage of true Religion, as it is a vital
Principle within, correspondent to the excellent Revelation on which
it is founded, that it furnishes real Christians with the most solid
Grounds of Comfort under the sharpest Trials, and disposes them
to the great Duty of Submission upon the highest Reasons.

It has pleased the All-wise Sovereign to call You to the Exercise
of that Faith and Resignation, that are supported by the divine
Principles of Christianity. His Hand has, of late, made frequent
Breaches in Your Family, and now again has touch'd You very sore.
I heartily condole with You the Loss of so valuable, and dear a
Relative: She is lost indeed to our World, but she is arrived to
immortal Glory, and everlasting Rest is her Gain.

It is the Will of God, that there should be so soon again an
additional Sorrow upon You, by the very sudden Death of one
(i.e. Sir Nathaniel Gould), nearly related to some of You, and

much valued by You all, a very excellent and useful Person; and great Loss it is not only to particular Relatives, but to the Publick.

May such afflictive Providences be very instructive to us who survive, that we may take a more close View of the eternal World, and be excited to the utmost Seriousness and Diligence in a religious Course, being Followers of them, who through Faith and Patience inherit the Promises.

It is an high Honour divine Grace has put upon Your Families, that there have been so many among them truly Pious, and some of them eminently distinguish'd for Their Faith and Holiness, and for Their great Usefulness. The Names of the Fleetwood's and Hartopp's have been for many Years past very honourable in the Churches of Christ, and it is with Pleasure we observe several Branches, and other Relatives of those worthy Families, treading the same Paths of serious Religion and Virtue.

It has been esteem'd a Favour of divine Providence to me, that my earliest Service in the Ministry was devoted to Your Family, wherein I lived many Years; and whatever spiritual Advantage has accru'd to any of You from that Service, I rejoice, and with You desire to ascribe the Glory of all the Success to our gracious God.

I acknowledge with great Thankfulness, the many Instances of that kind Respect I have received from You all, and shall always value the Friendship of Your Families, as a great Privilege and Pleasure of Life.

May the God of all Grace, and of all Comfort, inrich You all with Grace and Peace, comfort You under Your present Trials, and make You great Blessings to each other, in the Continuance of that exemplary Love that has long reign'd amongst You. May You still be more eminent in Piety and Holiness, and at last obtain the Crown of Life; which is the sincere Desire, and earnest Prayer of,

Your most faithful,
affectionate, humble Servant,

July 24, 1728.   JOHN ASTY."

Isaac Watts addressed a poem to Mr. C. and S. Fleetwood, Charles and Smith Fleetwood, sons of Smith Fleetwood: —

" To Mr. C. & S. Fleetwood

Fleetwoods, young generous Pair,
Despise the Joys that Fools pursue;
     Bubbles are light and brittle too,
     Born of the Water and the Air.
Try'd by a Standard bold and just
Honour and Gold are Paint and Dust;
How vile the last is and as vain the first?
     Things that the Crowd call great and brave,
With me how low their Value's brought?

Titles and Names, and Life and Breath,
Slaves to the Wind and born for Death;
    The Soul's the only Thing we have
    Worth an important Thought.

The Soul! 'tis of th' immortal kind,
Nor form'd of Fire, or Earth, or Wind,
    Out-lives the mouldring Corps, and leaves the Globe behind.
    In Limbs of Clay tho' she appears,
Array'd in rosy Skin, and deck'd with Ears and Eyes,
The Flesh is but the Soul's Disguise,
There's nothing in her Frame kin to the Dress she wears:
    From all the Laws of Matter free,
    From all we feel, and all we see,
She stands eternally distinct, and must for ever be.

Rise then, my Thoughts, on high,
Soar beyond all that's made to die;
Lo! on an awful Throne
Sits the Creator and the Judge of Souls,
    Whirling the Planets round the Poles,
Winds off our Threads of Life, and brings our Periods on.
Swift the Approach, and solemn is the Day,
    When this immortal Mind
Stript of the Body's coarse Array
To endless Pain, or endless Joy
    Must be at once consign'd.
The dull unwinding of Life's tedious Thread,
But burst the vital Chords to reach the happy Dead.

And now my Tongue prepares to join
The Harmony, and with a noble Aim
    Attempts th' unutterable Name,
But faints, confounded by the Notes Divine:
Again my Soul th' unequal Honour sought,
    Again her utmost Force she brought,
And bow'd beneath the Burden of th' unweildy Thought.
Thrice I essay'd, and fainted thrice;
Th' Immortal Labour strain'd my feeble Frame,
Broke the bright Vision, and dissolv'd the Dream;
    I sunk at once and lost the Skies:
    In vain I sought the Scenes of Light
    Rolling abroad my longing Eyes,
For all around 'em stood my Curtains and the Night."

This suggests that Watts was very well acquainted with the elder
Smith Fleetwood and his children, and that they were either still
resident in, or very frequent visitors at Fleetwood House up to 1700.
In 1693 Smith Fleetwood and Tobyas Loveday were elected surveyors

by the Parish Council. Fleetwood, however, declined the honour and Charles Deane, farmer, was appointed in his stead.

The statement that Smith Fleetwood, the younger, succeeded to the estates of his elder brother, Charles Fleetwood, is incorrect. In any event, the latter left his Norfolk estates to his sister, Anne Gosney, and Charles Fleetwood, in fact, survived his younger brother by about one year. Smith Fleetwood died in 1726, and Charles Fleetwood died between 30th May, 1727, and 25th November, 1728, though the exact date is not known.

$$\boxed{XI}$$

When in 1663 Charles Fleetwood married, as his third wife, Lady Mary Hartopp, the widow of the second Baronet, he brought with him to Fleetwood House, as we have seen, not only his own children by his first two marriages, but also Henry Ireton's daughters, Jane, Bridget and Elizabeth, who had become his responsibility when he married their mother, Bridget, daughter of Cromwell and widow of Ireton. Their brother Henry seems to have been looked after by his father's relatives and never to have lived at Stoke Newington. All three daughters married. Elizabeth, who was probably the eldest, in 1674 to Thomas Polhill, and Jane in 1668 to Richard Lloyd. Jane's Marriage Licence reads, " 1667-8, Jan. 22nd. Richard Lloyd of St. James's, Duke's Place, London, widower, 30, and Jane Ireton of Newington, Middx., Spinster about 20, her parents dead. Consent of Charles Fleetwood, here father-in-law: at Cheshunt, Herts, St. James's, Duke's Place or Newington, aforesaid." Bridget married Thomas Bendysh in 1669. " 1669, August 24th. Thomas Bendysh of Gray's Inn, Middx. Gent. Bach. about 24 and Bridget Ireton spinster about 19, her parents dead and she living with and at the disposing of Charles Fleetwood, Esq. her father-in-law of Stoke Newington, Middx. who consents: at Stoke Newington, Islington or St. Leonard's, Shoreditch, Middx."

All Cromwell's great qualities were transmitted to his daughters and their descendants and not to his sons, and none was of a more extraordinary character than Bridget Bendysh, who carried a real savour of the great Protector on into the eighteenth century. Mark Noble wrote, "If the reader wishes to know what figure Oliver, the protector, her grandfather would have made in petticoats, I would recommend him to read this lady's character." On one occasion she lay very ill of a fever and her aunt, Lady Mary Fauconberg, and others in the room thinking her asleep or insensible began to talk of the Protector in none too flattering a manner. Suddenly Bridget sat up and rounded on her aunt. " If I did not believe my grandmother to have been one of the most virtuous women in the world, I should consider your ladyship a bastard. I wonder how it could be possible that the daughter of the greatest and best man that ever lived could be so degenerate as not only to sit with patience to hear his memory so ill-treated, but to seem to assent to it." This outburst drove the fever out of her system and she was soon recovered. Dr. J. Brooke has left this description of her. " Splendid, indeed, she never was; her highest dress being a plain silk, but it was usually of the richest sort; though, as far as I can remember, of what is called a quaker's colour; and she wore besides a kind of black silk hood, or scarf, that I rarely, if ever, observed to be wore by ladies of her time; and though hoops were in fashion long before her death, nothing, I suppose, could have induced her to wear one. I can so far recollect her countenance as to confirm . . . her likeness to the best pictures of Oliver; and she no less resembled him in the qualities of enterprise, resolution, courage and enthusiasm. She looked upon him as the first and greatest of mankind, and also as the best; in talking of herself, on the mention of any good quality, she would say she learned it of her grandfather, and would add, if she had anything valuable, she learned it all from him . . . She might be safely trusted with any secret . . . this art of secret keeping, I have heard her say, she learned from her grandfather; for that when she was only six years of age she has sat between his knees when he has held a cabinet-council, and on very important affairs; and on some of them objecting to her being there, he has said 'there was no secret he would trust with any of them, that he would not trust with that infant,' and to prove that he was not mistaken, he has told her something as in confidence and under the charge of secrecy, and then urged her mother and grandmother to extort it from her by promises, caresses and bribes; and these failing by threatenings and severe whippings; but she held steady against all with amazing dispassionate firmness, expressing her duty to her mother, but her greater duty to keep her promise of secrecy to her grandfather, and the confidence he had reposed in her."

Once when travelling by coach she heard a gentleman abuse Oliver's character in the grossest terms. At the first stop she drew another passenger's sword, called the other a poltroon and a coward and challenged him to shew himself a man, and pay no attention to her sex. Needless to say she received a handsome apology.

She always took great interest in public affairs, and used to distribute papers supporting the cause of William of Orange. When he became King in 1688 she was presented to Queen Mary by Archbishop Tillotson. Her brother Henry married the daughter of the Speaker of the new House of Commons and was appointed a Gentleman of the Horse to King William. She was a friend of Dr. Isaac Watts and he wrote this poem, dated 1699, " To Mrs. B. Bendish— Against Tears

> Madam, persuade me Tears are good
>   To wash our Mortal Cares away;
> These eyes shall weep a sudden Flood,
>   And stream into a briny Sea.
>
> Or if these Orbs are hard and dry,
>   (These Orbs that never use to rain),
> Some Star direct me where to buy,
>   One sovereign Drop for all my Pain.
>
> Were both the golden Indies mine,
>   I'd give both Indies for a Tear:
> I'd barter all but what's divine:
>   Nor shall I think the Bargain dear.

But Tears, alas! are trifling Things,
  They rather feed than heal our Woe;
From trickling Eyes new Sorrow springs,
  As Weeds in rainy Seasons grow.

Thus Weeping urges Weeping on;
  In vain our Miseries hope Relief,
For one Drop calls another down,
  Till we are drown'd in Seas of Grief.

Then let these useless Streams be staid,
  Wear native Courage on your Face:
These vulgar Things were never made
  For souls of a superior Race.

If 'tis a rugged Path you go,
  And thousand Foes your steps surround,
Tread the Thorns down, charge thro' the Foe:
  The hardest Fight is highest crown'd."

No doubt she used to visit her old home at Fleetwood House where
Watts was acting as tutor to Sir John Hartopp's son. Watts wrote
another poem, dated 3rd September, 1701, addressed to her second
son, Henry Bendysh, upon his marriage, called "The Indian
Philosopher."

"Dear Sir,
  The following Song was yours when first compos'd: The Muse
then describ'd the general Fate of Mankind, that is, to be ill
match'd; and now she rejoices that you have escaped the common
Mischief, and that your Soul has found its own Mate. Let this
Ode then congratulate you Both. Grow mutually in more compleat
Likeness and Love: Persevere and be Happy.
  I persuade myself that you will accept from the Press what the
Pen more privately inscrib'd to you long ago; and I'm in no Pain
lest you should take Offence at the fabulous Dress of this Poem:
Nor would weaker Minds be scandaliz'd at it, if they would give
themselves leave to reflect how many divine Truths are spoken
by the Holy Writers in Visions and Images, Parables and Dream:
Nor are my wiser Friends ashamed to defend it, since the Narrative
is grave and the Moral so just and obvious.

Why should our Joys transform to Pain?
  Why gentle Hymen's silken Chain
A plague of Iron prove?
Bendysh, 'tis strange the Charm that binds
  Millions of Hands, should leave their Minds
At such a Loose from Love.

In vain I sought the wondrous Cause,
    Rang'd the wide Fields of Nature's Laws,
And urg'd the Schools in vain;
Then deep in Thought, within my Breast
My Soul retir'd, and Slumber dress'd
    A bright instructive Scene.

O'er the broad Lands, and cross the Tide,
    On Fancy's airy horse I ride,
(Sweet Rapture of the Mind!)
Till on the Banks of Ganges Flood,
In a tall ancient Grove I stood
    For sacred Use design'd.

Hard by, a venerable Priest,
    Ris'n with his God, the Sun, from Rest,
Awoke his Morning Song;
Thrice he conjur'd the murm'ring Stream;
The Birth of Souls was all his Theme,
    And half-divine his Tongue.

' He sang th' Eternal rolling Flame,
' That vital Mass, that still the same
    ' Does all our Minds compose:
' But shap'd in twice ten thousand Frames;
' Thence diff'ring Souls of differing Names,
    ' And jarring Tempers rose.

' The mighty Power that form'd the Mind
' One Mould for every Two design'd,
    ' And bless'd the new born Pair:
' This be a Match for this: (he said)
' Then down he sent the Souls he made,
    ' To seek them Bodies here:

' But parting from their warm Abode
' They lost their Fellows on the Road,
    ' And never join'd their Hands:
' Ah cruel Chance, and crossing Fates!
' Our Eastern Souls have dropt their Mates
    ' On Europe's barbarous Lands.

' Happy the Youth that finds the Bride
' Whose Birth is to his own ally'd,
    ' The sweetest Joy of Life;
' But oh the Crowds of wretched Souls
' Fetter'd to Minds of different Moulds,
    ' And chain'd t' Eternal Strife! '

> Thus sang the wond'rous Indian Bard;
> My Soul with vast Attention heard,
>   While Ganges ceas'd to flow:
> ' Sure then (I cry'd) might I but see
> ' That gentle Nymph that twinn'd with me,
>   ' I may be happy too.
>
> ' Some courteous Angel, tell me where,
> ' What distant Lands this unknown Fair,
>   ' Or distant Seas detain?
> ' Swift as the Wheel of Nature rolls
> ' I'd fly, to meet, and mingle Souls,
>   ' And wear the joyful Chain.' "

She had no sense of time and would visit her friends late at night in a chaise drawn by an old mare and without any servant in attendance. " God," she said, " was her guard and she would have no other." While driving, she would sing a psalm or one of Watts' hymns. " On such visits she generally stayed till about one in the morning. Such late visits, in these sober times, were considered by her friends as highly inconvenient, yet nobody complained of them to her. The respect she universally commanded, gave her a licence in this and many other irregularities. She would, on her visits, drink wine in great plenty; and the wine used to put her tongue into very brisk motion; but I do not remember that she was ever disgracefully exposed by it."

Mr. Bendysh died in 1707 and his wife in 1729. About twenty-five years later a Mr. Thomas Gardner, manager of the saltings at Southwold, found in a blacksmith's shop the dies of the first medal awarded to both officers and men of a victorious army, that for Dunbar. One of the dies bore the effigy of Oliver Cromwell. It was then remembered that Mrs. Bendysh had worked some saltings, near Yarmouth, some little distance up the coast, and no doubt the dies had once belonged to her. This effigy is one of the best likenesses of Cromwell and as his grand-daughter was said to be his " living image " the die is now, along with the stories collected by Mark Noble, the only surviving relic of an extraordinary and fascinating character.

Mrs. Bendysh's husband, Thomas Bendysh, of Southtown, near Yarmouth, was a distant relative of Sir Thomas Bendysh who had represented both Charles I and Cromwell as ambassador to Turkey. Sir Thomas Browne, author of " Religio Medici," who lived at Norwich, frequently refers to members of the Bendysh family in his letters. " I remember a woeman who being thirstie in a quartan ague, called for a bottle of beere in the windowe, butt the servant in hast brought her a bottle of Inck wch stood in the windowe, and she dranck a good draught and vomited much and black, and the ague left her. This was about the spring. She was my brother

Bendishes mother, who discovered not the error first, butt vomiting much black matter all her friends dispayred of her."

There were three children of Bridget Bendysh's marriage, Thomas, who died in the West Indies, and by his first marriage had a son, Ireton, who died young, Bridget, who died unmarried in 1736, and Henry, of Bedford Row, from whom the Berners family is descended.

★

Cromwell's daughter, Lady Mary Fauconberg, was a most amiable character, described by Bishop Burnet as both "a wise and worthy woman." Her sympathies seem to have inclined towards the Church of England and the Royalist cause. She and her husband had houses at Chiswick and in Soho Square, which are commemorated by a Fauconberg Road at Chiswick and Falconberg Mews, just off Soho Square. When in town she attended St. Ann's Church, Soho. Pepys, in his diary for 1663 wrote, "I saw my Lord Fauconberg and his Lady, who looks as well as I have known her, and well clad; but when the house began to fill she put on her vizard, and so kept it on all the play; which of late is become a great fashion among the ladies, which hides their whole face." Many years later John Macky described her at her Chiswick House, "I saw here that curious piece of antiquity, the daughter of Oliver Cromwell, still fresh and gay though of great age." She survived until 1713.

XII

After Watts' departure to the Minories Sir John Hartopp no doubt would have frequently invited him to Fleetwood House and gone to the City to hear his Sermons on Sundays. While Watts was still with Sir John the new Abney Chapel had been erected in 1700 on a site on the north side of Church Street, west of Lordship Road. The construction of the Abney House stables caused the first meeting house to be pulled down. Watts frequently preached in the new building, and delivered one of his sermons there on a very sad occasion, the deaths of Lady Hartopp and her daughter, Frances Gould. The final entry in Watts' diary reads: —

"My Lady Hartopp dyed, Nov. 9; and Mrs. Gould, Nov. 15th 1711."

In his funeral sermon Watts paid them this tribute: —

"May I be permitted here," says he, "to make a short reflection on that mournful providence that has joined two lovely relatives in death, and given occasion for the sad solemnities of this day. The pious mother led the way to heaven a few days before the pious daughter followed, each of them the parent of a reputable family, and the decendants from a progenitor whose name is in honour among the churches. As mutual affection joined their habitations in life, so the care of surviving friends has laid them to rest in their beds of earth together. I would copy a line from that most beautiful elegy of David, and apply it here with more justice than the psalmist could to Saul and Jonathan: 'Lovely and pleasant were they in their lives, and in death they were not divided.' Silent were they and retired from the world, and unknown except to their intimate friends. Humble they were, and averse to public show and noise; nor will I disturb their graves by making them the subject of public praise."

Sir John, however, still had six daughters at home to console him in his old age.

Some of Watts' finest sermons were preached on the subject of "Fear." John Flavel's "Treatise of Fear" was dedicated to Sir John Hartopp, and Watts gained inspiration from this work. He described the effect of fear on the body: "The hurry of the natural spirit shakes the whole network of the nerves in a moment; they throw all the blood into the face at once; or by a contrary operation, spread a universal chill and tremour over the body, and clothe the countenance in paleness and the image of death," and many of his hymns and sermons are strong encouragement for the fearful. In Sermon 30 he says: "The man of courage can despise the threatenings of the great, and the scoffs of the witty, conscious of his own integrity and truth. He can face the world with all its terrors and travel onwards in the paths of piety without fear. The righteous man is as bold as a lion."

Sir John Hartopp died in 1722 and was buried at Stoke Newington in St. Mary's on April 11th. Watts delivered his famous discourse on " The Happiness of Separate Spirits," in the Abney Chapel, during the course of which he paid this eloquent tribute to the character of his friend: —

" When I name Sir John Hartopp, all that knew him will agree that I name a gentleman, a scholar, and a Christian. He shone with eminence among persons of birth and title on earth; while his obliging deportment and affable temper rendered him easy of access to all his inferiors, and made him the delight of all his friends. He had a taste for universal learning, and ingenious arts were his delights from his youth. He pursued knowledge in various forms, and was acquainted with many parts of human science. Mathematical speculations and practices were a favourite study with him in younger years, and even to his old age he maintained his acquaintance with the heavenly bodies, and light and shade whereby time is measured. But the book of God was his chief study, and his divinest delight. His bible lay before him night and day, and he was well acquainted with the writers who explained it best. He was desirous of seeing what the Spirit of God said to men in the original languages; for this end he commenced some acquaintance with the Hebrew when he was more than fifty years old; and, that he might be capable of judging of any text in the New Testament, he kept his youthful knowledge of the Greek language in some measure to the latest period of life. Among the various themes of Christian contemplation he took peculiar pleasure in the doctrines of grace, in the display of the glories of the person of Christ, God in our nature, and the wondrous work of redemption by his cross. He adored him as his Lord and his God; and, while he trusted in his righteousness as the great Mediator, and beheld him as his crucified Saviour, he was ever zealous to maintain the honours due to his divine nature and majesty.

His conversation was pious and learned, ingenious and instructive. He was inquisitive into the affairs of the learned world, the progress of arts and sciences, the concerns of the nation, and the interests of the church of Christ, and upon all occasions was as ready to communicate as he was to inquire. There are many of his friends who will join with me to confess, how often we have departed from his company refreshed and advanced in useful knowledge; and I cannot but reckon it among the blessings of heaven, when I review those five years of pleasure and improvement which I spent in his family in my younger part of life, and I found much instruction myself where I was called to be an instructor. His zeal for the welfare of his country, and of the church of Christ in it, carried him out to the most extensive and toilsome services in his younger and middle age. He employed his time, his spirits, his interest, and his riches for the defence of this poor nation, when forty years ago it was in the utmost danger of popery and ruin. His doors were ever open, and his carriage always friendly and courteous, to the ministers of the gospel, though they were distinguished among themselves by names of different parties, for he loved all who loved Jesus Christ in sincerity. He chose indeed to bear a part in constant public worship with the Protestant dissenters, for he thought their practices more agreeable to the rules of the gospel. He joined himself in communion with one of their churches, which was under the pastoral care of the Rev. Dr. John Owen, where he continued an honourable member under successive pastors to the day of his death. Nor was he ashamed to own and support that despised interest, nor to frequent those assemblies, when the spirit of persecution raged highest in the days of King Charles and King James the Second. He was a present refuge for the oppressed, and the special providence of God secured him and his friends from the fury of the oppressor. He was always a devout and diligent attender on public ordinances till the last years of his life, when the infirmities of age coming upon him confined him to his private retirements. But if age confined him, death gave him a release. He is exalted now to the church in heaven, and has taken his place in that glorious assembly, where he worships among them before the throne. There he has no need to relieve his memory by the swiftness of his pen, which was his perpetual practice in the church on earth, and by which means he often entertained his family in the evening worship on the Lords day with excellent discourses, some of which he copied from the lips of some of the greatest preachers of the last age. There his unbodied spirit is able to sustain the sublimest raptures of devotion, which run through the worshippers in that heavenly state, though here on earth I have seen the pious pleasure too strong for him, and, while he has been reading the things of God to his household, the devotion of his heart has broken through his eyes, has interrupted his voice, and commanded a sacred pause and silence."

From an account in Walter Wilson's " History and Antiquities of Dissenting Churches," it seems that the eminent nonconformist divine, John Shower, retired to Stoke Newington in 1713, after partially recovering from a paralytic stroke, and was on intimate terms with Sir John Hartopp, and Sir Nathaniel Gould. He was, therefore, a visitor to Fleetwood House, and may even have stayed in it as a guest. Shower was born at Exeter in 1657, and received part of his education at Newington Green under Charles Moreton. Dr. Manton, rector of St. Mary's during the Protectorate, encouraged him to become a candidate for the ministry. In 1683 he made a tour on the continent with Sir Samuel Barnardiston's nephew. On his return James II succeeded to the throne, and he found it advisable once more to go abroad, this time to Holland, where he first resided at Utrecht, and then became lecturer to the English church at Rotterdam. In 1690, after the accession of William III he returned to England as assistant to Mr. John Howe in Silver Street. Soon after he became minister to a congregation in Jewin Street. He died in 1715 and was buried at Highgate.

In 1725 Watts began a theological duel with the Rev. Thomas Bradbury who held that Watts was a Socinian and a traitor to the faith and said, "I heard and saw the holy Sir John Hartopp, with tears running down his cheeks lament your opposition to Dr. Owen (i.e. to his doctrines) which he imputed to an instability in your temper and a fondness for your own inventions." Watts dealt satisfactorily with Bradbury's arguments, but made no mention of Sir John Hartopp in his reply.

Mr. Bradbury was a great supporter of the House of Hanover and never feared to speak out when he felt duty required him to do so. Queen Anne always called him, "bold Bradbury." He strongly objected to Watts' version of the psalms, and never allowed his own congregation to sing them. The clerk on one occasion unluckily gave out a stanza from Watts, and was reproved with the words, "Let us have none of Watts' whims." Bradbury thought Watts had taken too great liberties with the originals, and many dissenters were even opposed to choral services. As Dr. Speed wittily wrote: —

> "So far hath schism prevailed, they hate to see
> Our lines and words in couplings to agree,
> It looks too like abhorred conformity:
> A hymn so soft, so smooth, so neatly dress'd,
> Savours of human learning and the beast."

Once at a meeting of nonconformist ministers Watts, being in weak voice, had difficulty in making himself heard. Bradbury called out, "Brother Watts, shall I speak for you?" "Why Brother Bradbury," replied Watts, "you have often spoken against me."

{XIII}

Sir Nathaniel Gould was born in 1661, the son of John Gould of London and Bovingdon. The latter died in 1695, and was buried at St. Olave's, Hart Street, the church in which his son had been baptised on the 3rd December, 1661. In 1688, Sir Nathaniel married Frances Hartopp, daughter of the third baronet. He was a director of the Bank of England from 1697 to 1728, Deputy Governor from 1709 to 1711, and Governor from 1711 to 1713. In spite of his banking activities he also carried on business as a Turkey merchant in the parish of All Hallows the Great, and found time to represent Shoreham in Parliament from 1700 to 1727. He was knighted in 1721, and in 1726 his book " An Essay on the Public Debts " was published.

This little book, as might be expected, was of rather a technical nature being packed with figures to support the author's views, but the following short extract gives a glimpse of Sir Nathaniel's style : —

" It is vain to suppose that the necessary expences of a Government are to be supplied by any Taxes that are no ways burthensome to the whole or some part of the Community, and consequently to which some Objections may not be dressed up by persons interested in avoiding them; which Objections however, when such Taxes appear necessary, it is unreasonable to propose or aggravate. I shall not therefore point out any Inequality or Hardship that I may apprehend to be in the ordinary annual Provision made amongst us by a Land Tax; but content myself with making some observations, tending to recommend the greatest part of the Duties now appropriated to the Payment of our Debts, as the most convenient and reasonable Taxes to supply the ordinary Expence of our Government when redeemed by the Payment of those Debts."

Stoke Newington conferred on him an additional minor honour by electing him their surveyor in 1695. He was clearly a sound well-educated man with wide interests, and living in an age which had not succumbed to the curse of over specialisation was able to indulge those interests to the full.

Robinson in his " History of Stoke Newington " says that Sir Nathaniel Gould built an entirely new wing to Fleetwood House with the express purpose of leaving the Hartopps in undisturbed possession of the older part. Architectural evidence does not support this theory, though there is no doubt that large alterations and improvements were carried out about 1711. It is probable that Gould moved into the part of the house in which Fleetwood had lived soon after the latter's death, and that he was already installed by the time Isaac Watts came to live in the older part, for Watts addressed a poem to Gould in 1704 containing a reference to his business as a Turkey merchant : —

"To Nathanael Gould.

'Tis not by Splendour, or by State,
    Exalted Mien, or lofty Gait,
My Muse takes Measure of a King:
If Wealth, or Height, or Bulk will do,
She calls each Mountain of Peru
    A more Majestic Thing.
Frown on me, Friend, if e'er I boast
O'er Fellow-Minds enslav'd in Clay,
Or swell when I shall have engrost
A larger Heap of shining Dust,
And wear a bigger Load of Earth than they.
    Let the vain World salute me loud,
My thoughts look inward, and forget
    The sounding Names of High and Great,
The Flatteries of the Crowd.

When Gould commands his Ships to run
    And search the Traffick of the Sea,
His Fleet o'er takes the falling Day,
And bears the Western Mines away,
Or richer Spices from the rising Sun:
    While the glad Tenants of the Shore
Shout, and pronounce him Senator,*
Yet still the Man's the same:
For well the happy Merchant knows
    The Soul with Treasure never grows,
Nor dwells with airy Fame.

But trust me, Gould, 'tis lawful Pride
    To rise above the mean Controul
Of Flesh and Sense, to which we're ty'd;
This is Ambition that becomes a Soul.
We steer our Course up thro' the Skies;
    Farewel this barren Land:
We ken the heavenly Shore with longing Eyes,
There the dear Wealth of Spirits lies,
And beckoning Angels stand."

Gould enlarged the Fleetwood property by several purchases of
adjoining land and improved it in many ways. In the minutes of
the Vestry meetings held on the 15th August, and 26th of September,
1709, appear the following resolutions: "Agreed that this parish is
willing to settle four families of the Palatines, to the number not
exceeding 20 persons, at the rate of £5 per head, provided that
other parishes do the same. Sept. 26. Resolved, That the Churchwardens and Mr. Thomas Thompson do agree with some person to
build four houses in the parish field. Resolved, That Nathaniel

*M.P. for the Sussex port of Shoreham.

Gould, Esq. do choose two families of the Palatines to be inhabitants of two of the said houses."

The " Palatines " were poor destitute persons from Germany who had been driven from their homes by the military operations of the French. Most of them were Protestants. A great outcry was raised against their being settled in England.

" Those who advised the bringing in the Palatines," says Swift in one of his Examiners, " were enemies to the kingdom;" and in another of those papers he adds, " Some persons, whom the voice of the nation authorized me to call her enemies, taking advantage of the general naturalization act, had invited over a great number of foreigners of all religions, under the name of Palatines, who understood no trade or handicraft, yet rather chose to beg than labour; who, besides infesting our streets, bred contagious diseases, by which we lost in natives thrice the number of what we gained in foreigners. The House of Commons, as a remedy against this evil, brought in a bill for repealing that act of general naturalization; which, to the surprize of most people, was rejected by the lords. And upon this occasion I must allow myself to have been justly rebuked by one of my weekly monitors, for pretending in a former paper, to hope that law would be repealed; wherein the Commons being disappointed, took care however to send many of the Palatines away, and to represent their being invited over as pernicious counsel." To the same purpose, in his " History of the Four last Years of Queen Anne," the Dean repeats, " Whether bringing over the Palatines were a mere consequence of this law for a general naturalization; or whether, as many surmized, it had some other meaning; it appeared manifestly, by the issue, that the publick was a loser by every individual among them; and that a kingdom can no more be the richer by such an importation, than a man can be fatter by a wen, which is unsightly and troublesome at best, and intercepts that nourishment which would otherwise diffuse itself through the whole body."

The Palatines, however, or the great majority of them, were honest and hardworking and proved an asset wherever they settled.

In 1711 he lost his wife who died within a few days of her mother. There were two daughters of the marriage, Mary and Elizabeth.

Gould himself lived on till 1728, dying in Fleetwood House on 21st July. He lived an active public life until the end. He was buried at Bovingdon, where there is a monument, an altar tomb in the churchyard, with the sole inscription " Vir Honestus." Mr. J. R. Spratling in his " The Story of Church Street," says that the well-known writer, the Rev. Baring Gould, undertook to repair this tomb, but " found to his chagrin, when the work was finished, that he had spent his money on the grave of an entire stranger, for the families were in no way connected."

Sir Nathaniel Gould left his Stoke Newington property to his daughter Elizabeth, wife of Thomas Cooke, for life, and then to his male heirs.

★

Sir Nathaniel Gould's eldest daughter Mary married Sir Francis
St. John, Bart., of Longthorpe in the county of Northampton. This
marriage provided one more link with the family of Cromwell, for
Sir Francis St. John was the grandson of Oliver St. John, Lord
Chief Justice of the Common Pleas, and a cousin by marriage of the
Great Protector.

Oliver St. John received his education at Queen's College, Cambridge, and Lincoln's Inn. He soon became an eminent pleader, and
an opponent of all Charles I's arbitrary proceedings. He was, however, averse to the execution of his sovereign. Cromwell sent him to
Holland as ambassador, where he became embroiled with Prince
Edward, son of Elizabeth of Bohemia. Mark Noble relates that
Prince Edward met St. John at a turn-stile, at Verhout, where the
prince, with his sister Henrietta upon his arm, had walked out for
the air; he expected St. John, who came at that instant, to wait till
he and his sister had passed, but St. John regarded his quality as
ambassador, and to put a slight upon a prince of the blood,
endeavoured to force his way first, upon which the prince pulled off
his hat, calling him many opprobrious names, as dog and traitor, and
saying, " learn traitor to respect the relation of the King they lord."
St. John, with as little respect replied, " I regard neither thee nor
the person thou speakest of, but as a race fugitive," and it was with
difficulty they were prevented fighting.

When Charles II returned he is thought to have saved his life by
making heavy payments to the right persons, but was debarred from
holding any further public offices. He was married three times. His
first wife was the sole heir of Sir James Altham, maternally descended
from the Cromwells, by whom he had four children including Francis
St. John, father of the first baronet. His second wife was Elizabeth
Cromwell, daughter of the Protector's uncle, Henry Cromwell of
Upwood.

Sir Francis was High Sheriff of Northamptonshire in 1714 and
was created a baronet in the following year. By his wife, Mary
Gould, he had two daughters, Frances and Mary, the younger of
whom married Sir John Bernard, Bart. All published authorities
seem to be in agreement on the existence of these two daughters,
Frances and Mary, who are invariably stated to be the only children
of Sir Francis and his wife. In the Stoke Newington Registers,
however, appear the following two entries: —

" 1689-90. Elizabeth the Daughter of ffrancis St. John, Esq.
and Mary his wife was bapt. the 22nd January.

1696-7. Walter, the son of ffrancis St. John, Esq. was baptized
the 21st January."

These entries suggest that members of the St. John family were
frequent guests of Sir Nathaniel Gould at Fleetwood House.

Mr. Spratling assumed that the entries referred to the children of
Sir Francis St. John and Mary Gould. This is an impossibility for

Sir Nathaniel Gould had only married Frances Hartopp in 1788, and their daughter would not be of an age to be married until some years after 1700. Elizabeth and Walter St. John are clearly the children of Francis St. John by his second wife, Mary Foorth. The St. John pedigree is as follows: —

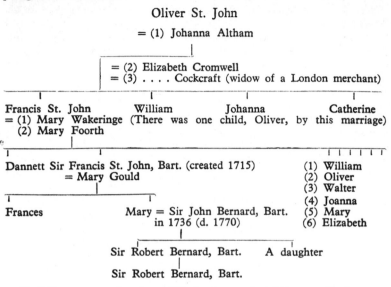

Gould's younger daughter Elizabeth married Thomas Cooke.

$$\boxed{XIV}$$

When Fleetwood House was demolished the following words were found cut with a diamond on the pane of an upper window, " I came into this house to live 12th December, 1728. Elizabeth Cooke." In addition there was a date, 21st July, 1728, and some characters in shorthand. Elizabeth Cooke was the daughter of Sir Nathaniel Gould, and it is thus certain that she and her husband, Thomas Cooke, moved into the part of the house formerly occupied by her father on the date mentioned. The second date is that of the death of Sir Nathaniel and the characters in shorthand probably referred to him.

Thomas Cooke was born in about the year 1672, the second son of Thomas Cooke of King's Thorpe, Northamptonshire, and Hackney. It is likely that he married Sir Nathaniel Gould's daughter in 1721. At any rate he became a Director of the Bank of England in this year, per haps with the assistance or at the suggestion of his father-in-law, and on 3rd November, 1728, his elder daughter, Frances, died aged six, and was buried in the parish church. He remained a Director of the Bank until his death in 1752, was Deputy Governor from 1735 to 1737, and Governor from 1737 until 1740. He was also a Justice of the Peace for Middlesex and High Sheriff of Northamptonshire in 1733. He carried on business in London as a Turkey merchant just as did his father-in-law, and in about 1713-1714 was in residence at Constantinople in connection with his trading affairs.

★

At this time Charles XII of Sweden was an exile in Turkey, or perhaps almost a prisoner, living in the utmost poverty with all his enterprises at their lowest ebb. From the time of Gustavus Adolphus' entrance into the Thirty Years War the Swedes had proved themselves the greatest soldiers in Europe. Charles XII was a born Commander. When only a boy his tutor asked him what he thought of Alexander the Great, and he replied, " I would like to be like him." " But," said the tutor, " he only lived thirty-two years." " Ah! " answered the Prince, " and is that not long enough when one has subdued kingdoms? " Before he was ten he was hardening himself by sleeping in mid-winter on the bare boards. His Spartan powers of endurance made him the idol of his soldiers. In his very first speech to his Parliament he declared " I am resolved never to begin an unrighteous war, but I am also resolved never to finish a righteous war until I have completely humbled my enemies." The first nine years of his reign, spent almost entirely in the field, were distinguished by an apparently endless succession of victories, with the exception of a strategic retreat from the charms of the beautiful Countess Aurora von Königsmark. Augustus of Saxony finding himself likely to be involved in war with Sweden prevailed on her to go to Stockholm on a diplomatic mission. Voltaire has described it. " The Countess, among the talents which made her one of the most delightful persons in Europe, had a gift for speaking several languages like a native, and would sometimes amuse herself by making French verses which might have been written at Versailles. She made some for Charles XII. She introduced the gods of antiquity, praising his different virtues, and ended as follows: —

' Enfin chacun des Dieux discourant à sa gloire,
Le plaçait par avance au temple de memoire:
Mais Venus ni Bacchus n'en dirent pas un mot.'

All her wit and charm were lost on such a man as the King of Sweden; he obstinately refused to see her. She planned to intercept him when he was taking his usual horse-exercise. Thus meeting him one day in a very narrow lane she alighted as soon as she saw him. The King bowed without a word, turned his horse and rode straight back, so that the only satisfaction that the Countess got from her journey was the conviction that she was the only person of whom the King was afraid."

As she herself said, " She was very unlucky to be the only person in the world on whom that great prince had turned his back." Her son, Marshall Maurice de Saxe, was later to be the greatest commander of his age.

Judged simply as a military hero Charles XII was beyond compare. As Lamberty wrote, " he risked an army as a gentleman might risk his life in a duel." When commanding at Narva, he said, " Now is our time, with the storm at our backs. They will never see how few we are." Dr. Johnson was well aware of his magnetic personality, and Boswell recorded him as saying: —" No Sir: were Socrates and Charles XII of Sweden both present in any company, and Socrates to say ' Follow me, and hear a lecture in philosophy,' and Charles laying his hand on sword to say ' Follow me, and dethrone the Czar '; a man would be ashamed to follow Socrates." When the great Duke of Marlborough visited him at Alt-Ranstadt in 1707, he said: —" I present to your Majesty a letter not from the Chancery but from the heart of the Queen, my mistress, written with her own hand. Had not her sex prevented it, she would have crossed the sea to meet a Prince admired by the whole universe. I am, in this respect, more fortunate than the Queen, and I wish I could serve some campaign under so great a general as Your Majesty, that I might learn what I yet do not know in the art of war." This compliment would appear to be sincere, for after Charles' affairs had taken an unfortunate turn Marlborough said: —" Having once seen the King of Sweden I am very much touched by the misfortune to that young King."

That delightful character, Baron Charles Louis von Pöllnitz, was also at Alt-Ranstadt at this time and wrote: —" The King was always booted and spurred, with the tails of his coat buttoned up, as if ready to mount his horse. He was well built, above ordinary height, supple below; he had broad shoulders, and altogether was a fine man. He held himself very upright, and had an imposing air; when he walked he dragged one leg a little, since in consequence of a fall from his horse at Cracow, he broke his thigh. No one sat a horse better than he did. He covered eight to ten German miles a day simply for a ride."

Charles was fortunate to command the finest soldiers in Europe. Marshall Maurice de Saxe, the victor of Fontenoy, described the bravery of the Swedish Infantry as astounding. Magnus Stenbock the greatest of Charles' commanders said: —" Such soldiers and such subjects are not to be found the wide world over, except in Sweden. Never have I seen such a combination of uncontrollable dash and perfectly controlled discipline." The great line of Swedish commanders begun under Gustavus Adolphus continued under Charles XII, who was surrounded by captains in every way worthy of comparison with Napoleon's immortal marshals. Greatest of all was Magnus Stenbock. Born at Stockholm in 1664, he was trained under William of Orange. He idolised his King and copied his tactics. He won his marshal's baton at Gadebusch. He was a man of cheerful and engaging personality. One of the King's hangers-on, Lagercrona, said that Stenbock had drunk too much at a banquet and become noisy and incoherent. Charles replied: —" You only mean to blacken Stenbock but let me tell you that Stenbock drunk is more capable of giving orders than Lagercrona sober." Emanuel Swedenborg, the great philosopher and mystic, celebrated Stenbock's victory at Helsingborg in an ode translated by Francis Barham: —

> " Though Swedish Charles, our hero King's afar
> In Russian battles—his bright valour fills
> The heart of Stenbock—the victorious one;—
> These names of Charles and Stenbock like a spell
> Created armaments, and hurled pale fear
> Among our foes.—Stenbock! thy red right hand
> Hath smitten down the spoiler; and in thee
> Another Charles we honour,—and rejoice
> To hail thee hero of they grateful country."

Carl Gustaf Rehnskjöld described by Charles as " a valiant stout hearted soldier," had also served with William of Orange. Victorious in twelve pitched battles, including Franstadt, and thirty engagements he was a leader of immense dash.

Adam Ludwig Levenhaupt was an excellent general when acting alone. He belonged to the cautious Dutch school of tactics, and after Stenbock was perhaps the soundest of all Swedish commanders. Charles called him his " Latin Colonel," as he could negotiate in that language. Arvid Bernhard Horn came of poor but noble Finnish stock. In his own words he was " taken out of the mire to be set among princes." He loved the King but did not agree with his policy.

A Dutchman, Van Effen, travelling in south Sweden noticed the almost total absence of men between the ages of twenty and forty. Horn did not wish to see " Sweden shed her last drop of blood as a libation to Charles XII's caprices." Later he played a leading part in restoring his country to prosperity.

A later King of Sweden, Gustavus III, and Charles' great rival, Peter of Russia, both left acute impressions of his character. Gustavus III wrote " Charles XII was rather extraordinary than great. He certainly had not the true conquering temperament which simply aims at acquisition of territory. Charles took dominions with one hand only to give them away with the other. Superior to Alexander, with whom it were an injustice to compare him, he was as much inferior to his rival Peter in the qualities that make a great ruler as he excelled him in those qualities which go to make a great hero." Peter the Great said :—" I believe that from the beginning of the world, there has never been so perfect a man and hero as brother Charles; though he was therefore not the happiest of men, for he was too great to reign over people. As he possesed more than normal courage, he believed that all who served him should possess the same, but in this he was mostly disappointed. He wished that all should act honourably without danger of punishment, thinking that they would follow his example; but such hopes proved often futile. Because he was faithful and honest, he thought that everybody should be so; but he was often cheated both by his neighbours and his subjects. When he gave a promise he kept it, should it cost him even his crown, Kingdom, and life; and to this his neighbours did not always respond. Therefore that man succeeds better in reigning over others who is himself conscious of human limitations."

The Swedes, however, were a small nation in numbers, and though repeatedly successful against enormous odds, it was not possible for them to make good their huge losses. In 1709 was fought the battle of Pultowa, and Charles received a terrible defeat from Peter the Great of Russia, which forced him to withdraw to Turkey. It was then that Thomas Cooke came to his assistance, and contributed generously to his financial relief, on one occasion presenting him with his whole sideboard of plate. " Mr. Cooke well knew the Divan wished to get rid of the King, their prisoner, who always pleaded poverty and inability to pay his debts, and they having lent him money, were afraid to lend any more. He devised a scheme to assist him, and applied to the high treasurer upon the subject, who heard the proposal with great satisfaction, but was surprised to be told 'Your Excellency must find the money.' To this he answered by putting a very natural question: 'How will you ever pay us?' Mr. Cooke replied they were building a mosque, and would stand in need of lead to cover it, which he would engage to supply. The treasurer replied, he would speak to the grand vizier, and directed him to call again, which he did the next morning, when the proposal was accepted and the arrangements concluded on. Mr. Cooke then treated with the King of Sweden, and offered him a certain sum of money upon condition of being paid in copper, the exportation of which from Sweden had been for some time prohibited, at a stipulated price. The offer was accepted, the money paid to the King by the hands of La Mortraye, the well-known author of several volumes of travels, and Mr. Cooke received an order upon the states of Sweden to be paid in copper, which he sold to a house in that Kingdom, at an advance of £12,000 sterling, upon the first cost, besides the profit he obtained upon the sale of his lead."* No doubt this financial assistance contributed to Charles' ability to return to Sweden in 1714. He continued to be involved in wars and eventually perished in mysterious circumstances at the siege of Frederickshall in 1718.

Mary Wollstonecraft, who lived for a time at Newington Green, visited this place when on her Scandinavian tour. "Arriving at Fredericshall at the siege of which Charles XII lost his life, we had only time to take a transient view of it, whilst they were preparing us some refreshment.

"Poor Charles! I thought of him with respect. I have always felt the same for Alexander; with whom he has been classed as a madman by several writers, who have reasoned superficially, confounding the morals of the day with the few grand principles on which unchangeable morality rests. Making no allowance for the ignorance and prejudices of the period, they do not perceive how much they themselves are indebted to general improvement for the acquirements, and even the virtues, which they would not have had the force of mind to attain, by their individual exertions in a less advanced state of society."

Some writers have suggested assassination, but Voltaire writing only ten years after the event says: —" The King stood with half his body exposed to a battery of cannon directed precisely at the angle where he stood. No one was near him but two Frenchmen: one was M. Siquier, his aide-de-campe, a man of capacity and energy, who had entered his service in Turkey, and was particularly attached to the Prince of Hesse; the other was the engineer. The cannon fired grape shot, and the King was more exposed than any of them . . . at this moment Siquier and Megret saw the King fall on the parapet, with a deep sigh; they came near, but he was already dead. A ball weighing half a pound had struck him on the right temple leaving a hole large enough to turn three fingers in; his head had fallen over the parapet, his left eye was driven in and his right out of its socket; death had been instantanous, but he had had strength to put his hand to his sword and lay in that posture. At this sight, Megret an extraordinary and feelingless man, said ' Let us go to supper. The play is done '." Dr. Johnson summed up his career in a few superb lines: —

" On What foundation stands the warrior's pride,
How just his hopes let Swedish Charles decide;
A frame of adamant, a soul of fire,
No dangers fright him, and no labours tire;

*Robinson—" History of Stoke Newington."

O'er love, o'er fear, extends his wide domain,
Unconquer'd lord of pleasure and of pain;
No joys to him pacific sceptres yield,
War sounds the trump, he rushes to the field;
Behold surrounding kings their powers combine,
And one capitulate, and one resign;
Peace courts his hand, but spreads her charms in vain;
' Think nothing gain'd, (he cries) till nought remain;
On Moscow's walls till Gothic standards fly,
And all be mine beaneath the polar sky.'
The march begins in military state,
And nations on his eye suspended wait;
Stern Famine guards the solitary coast,
And Winter barricades the realms of Frost:
He comes; not want and cold his course delay;—
Hide, blushing Glory, hide Pultowa's day:
The vanquish'd hero leaves his broken bands,
And shows his miseries in distant lands;
Condemn'd a needy supplicant to wait;
While ladies interpose, and slaves debate.
But did not Chance at length her error mend?
Did no subverted empire mark his end?
Did rival monarchs give the fatal wound?
Or hostile millions press him to the ground?
His fall was destin'd to a barren strand,
A petty fortress, and a dubious hand;
He left the name, at which the world grew pale,
To point a moral, or adorn a tale."

★

Many biographers of Charles XII make no mention of the help given him by Thomas Cooke. The Hon. Eveline Godley, in "Charles XII of Sweden," however, wrote, " An English merchant in Constantinople (prophetically named Thomas Cook!) facilitated the king's travels by advancing various sums and transacting the necessary exchange of coinage." There also exists in the Royal Archives at Stockholm a series of letters known as the " Thomas Cooke File." These letters, written in French, relate to the attempts Cooke made to recover the money advanced to Charles XII from the Swedish Chancellor. Slightly more than half the letters are from Thomas Cooke, and the rest from J. W. Cooke, who was perhaps a brother and partner in the business.

It is of interest to try and determine to what extent Thomas Cooke was out of England visiting Constantinople to further his business as a Turkey Merchant, for Mrs. Valerie Pirie in her life of Theodore von Neuhoff, " His Majesty of Corsica," links the name of Cooke— " Mr. Cook the banker "—with that of von Neuhoff. The first reference to Cooke shows him a resident at Constantinople during the time

Charles XII was attempting to raise money for his return to Sweden. This " Mr. Cook," as we have seen, was Thomas Cooke. " Mr. Cook " is then said once more to have been at Constantinople in 1732, when Theodore von Neuhoff arrived to seek the help of the Sultan in his attempt to free the Corsicans from the Genoese and make himself King of Corsica.

Theodore von Neuhoff was one of the most engaging of the many political adventurers of the eighteenth century. When he arrived at Constantinople he called on " Mr. Cook," whom he had known previously, and Cooke at once invited him to stay in his own house, and offered to find him work at the bank. This von Neuhoff refused, as he was determined to stake everything on his Corsican adventure. Cooke also supplied him with native clothes so he could wander through the bazaars without attracting attention. In 1735 von Neuhoff left Constantinople for Morocco, and found there the man who had once employed him in Spain, Baron Ripperda. He, too, was a political adventurer and a fascinating character. Born at the staid Dutch town of Groningen and brought up a Roman Catholic, he had changed his religion as often as he thought it would further his career. In 1735 he was a Moslem, and at the time of his death was busy trying to found a religion of his own. For a time he had lived in Lady Mary Fauconberg's old house in Soho Square. From Morocco von Neuhoff sailed for Corsica, and in 1736 was actually crowned King. His " reign " did not last long, and he eventually died in Soho, and was buried in a pauper's grave in the churchyard of St. Anne's. Horace Walpole wrote a clever but unkind epitaph, which was placed on an exterior wall of the church. The original stone decayed and was replaced, and the epitaph, surmounted by a crown, can still be read on the wall of the church facing Wardour Street: —

" Near this place is interred

THEODORE, KING OF CORSICA

Who died in this parish December 11th, 1756
immediately after leaving the King's Bench prison
by the benefit of the Act of Insolvency;
in consequence of which he registered
His Kingdom of Corsica
for the use of his creditors.

———

The grave, great teacher, to a level brings
Heroes and beggars, galley slaves and kings.
But Theodore his moral learned ere dead;
Fate poured its lessons on his living head,
Bestowed a kingdom, and denied him bread."

For a long period of years Thomas Cooke was a member of the Stoke Newington Vestry, and also, for a time, Churchwarden. The oldest surviving volume of minutes is inscribed: —

" Stoke Newington
MIDDLESEX
Thomas Cooke
John London
Esqs.
Church Wardens
ANNO DOMINI
1730 "

Cooke signed the minute book for the first time on 12th March, 1721, and again on 24th July, 1721. He was also present on 26th March, 1722. At that time a David Cooke was regularly attending the vestry meetings. Perhaps he was a relative. Thomas Cooke did not attend a meeting again until 26th December, 1726. In the following year he was twice at meetings, in 1728 three times, and in 1729 eight times. During 1730 and 1731 he attended every meeting—nine in all. The final meeting for 1731 was held on 27th December. Cooke was then absent from the next two meetings held on 20th April, and 1st May, 1732. At the second of these, however, he was appointed one of the auditors of the parish accounts. He was again present at the September meeting, held on the 24th of that month, and the December meeting, missed the March, April and July meetings in 1733, but attended the final meetings held on 11th and 26th December. He then attended regularly until May, 1735, during which time he was much concerned with the adaptation of a house in Church Street, leased to the churchwardens by Joseph Baily and others, for use as a workhouse. Thereafter he was not again present until 28th March, 1743. He was, however, in Stoke Newington during 1738 and 1739 as he helped the vagrant Mary Le Brun and fell out with his fellow vestrymen over her case.

It will thus be seen that from the end of 1726 until May, 1735, Thomas Cooke could not have been out of England for any great periods of time, travel being very slow in those days. Presumably he was in charge of the London end of his merchant business. Was the " J. W. Cooke," who had written many of the letters to the Swedish Chancellor, representing the firm in Turkey? If so, it may have been J. W. Cooke with whom von Neuhoff was on such good terms. On the other hand, Thomas Cooke was absent from all meetings of the vestry from December, 1731, until nearly the end of September, 1732, and so had the opportunity of travelling to Turkey, meeting von Neuhoff, attending to his business and returning to Stoke Newington.

✳

A few years after returning from Turkey, Cooke married and settled down in Stoke Newington, first in the house built by Thomas Gunston next door to Fleetwood House, later to be Abney House, and then on the death of his father-in-law, in Fleetwood House itself. In 1739 he became engaged in a dispute with the Churchwardens over a vagrant and her children. For some time he fed them from his own table. The following account of the episode appears in the Minutes of the Vestry: —

"*May 7th*, 1739.

The Churchwardens informed the Vestry that Mr. Cooke having sent a warrant to command them to attend him on Sunday last to shew cause why they should not releive one Mary Le Brunn and her 5 Children and Monday following having by his warrant commanded them to pay the said Mary Le Brunn five shillings every Tuesday morning for the support of herself and five children and the said Mary Le Brunn being a vagrant within the intent and meaning of the Act of the 12th of Queen Anne and the said Mr. Cooke having refused to grant a pass to send the said Vagrant out of this parish they had taken the opinion of Councell for their direction and which they prayed might be read and the same was read and was as follows.

Case. About Wednesday 21st March 1738 One Mary Le Brun and her 5 Children came into the Parish of —————— in Middx without any pass as she pretended and applyed to the Overseers of the Poor of said Parish for Relief and said her Husband had been a Carpenter and worked Journey work at Lambeth was Dead 14 days before and she was travelling down to Thorney ffenn in Cambridgeshire to a brother of her husbands (as she said) The overseers would have relieved her if she would have gone through the parish but she insisted on having a pass. The Overseer applyed to a Justice in the Parish but he refused to grant a pass or to take her Examination on oath and being towards evening the officer put her into a stable of His own that heppened to be in another Parish and there the Justice in A sent her Relief from time to time from his own house but though after applyed to Refused to grant her a Pass and told the Parish officers the Parish was Rich enough and they might keep her—Note it did not appear she had any settlement.

The Justice in A refusing a pass the officers applied to two other Justices in the County and got the woman a pass to go to Dover in her way to St. Omers where she said she was born and offered her the Pass and 5/- for Relief and would have taken her away in a coach and carryed her to the next parish, but tho' she had often said she would go if she could have a pass (yet when at a Great Deale of trouble and expense) the officers had gott one she refused to take either Pass or money or stir out of the Parish after the encouragement she had met with from the Justice in A.

The Justice in A on Sunday last sent a Warrant under Seal to the Constable of the Parish requiring the two Churchwardens of A to appear before him at 6 that evening to show cause why they should not relieve Mary Le Brun and Her five children—(Copy warrant annexed) and according the Churchwardens and Constable attended the Justice and told him they had offered to Relieve her and give Her a pass but she refused to take relief and go out of the Parish.

On same evening the Justice Ordered the woman and her 5 Children to be put into a House held by the Parish for accomodating the poor of said parish and on the Monday sent the warrant (copy annexed) by the constable to the Chuchwardens.

Now the woman having told the officers her Husband had worked and Dyed at Lambeth they went and enquired there and could hear nothing of Her or Her Husband and the Justice in A then examining her on Oath she confessed her Husband dyed at Battle in Sussex.

The Parishioners think the Justice has in this affair used them exceedingly Ill and are Desiours of having a Redress if they can by Law.

In what manner the Parish are to get Ridd of this Woman and her 5 Children? and if the officers are Bound to obey the Warrant? And if they should not what would be the Consequences? If the Justice has acted in this affair beyond his Authority then what Method is advisable for the Parish to Have Reliefe.

Now the Parish officers being intimidated by the Justice have paid the first 5/- to the woman.—

The Parish has no way to get rid of this Pauper and Child by a vagrant Pass (if neither her Husbands Settlement nor hers nor Parents can be found) to the place where she or They were found last begging and passed unapprehended.

I am further of Opinion that the Officers ought in prudence to obey the warrant tho' It is a very irregular one and a very unjustifiable one and my Reason is that It is a warrant granted on a Complaint over which the Justice has Jurisdiction (this Being to be considered as the case of an accidental pauper) I don't mean that They are Bound in Strictness of Law to obey this Warrant but only that 'tis prudent for them so to do lest by their Negligence the pauper should be starved and They be liable to an expensive prosecution and a fine. But as this Warrant is penned I do not conceive that They are strictly Bound to obey. If they Disobey It They are liable to be bound over to the Sessions for a Contempt of the order and on an Indictment found for that the validity of the order will be the only question.

As to the Justices behaviour on this Occasion it is (as I conceive) very unjustifiable and such a gross abuse of his office as would scarecely be construed as to be owing to an Error of his Judgment only, and tho' the Court of Kings Bench is very tender of granting Informations against Justices of the Peace where there is any reasonable presumption of Ignorance and not wilfullness in them yet I think it would be advisable in a case so grossly circumstanced as this is for the Parish to move that court (on proper Notice of Motion) for leave to file an Information against him.

Richard Lloyd. Chancery Lane.

May 3, 1739.

The said Mary Le Brun coming into the Vestry and declaring

she was immediately goeing out of the parish with her children 'No order was made concerning her.'
Ralph Thoresby Rector.

William Pickett Church Warden."

In 1740 Thomas Cooke obtained the lease for ninety-nine years of a piece of waste land forming part of the common of Stoke Newington in the parish of Hackney. On this land he built a large house, which was divided into eight apartments. Each of these apartments he let to poor families at a nominal rent of two or three shillings a year. By his will dated 25th March, 1751, he devised certain houses and land at Eltham in Kent to his wife, on trust, to apply the income therefrom in keeping the house and apartments in a good state of repair. This devise eventually turned out to be void by the statute of mortmain and the property became vested in Cooke's eventual heiress-at-law Margaret Fremeaux. She executed a deed reciting Cooke's will and carried out its terms as he had intended, but the deed was never of legal effect, having been executed by a married woman without the precaution of levying a fine. Mrs. Fremeaux' daughter Susannah, and her husband Thomas Reeve Thornton, however continued to carry out the terms of Cooke's will.

Cooke was a very rich man, worth perhaps £100,000, equal to half a million to-day. By his will he bequeathed £1,000 to the clerks in the Bank of England. In the month of February preceding his death he decided to give them the money while he was still alive, and had it distributed in the proportion of one guinea for each year of service in the Bank, and £3 to each porter. He died in Fleetwood House on 12th August, 1752, aged about eighty. The following account of his funeral appeared in the " Gentleman's Magazine " for that year : —

"*12th August.* Tho. Cooke, Esq; a director of the Bank, and one of the trustees of Sir John Morden's college, Blackheath, aged 80; a gentleman of extensive charity.—Agreeable to his own directions, he was attended to the grave by 12 poor house-keepers, belonging to a box club at Newington, of which he had long been a generous and useful member: they were each bequeathed a guinea and a suit of cloaths, and as much victuals and drink as they would have; but if any of them appeared to be fuddled after his interment, they forfeited his legacy, and were only to have half a crown for their days work.—His corpse was wrapped in a clean blanket, sew'd up, and being put into a common coffin, was conveyed, with the above attendants in three coaches, to the grave at Morden college, when the corps was taken out of the coffin and buried in a winding sheet, according to the Eastern custom. The coffin was left in the college for the first pensioner it would fit."

He was survived by his widow. A second daughter, Margaret, had died aged 23 on 20th November, 1749. Mrs. Elizabeth Cooke lived on until 15th January, 1763, dying in Fleetwood House, which her father had left to her for life with a reversion to his male heirs. In the older part of the house her aunts and the Hurlocks had been living. Mrs. Cooke had, however, procured a lease of that part of the house for a further seven years to protect her aunt's interests. Miss Anne Hartopp, the last of these aunts' survived only one more year and died on 6th April, 1764.

XV

Sir John Hartopp (1682-1762), Watts' pupil, the fourth and last baronet succeeded in 1722 to the title. Until the death of his father he appeared to be treading in his footsteps, but it seems that for the remainder of his life his connnection with the nonconformists was not very close or frequent. He lived a quiet retired life and showed no inclination to embark on a public career.

In 1724, John Eames, tutor at the Moorfields Nonconformist Academy persuaded Watts to publish his " Logic " and it was printed in the same year and came out with a dedication to Sir John: —

"It is fit the public should receive through your hands what was written originally for the assistance of your younger studies, and was then presented to you. It was by the repeated importunities of our learned, friend, Mr. John Eames, that I was persuaded to revise the Rudiments of Logic. I will not presume that this little book is improved since its first composure in proportion to the improvements of your manly age; but when you shall please to review it in your retired hours, perhaps you may refresh your own memory in some of the early parts of learning."

This book attained great popularity, was used as a text-book at the universities, and can be said to be one of the few readable books on its subject.

Watts in the dedication of his " Death and Heaven " again addressed his former pupil: —

"Forgive me, if I take the liberty of saying, it is with a sort of fond pleasure that I have beheld your victories over the most dangerous scenes and temptations of youth; and every step in your progress towards perfect triumph is an addition to my joy. The world and the church hold their eyes fixed upon you; and, perhaps, the souls of your sacred ancestors look down from on high to observe your conduct. You know I pretend to no authority to pronounce effectual blessings upon you; but you will accept the sincere good wishes of a man who loves you, and is zealous for your felicity in the upper and lower worlds. May the best of mercies descend daily on yourself, your lady, and your little offspring. May the closet, the parlour, and public assemblies, be constant witnesses of your piety; and the house where a Sir John Hartopp dwells, be a house of prayer and of praise in every generation. Such a lovely scene, with such a long and joyful prospect, will advance the satisfactions of my life, and give pleasure, even in a dying hour, to him who had once the honour to be your affectionate monitor."

In 1718 Watts had published his " The Psalms of David Imitated," of which he wrote, " 'Tis not a translation of David that I pretend, but an imitation of him, so nearly in Christian hymns that the Jewish Psalmist may plainly appear and yet leave Judaism behind." It is interesting to compare Watts' version of the 9th and 10th verses of the 18th psalm with the version of Sir Philip Sidney whose death at Zutphen has been earlier referred to. Sir Philip Sydney's translation runs: —

> " He bowed the heavens, and from the bow'd heavens did descend
> With hugy darkness, which aboute his feete did wend.
>
> The cherubims their backs, the windes did yield their wings,
> To beare his sacred flight; in secrete place then clos'd;
> About which he dimme cloudes, like a pavillion brings
> Cloudes, even of waters darke, and thickest aire compos'd;
> But streight his shining eyes this misty masse disclos'd:
> Then haile, then firie coales, then thund'red heav'nly Sire,
> Then spake he his lowd voice, then hailstones, coles and fire."

Watts' free adaptation is as follows: —

> " When God, our leader, shines in arms,
> What mortal heart can bear
> The thunder of his loud alarms,
> The light'ning of his spear?
>
> He rides upon the winged wind,
> And angels in array,
> In millions wait to know his mind,
> And swift as flames obey."

★

Sir John married Sarah, daughter and co-heiress of Sir Joseph Woolfe of Hackney, an Alderman of London, with a fortune of £30,000. On his marriage the elder Sir John is said to have made over to his son the family estates on condition that he settled on his maiden sisters, who all lived and died in Fleetwood House, an annuity of £500. The former is said, in one publication, to have left £10,000 for the instruction of young men for the dissenting ministry, but his " heirs " taking advantage of a defect in the conveyance appropriated the bequest to themselves. Nearly one half of the legacy is said to have been later restored and applied to the purposes for which it was intended. This story, however, does not seem very probable. By his marriage the younger Sir John had two daughters, Elizabeth and Sarah, born in 1717 and 1719 respectively.

Sir John and his wife and children no doubt were frequently in residence at Fleetwood House and varied their existence with visits to their estates at Freeby and Buckminster. His sisters lived in Fleetwood House and probably accompanied him on occasions to Leicestershire, but nothing is recorded of them except their deaths. Martha died in 1739, Bridget in 1741, Mary in 1749, Elizabeth in 1754, Dorothy in 1755 and Anne in 1764. An earlier Anne had died in 1674. It can seldom have happened that two sisters bearing the same name have died at a distance of ninety years from one another. Watts died on Friday, the 25th of November, 1748, during the afternoon. By his will dated 26th July, 1746, he left £10 " to his friend, Sir John Hartopp," which can be taken as a token of friendship given by a poor man to a rich one, for his estate only totalled about £2,000. Sir John assisted Lady Abney in erecting a memorial to Watts in Bunhill Fields.

Sir John lost his first wife in 1730, aged thirty-five, and she was buried in the parish church at Stoke Newington. In the same year he gave three guineas towards the erection of a singers' gallery in the church at Buckminster. A good many years later he married Sarah Marsh, said to have been his nurse. There were no children of this second marriage. He himself died on 15th January, 1762, at Bath, where perhaps he had gone for reasons of health. He was buried in St. Mary's on 28th January. His widow proved his will, under which she received the Buckminster estate, which she sold in 1763 to Lord William Manners. She died in the same year and was buried at Stoke Newington in the parish church.

Sir John Hartopp was survived by his two daughters. Elizabeth had married, about December, 1759, Timothy Dallowe, M.D., whom she survived but by whom she left no issue. The younger daughter, Sarah, married Joseph Hurlock in June, 1755. She died on 27th March, 1766, aged 47 and was buried at Stoke Newington, leaving only one child, a daughter, Anne. The direct male line of the Hartopps had come to an end with the death of the fourth baronet, and with his grand-daughter the family's connection with Fleetwood House and Stoke Newington likewise terminated.

Anne Hurlock married Edmund Bunney (1749-1833) of Four-Oaks Hall, Warwickshire, on 8th August, 1777. He was the son of Joseph Bunney and Mary Cradock. He was permitted to take the name and arms of Hartopp by special Act of Parliament in 1778, and took the name and arms of Cradock in pursuance of the will of his uncle Joseph Cradock. He was created a baronet in 1796, was High Sheriff for Leicester in 1781, and Member of Parliament in 1798 and 1802. His wife is said by Robinson in his " History of Stoke Newington " to have become " heiress and representative of the families of Hartopp and Fleetwood, and by the will of Mrs. Jane Fleetwood, came into possession of the estates of that family in the county of Norfolk." As regards the Hartopp estates, however, a moiety of the Freeby estate passed to Edward Hartopp-Wigley (1758-1808) of Little Dalby, under the will of Mrs. Elizabeth Dallowe who died in 1789.

Edward Hartopp-Wigley was descended from George Hartopp, a younger brother of the first baronet. He, too, was High Sheriff of Leicester in 1790, a position which the family seem almost to have monopolised. He took the name of Wigley in 1781 in pursuance of the will of his great uncle, James Wigley of Scraptoft. In 1776 he inherited Potters-Marston from his uncle Thomas Boothby. He married Juliana, daughter of George Evans, third Lord Carbery, and died at Matlock in 1808.

From Anne Hurlock and Edmund Bunney is descended the Cradock-Hartopp family which still flourishes and has not forgotten the memory of Charles Fleetwood, as is shown by the name of the eighth baronet, Sir George Francis Fleetwood Cradock-Hartopp, who died on 6th September, 1949. He was the owner of Southside House, Wimbledon Common, a fine house of a size but different appearance from Fleetwood House.

★

In the Stoke Newington parish church is a very handsome monument by Banks erected by Anne Cradock-Hartopp: —

Humanitate.

Joseph	Sarah
Hurlock	his wife
died	died
August 10th,	March 27th,
1793	1766
aged 70.	aged 47.

To the memory of the above
Joseph and Sarah Hurlock,
her immediate parents,
and of the late Sir John Hartopp,
of Freathby, in the county of Leicester, Baronet,
and Sarah his first wife,
her maternal grandfather and grandmother,
whose remains are deposited in a vault
in this church;
This monument is inscribed
by Anne, the wife of Edmund Cradock Hartopp,
of Fouroaks Hall, in the county of Warwick, Esq.
heiress and sole survivor
of that branch of the Hartopp family.

On the pavement of the church are tombstones on which appear the following inscriptions: —

Mrs Sarah Hurlock, late wife of Joseph Hurlock, Esq. eldest daughter of the under-mentioned Sir John and Dame Sarah Hartopp, ob. 27 March, 1766, ae. 47.

Faith hath an overcoming pow'r,
It triumphs in the dying hour;
Christ is my life, my joy, my hope,
Nor can I sink with such a prop.
Dr. I. Watts.
Dame Sarah Hartopp,
daughter of Sir Joseph Woolfe,
knt. ob. 12 Sept. 1730, ae. 35.

(The above three lines on the late stone.)

Sir John Hartopp, Bart. ob. 15 Jan. 1762, ae. 82. Mrs Anne Hartopp, sister of the above said Sir John, ob. 17 March, 1764, ae. 81.

Mrs. Elizabeth Cooke, obiit 15 Jan 1763, aetat. 63
                    Eternity!   Eternity!   Eternity!
Waiting for a glorious triumph over her last enemy, Here lyeth the precious remains of Miss Margaret Cooke, daughter of Thomas Cooke, Esq. and Elizabeth his wife: she departed this life 20 Nov. 1749, in the 23rd year of her age.

> If sin be pardon'd, I'm secure,
> Death hath no sting beside:
> The law gives sin its damning pow'r,
> But Christ my ransom dyed.
> Now to the God of victory
> Immortal thanks be paid,
> Who makes us conqu'rors while we die,
> Though Christ our living head.
>   Dr. I. Watts.

And also in memory of Miss Frances Cooke, who departed this life 3 Nov. 1728, aged 6 years.

$$\boxed{\text{XVI}}$$

Joseph Hurlock came to live in Fleetwood House as a result of his marriage with Sarah Hartopp, daughter of the fourth and last Hartopp baronet in 1755. He had returned to England from the Far East in 1752.

He entered the service of the East India Company on the 23rd October, 1730, as a Writer for Bencoolen. He was probably born in about the year 1714, as in a list of the Honourable Company's servants on the West Coast of Sumatra for the year 1748 his age is given as thirty-four years. At the time of his first appointment Joseph Hurlock of Coleman Street, Surgeon, and Philip Constable also of Coleman Street, Corn Chandler, were approved as sureties for him in the sum of £500. Joseph Hurlock was perhaps his father, or an uncle.

The East India Company came into existence on 31st December, 1600, when Queen Elizabeth established the first Incorporated Company, the London East India Company. After a long series of losses and disasters the Company obtained powers, at great expense, of conducting a limited trade in certain parts of India and Persia, and of establishing small settlements or Houses of Trade, called Factories, for the residence of their factors and servants. At first the charters of the Crown and the powers which they conveyed were not thought to require Parliamentary sanction. It was not until after the restoration of Charles II that the rights conferred by these charters were called in question, and only then doubtless for the reason that the Company had at last become prosperous, and its profits excited envy. Many attempts were made to get the charters revoked, and ultimately some distinction was drawn between places which had been acquired by actual conquest or influence of arms and to which the nation had some claim of right, and those places which the Company had purchased from the native powers. The settlement at Bencoolen was established in 1684, as a result of purchase, under the name of York Fort. This was moved in 1714 to a more healthy site in the same district, and the name of Fort Marlborough was given to the new building. The agency which had previously been subordinate to Madras, was raised in 1703 to the rank of a Presidency, with a Governor and Council. In 1785 the settlement was reduced to a Residency and placed under the Government of Bengal. Finally in 1825 all the British possessions in Sumatra were made over to the Dutch, under a treaty signed in 1824, in exchange for Malacca and the Dutch Settlements in India.

Joseph Hurlock arrived on the west coast of Sumatra on 12th July, 1731, and after occupying various positions was eventually made Deputy Governor of Fort Marlborough on 12th March, 1746. He finally returned to England in 1752 on the East India Company's

ship " Onslow " (Captain Thomas Hinde). He was elected a Director of the East India Company·for the years 1768, and 1770 to 1773 inclusive. He seems to have remained associated with the East India Company, for in 1778 the following letter was sent to Warren Hastings from the Company dealing with one of the usual malpractices of eastern trade and Hurlock is one of the signatories: —
" Warren Hasting Esq.
    Our President and Governor of Bengal.
Par. 1. Notwithstanding we have so often expressed to the successive Governors and Councils of our Presidency of Bengal our solicitude to promote the prosperity and happiness of the Natives of those Provinces, from which the Publick as well as the Company derives such great advantages; and that to effect the same we have repeatedly given the most peremptory orders for laying open to the Natives the several Articles of the Inland Trade, more particularly those of Salt, Beetle Nut and Tobacco, which are considered by them as the nescessaries of life, yet we are at length constrained to believe that our intentions have been counteracted and our Orders disobeyed, even by some of our Servants whose stations we had reason to hope would have prevented them from pursuing their private Emolument by any indirect and unwarrantable means.
2. We therefore shall not hesitate to declare that we have received such Information as will not permitt us to doubt but that several of our Council who were Members of that Board at the time of the dispatch of the Lord Mansfield in April '77 and many of our Servants in the different districts of the Country appointed as Supervisors of the Collection of our Revenues had, in manifest violation of our Orders entered into a combination, and unduly exercised the power and influence derived from their stations in order to carry on a Monopoly in the several articles of Salt, Beetle Nut, and Tobacco, and that they had been so far lost to the principles of Justice and humanity as to include rice and other grain in the same destructive Monopoly, by which an Artificial scarcity was made of an Article so necessary to the very being of the inhabitants.
3. As upon a charge of this nature we cannot but apply every means in our power to detect the guilty and by exemplary punishment prevent the continuance of such proceedings as are not only a dishonour to our Service, but a reproach to human Nature; And as we repose the most perfect confidence in your Abilities, Integrity and Zeal for our Service, we have thought fit to commit to your sole care the detection of those crimes which have been charged on the servants of the Company. . .
. . . It is therefore our pleasure and command that you enter without delay into a strict scrutiny of the Conduct of the several Members who composed our Council at the time of the Lord Mansfield's departure from Bengal in April '77, And of the Persons appointed to supervise, in the different districts of the Country, the Collection of the Revenues in respect to their having been

138

engaged in a Monopoly of Salt, Beetle Nut, Tobacco, and Grain. And in this investigation we most seriously enjoin you, not to suffer any bias of friendship to interrupt or weaken your research; and thus we have the greater reason to expect, since the result of your Enquiries may bring due chastisement upon the Offenders and thereby conciliate the Minds of the Natives to our Government, and restore prosperity to those extensive Provinces, which are entitled to our utmost care, both from the ties of Interest and Humanity.

4. Relying therefore upon your judgment and impartiality, and not doubting but they will lead you to the means of obtaining full evidence of those Enormities which may have been committed we hereby direct, that if it shall appear to you that any Member or Members of our before mentioned Council or any of our Servants, appointed to Supervise the collection of our Revenues or any other Persons in our Service, Civil or Military have been any ways concerned in these unwarrantable Monopolys such Servant or Servants be forthwith dismissed our Service, and we hereby declare them to be actually so dismissed as unworthy of holding any office or employment under the Company.

We are
Your loving friends.
(18 signatures, including that of J. Hurlock).

London,
8th December, '77.

Postcript

Since writing the above being well assured that the Resident of Hughley in '70 and '77 has been particularly engaged in the Monopoly of Rice complained of in the above 2nd Para., and although this greviance was of such a degree it appears that the Governor only reprimanded him for it, you are therefore especially to make his conduct one of the immediate objects of your enquiry and if he shall have been a Delinquent in that respect he must be punished in the manner we have ordered other defaulters to be.

We are your loving Friends,
(Signatures including that of J. Hurlock).

London,
8th Decem. '77."

This letter is in the Department of Manuscripts at the British Museum (Add. Ms. 29132, f. 469) and has not apparently been quoted before. The Museum also has a signed " state of receipts," 1771-1778 of Bencoolen (Add. Ms. 38406, f. 181).

Hurlock must have come to live in Fleetwood House immediately on his marriage in 1755, for at Christmas in that year Mrs. Abney made a grant of the Dissenting Meeting House in Church Street for ninety years at five shillings per annum to eleven persons as trustees. In 1783 six of the trustees were dead, the survivors being the Rev. Meredith Townsend, John Howard, John Walbank, Joseph Parker and Joseph Hurlock. The part of the house occupied by Hurlock and his wife was the older part, which was shared with the surviving daughters of Sir John Hartopp, the third baronet. In 1766 Hurlock's wife died and was buried in St. Mary's. He then seems to have left Stoke Newington and gone to live at Chelsea. The survey of London lists him as the tenant of 99, Cheyne Walk (Lindsey House) in 1792. In August of the following year he died. In the Moravian Burial Ground, Chelsea, was buried Elizabeth Hurlock (died in January, 1800, aged 77) and there were tombstones inscribed P. Hurlock and Ann Trypheria Hurlock (1758-1806) in the same burial ground. It is possible that these were all related to Joseph Hurlock.

One page 82 of Robinson's "History of Stoke Newington" (the first line in both editions) it is said that "on August 10th, 1793, the estate came into the plenary possession of John Gould Esq., nephew to Sir Nathaniel. The family of Hurlock quitted it and Mr. Gould soon after sold to George Perrott Esq., one of the Barons of the Exchequer, who resided for several years in Sir Nathaniel Gould's house." The year "1793" is a misprint and clearly must read "1763" or "1764" to make any sense.

George Perrott was born in 1710, the heir and second of the eleven children, of the Rev. Thomas Perrott, Rector of Welbury and Martin-cum-Gregory in Yorkshire, and a Prebendary of Ripon, by Anastasia, daughter of George Plaxton Esq., of Berwick. He was a student of the law at the Inner Temple, being admitted in November, 1728, and called in 1732. He became a bencher in May, 1757, and two years later King's Counsel.

In 1760, with the Attorney-General leading, he opened the case for the Crown against Lord Ferrers, when tried for murder by the House of Lords, one of the most sensational trials of the whole 18th century. Perrott's opening speech, reading the indictment with its quaint phraseology was: —

"May it please your Lordships; this noble lord Lawrence earl Ferrers, the prisoner at the bar, stands indicted for the felonious killing and murder of one John Johnson; and the indictment sets forth, That the right honourable Lawrence earl Ferrers, viscount Tamworth, on the 18th day of January, in the 33rd year of his present majesty's reign, with force and arms, at the parish of Breedon, in the county of Leicester, in and upon one John Johnson, feloniously, wilfully, and of his malice aforethought, did make an assault; and that a certain pistol then and there being charged with gunpowder and a leaden bullet, which pistol he the said Lawrence earl Ferrers then and there held in his hand, at, against, and upon him the said John Johnson, then and there feloniously, wilfully, and of his malice aforethought, did discharge and shoot off; and with the leaden bullet aforesaid, by force of the gunpowder aforesaid, out of the said pistol by him so discharged and shot off, the said John Johnson in and upon the left side of the said John Johnson, a little under his lowest rib, then there feloniously, wilfully, and of his malice aforethought, did strike and wound, giving to the said John Johnson then and there with the leaden bullet aforesaid, out of the said pistol so as aforesaid discharged and shot off, in and upon the said left side a little under the lowest rib of the said John Johnson, one mortal wound, of the breadth of one inch, and depth of four inches; of which said mortal wound the said John Johnson did languish, and languishing did live, until the 19th day of the same month of January, in the 33rd year aforesaid; on which day, about the hour of nine of the clock in the morning, he, the said John Johnson, of the mortal wound aforesaid, died; and so the jurors, upon their oath, do find, that the said Lawrence earl Ferrers, the said John Johnson, in manner aforesaid, feloniously, wilfully and of his malice aforethought, did kill and murder against the peace of our lord the king, his crown and dignity.

To this indictment the noble lord, the prisoner at the bar, hath pleaded Not Guilty, and for his trial hath put himself upon your lordships, his peers here present.

We, who have the honour to serve the crown in this prosecution, shall call our evidence; and, if we prove the fact charged by this indictment, we doubt not but your lordships will find him guilty, and give such judgment for the same as shall be just."

Lord Ferrers was an extraordinary character even by the standards of those times and to-day would almost certainly have been found insane. Horace Walpole wrote to his friend, Sir Horace Mann in Florence on 21st March, 1758: —

" The most particular thing I know is what happened the other day: a frantic Earl of Ferrers has for this twelvemonth supplied conversation by attempting to murder his wife, a pretty harmless young woman, and everybody that took her part. Having broken the peace to which the House of Lords tied him last year, the cause was trying again there on Friday last. Instead of attending it, he went to the assizes at Hertford to appear against a highwayman, one Page, of extraordinary parts and escapes. The Earl had pulled out a pistol, but trembled so that the robber laughed, took it out of his hand quietly and said, ' My lord, I know you always carry more pistols about you; give me the rest.' At the trial Page pleaded that my Lord was excommunicated, consequently could not give evidence, and got acquitted."

Two years later Lord Ferrers was again in the news and Walpole on 3rd February, 1760, wrote to tell his friend about it, though professing not to be very interested in the matter: —

" There will soon be another trial of another sort on another madman, an Earl Ferrers, who has murdered his steward. He was separated by Parliament from his wife, a very pretty woman, whom he married with no fortune, for the most groundless barbarity, and now killed his steward for having been evidence for her, but his story and person are too wretched and despicable to give you the detail. He will be dignified by a solemn trial in Westminster Hall."

Walpole's interest, however, was soon to be awakened and three months later he sent Mann a superb account of the trial: —

" What will your Italians say to a peer of England, an Earl of one of the best families, tried for murdering his servant, with the utmost dignity and solemnity, and then hanged at the common place for execution for highwaymen and afterwards anatomized? This must seem a little odd to them, especially as they have not

lately had a Sixtus Quintus. I have hitherto spoken of Lord
Ferrers to you as a wild beast, a mad assassin, a low wretch, about
whom I had no curiosity. If I now am going to give you a
minute account of him, don't think me so far part of an English
mob, as to fall in love with a criminal merely because I have had
the pleasure of his execution. I certainly did not see it, nor should
have been struck with mere intrepidity—I never adored heroes,
whether in a cart or a triumphant car—but there has been such
wonderful coolness and sense in all this man's last behaviour that
it has made me quite inquisitive about him—not at all pity him.
I only reflect, what I have often thought, how little connection
there is between any man's sense and his sensibility—so much so,
that instead of Lord Ferrers' having any ascendant over his
passions, I am disposed to think that his drunkenness, which was
supposed to heighten his ferocity, has rather been a lucky circumstance—what might not a creature of such capacity, and who stuck
at nothing, have done, if his abilities had not been drowned in
brandy? I will go back a little into his history. His misfortunes,
as he called them, were dated from his marriage, though he has
been guilty of horrid excesses unconnected with matrimony, and
is even believed to have killed a groom who died a year after
receiving a cruel beating from him. His wife, a very pretty woman
. . . had no fortune, and he says, trepanned him into marriage,
having met him drunk at an assembly in the country and kept him
so until the ceremony was over. As he always kept himself so afterwards, one need not impute it to her. In every other respect, and
one scarce knows how to blame her for wishing to be a countess,
her behaviour was unexceptionable. He had a mistress before and
two or three children, and her he took again after the separation
from his wife. He was fond of both, and used both ill: his wife
so ill, always carrying pistols to bed, and threatening to kill her
before morning, beating her, and jealous without provocation, that
she got separated from him by Act of Parliament, which appointed
receivers of his estate in order to secure her allowance. This he
could not bear. However, he named his steward for one, but
afterwards finding out that this Johnson had paid her fifty pounds
without his knowledge, and suspecting him of being in the con-
federacy against him, he determined, when he failed of opportunities of murdering his wife, to kill the steward, which he effected
as you have heard. The shocking circumstances attending the
murder I did not tell you—indeed, while he was alive, I scarce
liked to speak my opinion even to you; for though I feel nothing
for him, I thought it wrong to propagate any notions that might
interfere with mercy, if he could be thought deserving it—and
not knowing into what hands my letter might pass before it reached
yours, I chose to be silent, though nobody could conceive greater
horror than I did for him at his trial. Having shot the steward
at three in the afternoon, he persecuted him till one in the morning,
threatening again to murder him, attempting to tear off his bandages

and terrifying him till in that misery he was glad to obtain leave
to be removed to his own house, and when the Earl heard the poor
creature was dead, he said he gloried in having killed him. You
cannot conceive the shock this gave the court—many of the lords
were standing to look at him—at once they turned from him with
detestation. I had heard that on the former affair in the House
of Lords, he had behaved with great shrewdness—no such thing
appeared at his trial. It is now pretended that his being forced
by his family against his inclination to plead madness, prevented
his exerting his parts—but he has not acted in anything as if his
family had influence over him—consequently his reverting to much
good sense leaves the whole inexplicable. The very night he
received sentence, he played at picquet with the warders and would
play for money, and would have continued to play every evening
but they refused. Lord Cornwallis, governor of the Tower,
shortened his allowance of wine after his conviction, agreeably to
the late strict acts on murder. This he much disliked, and at last
pressed his brother, the clergyman, to intercede that at least he
might have more porter; for, said he, what I have is not a draught.
His brother represented against it, but at last consenting (and he
did obtain it)—then said the Earl, ' Now is as good a time as any
to take leave of you—adieu!' A minute journal of his whole
behaviour has been kept to see if there was any madness in it.
Dr. Munro since the trial has made an affidavit of his lunacy.
The Washingtons were certainly a very frantic race, and I have
no doubt of madness in him but not of a pardonable sort. Two
petitions from his mother and all his family were presented to the
King, who said, as the House of Lords had unanimously found him
guilty he would not interfere. Last week my Lord Keeper very
good-naturedly got out of a gouty bed to present another: the
King would not hear him. ' Sir,' said the Keeper, ' I don't come
to petition for mercy or respite; but that the four thousand pounds
which Lord Ferrers has in India Bonds may be permitted to go
according to his disposition of it to his mistress, children, and the
family of the murdered man.' ' With all my heart,' said the
King. ' I have no objection; but I will have no message carried
to him from me.' However, this grace was notified to him and
gave him great satisfaction, but unfortunately it now appears to be
law that it is forfeited to the sheriff of the county where the fact
was committed; though when my Lord Hardwicke was told that he
had disposed of it, he said to be sure he may before conviction.
   Dr. Pearce, Bishop of Rochester, offered his service to him: he
thanked the Bishop but said, as his own brother was a clergyman,
he chose to have him. Yet he had another relation who has been
much more busy about his repentance. I don't know whether you
have ever heard that one of the singular characters here is a Countess
of Huntingdon, aunt of Lord Ferrers. She is the Saint Theresa of
the Methodists. Judge how violent bigotry must be in such mad
blood! The Earl, by no means disposed to be a convert, let her visit

him, and often sent for her, and complained that she was enough
to provoke anybody. She made her suffragan, Whitfield, pray for
and preach about him, and that impertinent fellow told his
enthusiasts in his sermon that my Lord's heart was stone. The
Earl wanted much to see his mistress: my Lord Cornwallis, as
simple an old woman as my Lady Huntingdon herself, consulted
her whether he should permit it. ' Oh! by no means; it would be
letting him die in adultery! ' In one thing she was more sensible
He resolved not to take leave of his children, four girls, but on
the scaffold, and then to read to them a paper he had drawn up,
very bitter on the family of Meredith, and on the House of Lords
for the first transaction. This my Lady Huntingdon persuaded him
to drop, and he took leave of his children the day before. He wrote
two letters in the preceding week to Lord Cornwallis on some
of these requests: they were cool and rational, and concluded with
desiring him not to mind the absurd requests of his (Lord Ferrers')
family in his behalf. On the last morning he dressed himself in his
wedding clothes, and said he thought this, at least, as good an
occasion of putting them on as that for which they were made.
He wore them to Tyburn. This marked the strong impression on
his mind. His mother wrote to his wife in a weak angry style,
telling her to intercede for him as her duty, and to swear to his
madness. But this was not so easy: in all her cause before the
Lords she had persisted that he was not mad. Sir William Meredith, and even Lady Huntingdon, had prophesied that his courage
would fail him at the last, and had so much foundation, that it
is certain Lord Ferrers had often been beat: — but the Methodists
were to get no honour by him. His courage rose where it was
most likely to fail—an unlucky circumstance to prophets, especially
when they have had the prudence to have all kind of probability
on their side. Even an awful procession of above two hours, with
that mixture of pageantry, shame and ignominy, nay, and of delay,
could not dismount his resolution. He set out from the Tower at
nine, amidst crowds, thousands. . ."

Lord Ferrers was convicted and the account of his execution is a
vivid commentary on the manners of the time: —

" The procession was conducted with the utmost solemnity; but
moved so very slow, that it did not reach the place of execution
till a quarter before twelve, so that his lordship was two hours and
three quarters in the landau; during the whole of which time he
appeared to be perfectly easy and composed, and his decent deportment seemed greatly to affect the minds of all that beheld him;
insomuch that although his lordship thus passed through many
hundred thousand spectators, yet so respectful was the behaviour of
all towards him, that not the least affront or indignity was offered
to him by any one; but, on the contrary, many persons saluted him
with their prayers for his salvation.

His lordship asked the Sheriff, If he had ever seen so great a
concourse of people before? and upon his answering that he had

not; I suppose, said his lordship, it is because they never saw a lord hanged before. He said, that he had wrote to the king, to beg that he might suffer where his ancestor the earl of Essex had suffered; and that he was in the greater hopes of obtaining that favour, as he had the honour of quartering part of the same arms, and of being allied to his majesty, and that he thought it was hard that he must die at the place appointed for the execution of common felons. But whatever his lordship's thoughts were on that account, those considerations will forever throw an additional lustre on his majesty's impartiality and justice.

Mr. Humphries, the chaplain, who, it seems, had not attended his lordship until this morning, took occasion to observe, that the world would naturally be very inquisitive concerning the religion his lordship professed; and asked him, If he chose to say anything upon that subject? To which his lordship answered, That he did not think himself at all accountable to the world for his sentiments on religion; but that he had always believed in, and adored one God, the maker of all things; that whatever his notions were, he had never propagated them, or endeavoured to gain any persons over to his persuasions; that all countries and nations had a form of religion by which the people were governed, and that whoever disturbed them in it, he looked upon him as an enemy to society; but that, if he himself was wrong in his way of thinking, he was very sorry for it, That he very much blamed my lord Bolingbroke for permitting his sentiments on religion to be published to the world. That the many sects and disputes which happen about religion, have almost turned morality out of doors. That he could never believe what some sectaries teach, that faith alone will save mankind; so that if a man, just before he dies, should say only, I believe, that that alone will save him; ' Shew me thy faith '— Here his lordship stopped; but by which quotation he plainly meant, according to the holy writer (St. James, chap. ii. v. 18) whose words they are, that faith without works is a dead faith.

Concerning the unfortunate and much-to-be-lamented Mr. Johnson, whose death, occasioned the trouble of this day, his lordship declared, That he was under particular circumstances; that he had met with so many crosses and vexations he scarce knew what he did; and most solemnly protested, that he had not the least malice towards him.

The slowness of the procession made this journey appear so very tedious to his lordship, that he often expressed his desire of being got to the end of it, saying, that the apparatus of death, and the passing through such crowds of people, were ten times worse than death itself; but upon the sheriff's taking notice to his lordship, that he was glad to see that he supported himself so well, his lordship replied, I thank you, Sir, I hope I shall continue so to the last.

When his lordship had got to that part of Holborn which is near Drury Lane, he said, he was thirsty, and should be glad of a glass of wine and water; but upon the sheriff's remonstrating to him, that a stop for that purpose would necessarily draw a greater crowd about him, which might possibly disturb and incommode him, yet if his lordship still desired it, it should be done; he most readily answered—That's true, I say no more, let us by no means stop.

When they approached near the place of execution, his lordship told the sheriff, That there was a person waiting in a coach near there, for whom he had a very sincere regard, and of whom he should be glad to take his leave before he died; to which the sheriff answered, That if his lordship insisted upon it, it should be so; but that he wished his lordship, for his own sake, would decline it, lest the sight of a person, for whom he had such a regard, should unman him, and disarm him of the fortitude he possessed.—To which his lordship, without the least hesitation, replied, Sir, if you think I am wrong, I submit; and upon the sheriff's telling his lordship, that if he had any thing to deliver to that person, or any one else, he would faithfully do it; his lordship thereupon delivered to the sheriff a pocketbook, in which was a bank-note, and a ring, and a purse with some guineas, in order to be delivered to that person, which was done accordingly.

The landau being now advanced to the place of execution, his lordship alighted from it, and ascended upon the scaffold, which was covered with black baize, with the same composure and forti-tude of mind he had enjoyed from the time he left the Tower; where, after a short stay, Mr. Humphries asked his lordship, if he chose to say prayers? which he declined; but upon him asking him, if he did not choose to join with him in the Lord's Prayer? He readily answered, He would, for he always thought it a very fine prayer; upon which they knelt down together upon two cushions; covered with black baize, and his lordship with an audible voice very devoutly repeated the Lord's Prayer, and afterwards, with great energy, the following ejaculation, O God, forgive me all my errors—pardon all my sins.

His lordship then rising, took his leave of the sheriffs and the chaplain; and after thanking them for their many civilities, he presented his watch to Mr. Sheriff Vaillant, which he desired his acceptance of; and signified his desire, That his body might be buried at Breedon or Stanton, in Leicestershire.

His lordship then called for the executioner, who immediately came to him, and asked him forgiveness; upon which his lordship said, I freely forgive you, as I do all mankind, and hope myself to be forgiven. He then intended to give the executioner five guineas, but, by mistake, giving it into the hands of the executioner's assistant, an unseasonable dispute ensued between those unthinking wretches, which Mr. Sheriff Vaillant instantly silenced.

The executioner then proceeded to do his duty, to which his lordship, with great resignation, submitted.—His neckcloth being taken off, a white cap, which his lordship had brought in his pocket being put upon his head, his arms secured by a black sash from incommoding himself, and the cord put around his neck, he advanced by three steps upon an elevation in the middle of the scaffold, where part of the floor had been raised about eighteen inches higher than the rest; and standing under the cross-beam which went over it, covered with black baize, he asked the executioner, Am I right?—Then the cap was drawn over his face: and then, upon a signal given by the sheriff (for his lordship, upon being before asked, declined to give one himself) that part upon which he stood, instantly sunk down from beneath his feet, and left him entirely suspended; but not having sunk down so low as was designed, it was immediately pressed down, and levelled with the rest of the floor.

For a few seconds his lordship made some struggles against the attacks of death, but was soon eased of all pain by the pressure of the executioner."

From the point of view of the unfortunate person who has to die a public execution may be the most merciful, for at least he has to put on a brave show and reveal no sign of weakness, and this necessity may distract his mind.

On 24th May, 1760, Walpole writing again to Mann has a last word to say on Lord Ferrers, who has now become " that wonderful creature," so fascinated is Walpole by his character: —

" That wonderful creature Lord Ferrers of whom I told you so much in my last, and with whom I am not going to plague you much more, made one of his keepers read 'Hamlet' to him the night before his death after he was in bed—paid all his bills in the morning as if leaving an inn, and half an hour before the sheriffs fetched him, corrected some verses he had written in imitation of the Duke of Buckingham's epitaph.

. . . What a Noble Author have I here to add to my ' Catalogue '."

On 24th January, 1763, Perrott obtained a seat on the bench as a Baron of the Exchequer. Barons of the Exchequer were formerly six judges (a chief baron and five puisne barons) to whom the administration of justice was committed in causes between the King and his subjects in matters of revenue. The title became obsolete in 1875, when the Court of Exchequer was merged in the High Court of Judicature. During the years 1762-63 the Government was trying to settle the terms of peace with France and Spain, and these proved unpopular. Mr. Pitt called the peace " inadequate." Horace Walpole in his " Memoirs of George III " wrote: —

" The Court at the same time met with some mortification in their pursuit of congratulatory addresses on the peace, which they sedulously promoted. One, Judge Perrott, was so servile as to recommend it from the bench on circuit."

This was certainly an unusual course for a Judge to take.

In a trial at Exeter as to the right to a certain stream of water, Perrott concluded his summing-up thus: —

148

" Gentlemen, there are fifteen witnesses who swear that the water-course used to flow in a ditch on the north side of the hedge. On the other hand, gentlemen, there are nine witnesses who swear that the watercourse used to flow on the south side of the hedge. Now, gentlemen, if you subtract nine from fifteen there remain six witnesses wholly uncontradicted; and I recommend you to give your verdict accordingly for the party who called those six witnesses."

George Perrott married in 1742, Mary, daughter of William Bower of Bridlington in Yorkshire, the widow of Peter Whitton, Lord Mayor of York in 1728, but left no issue. It was during the period that he was a Baron of Exchequer that he lived in Fleetwood House. His judicial career was terminated by an attack of palsy with which he was seized at Maidstone during the Lent Assizes in 1775. He resigned in the following May. "The Gentleman's Magazine" records under 16th June of the same year:—"A grant passed the Great Seal to George Perrott, Esq., late one of the Barons of the Exchequer of a pension of £1,200 a year for the signal services he has rendered his country."

He was never knighted.

He now purchased the manor of Fladbury in Worcestershire and retired there to live in Craycombe House. He did not entirely give up his legal interests as he acted as a local magistrate. He died on the 28th January, 1780, at Pershore, Worcestershire, and was buried at Laleham, Middlesex, where a monument was erected in the church. His wife survived until 7th March, 1784, dying also at Pershore.

The following inscription appears on the Perrott monument in Laleham Church:—

" Sacred to the Memory of
GEORGE PERROTT Esqr.
Late one of the Honble. Barons
of his Majesty's Court of Exchequer,
who departed this Life on the 28th Day of January 1780
in the 70th Year of his Age
By whose Death
The Revenue lost a most able Assertor
of its legal Rights
The Subject a firm Protector against Oppression,
The Publick an able & upright Minister of Justice,
And
the industrious & infirm Poor,
a ready and comfortable Support.

To perpetuate her Esteem, for such amiable Qualities,
his truely afflicted Widow MARY PERROTT
By her last Will caused this Monument to be erected.
Having passed a Life in the continual Exercise of
Religion, Humanity, & Friendship,
(And most deservedly lamented by all who knew her,)
She exchanged this Life for a better,
On the Seventh Day of March 1784
in the 83rd Year of her Age.
She was the only Daughter
of JOHN BOWER Esqr. of BRIDLINGTON KEY
by CATHARINE Daughter of EDWD. TROTTER Esqr.
of SKELTON CASTLE in the NORTH RIDING
in the COUNTY of YORK."

XVIII

The house, after the departure of Baron Perrott, passed into the ownership and occupation of some very shadowy persons who are little more than names. Clearly it was ceasing to attract as a residence.

Mr. James Stewart Tulk succeeded the Baron of the Exchequer as occupier of the more modern part, but by 1782 Mr. John Eade, described as a Ship Chandler from Wapping, had become the tenant. Baron Perrott had left the property by will to his sister Mary, widow of the Rev. John Territt, M.A., Vicar of South Weald in Essex, with reversion to his nephew Mr. Robert Perrott, and in 1791, Mr. John Robley being then in occupation, managed to purchase the property from him, the reversion having fallen in. Robley and his wife lived in the house for some time, and after his death she continued in occupation and was still there in 1824. She also had about fifteen acres of land, some of which had once belonged to Abney House. There were fine trees at the back of the house, including a cedar, said by Robinson "to have been planted in Fleetwood's time; a singular circumstance attaches to this tree;—many years ago a scythe was hung up in the fork of the tree, and was left there unnoticed and untouched for several years, till at length the body of the tree completely overgrew it, and enclosed the blade so fast, that it could not be removed. It is at this day to be seen, the point of the blade on the one side, and the end on the other."

In 1766 the older part of the house was taken by Mr. Henry Guinand, Mr. Hurlock having left on the death of his wife. Guinand is described as a successful stockbroker, and sometimes as a merchant. Although he only remained in occupation for three years he played an important part in the story of the house, for he pulled down the entire front of the old part and rebuilt it in the Palladian style. Unfortunately the "Gentleman's Magazine" of 1769 records him as among the bankrupts for that year: —"B--kr--ts, Henry Guinand of London, merchant." Perhaps the expense of the building work had been a contributory cause of his failure. An apothecary called T. Arndell then occupied the property for a short time, as did Mr. Charles Rebotier who had married Guinand's daughter, Magdalen. Mrs. Crisp eventually used the house for many years as a boarding school for girls, and was certainly there in 1795, the year of publication of Lyson's "Environs of London," as this author specifically mentions her. She was succeeded by Miss Jefferies.

Miss Crisp's school was evidently well established by 1772, for in July of that year Martha Rogers, sister of the celebrated banker-poet, Samuel Rogers, was sent to it as a day pupil. The Rogers lived in a big house at Newington Green, the site of which is to-day marked by Ferntower Road. Thomas Rogers, a Stourbridge glass manufacturer, had entered into partnership with Daniel Radford, a warehouseman in Cheapside, whose house was at Newington Green. The partnership turned out well, and Thomas Rogers' son, Thomas the second, married Radford's only child, Mary, in 1760. The Rogers were on excellent terms with Dr. Richard Price, the famous nonconformist preacher, who also had a house on the Green, and in the summer of 1772 Thomas Rogers went on a trip with Price to the latter's native district in South Wales.

Mary Rogers wrote to her husband on 11th July: —" My ever dear T.R., . . . I called on Saturday morning on Miss Crisp, and agreed for Patty to go to day-school: £1 1s. 0d. entrance and £2 12s. 6d. per quarter, for which she learns reading and working(?), and has five dinners per week. She began on Wednesday, and seems at present very happy with it . . . " In August, 1773, Mr. Rogers again went off on a tour, and on the 17th his wife wrote, ". . . Mrs. Bowles took Patty to London on Sunday. She has got the measles in a very favourable way. Mr. Field attends her . . ." Mr. Field was John Field, who married a descendant of Richard Cromwell. He was an apothecary and founder of the London Annuity Society, and lived at Stoke Newington. On the 23rd September she again wrote to Thomas Rogers: —" Pray tell Mrs. Bowles that all her young folks dined with us yesterday, and were very well and very merry. We had, also, two of the young ladies from Miss Crisp's, and they were altogether a joyous party."

Martha Rogers (Patty) was born in 1755 and lived until 1837. She married John Towgood.

In 1820, or thereabouts, Mr. Joseph Graves was the occupant of Fleetwood House, and soon after a school for Quaker girls was established in it. This must be the school mentioned by Robinson as being " established by the Quakers where a number of girls, the daughters of Quakers, are educated. They, however, support the establishment by needle-work."

Prior to the alterations carried out by Henry Guinand the other part of the house was red brick with large casement windows. The glass of these windows was ornamented with the arms of Fleetwood, Hartopp and Cooke. When Mr. Hurlock vacated the house, he had all the painted panes removed and left them in the care of a local resident. Later he sent a man on horseback from Chelsea to fetch them, but they never reached him intact, being broken to pieces on the journey. In the upper part of the house there was said to be a little secret room used for hiding persecuted nonconformists during the reign of Charles II. The loss of the painted glass windows was unfortunate, but if Mr. Hurlock had not removed them, Guinand's builders might well have smashed them, and they would hardly have survived the final demolition.

{ XIX }

On 5th November, 1913, Miss I. P. Moline gave a lecture to the Stoke Newington Mothers' Union which was printed and published as " Old Stoke Newington " in the same year. In it occurs the following passage: —

" Where Fleetwood Street stands, I remember a large house with a beautiful garden, where I have often played croquet. More than 200 years ago it was inhabited by Colonel Fleetwood, son-in-law of Oliver Cromwell. It was later divided into two and in one half there used to be a school for little Quaker girls. My aunt went there nearly ninety years ago and she often told me of the strict discipline enforced. All the pupils were obliged to wear the plainest Friends' dress. She was greatly interested in an underground passage beneath the house, which was said to extend to the Birdcage Walk, at the foot of Stamford Hill. Once a small part of it was cleared out, and the girls allowed to go a little way into it. It is an interesting link with the past that my aunt well remembered Ugo Foscolo, who taught at the school. He was an Italian refugee, a great authority on Dante and a most interesting man. In his youth he was devotedly attached to the Countess of Albany the widow of Charles Edward Stewart, the Young Pretender, the hero of the rebellion in Scotland in 1745. I have seen the grave of Ugo Foscolo in the Church of Santa Croce, in Florence, which is by his own desire as close as possible to that of his beloved Countess."

It is impossible to rate too highly the value of personal reminiscence in biographical and historical matters. As Dr. Johnson said, " the necessity of complying with times, and of sparing persons, is the greatest impediment of biography. . . . What is known can seldom be immediately told: and when it might be told, it is no longer known."

But for a conversation between an old lady and a young girl, who subsequently took the trouble to write it down, it might never have been known that Ugo Foscolo, that stormy petrel of Italian poetry, had ever crossed the threshold of Fleetwood House. How many other fascinating associations may have been lost for want of a recorder? From one of Foscolo's letters in which he says he is teaching pupils at half a crown a head a lesson, eight of them, all living " in the same village " it is possible to fix the year in which he was teaching at Fleetwood House as 1826. Although making it clear that he was at a school for Quaker girls, he does not indicate the locality of its situation. Miss Moline has somewhat exaggerated the romantic attachment of Foscolo to the Countess of Albany, and perhaps confused him with another famous Italian poet, Alfieri. It is worth briefly following their story.

The Countess of Albany (1752-1824), before her marriage, Louise, Princess of Stolberg-Gedern, was married to Charles Edward Stuart, the Young Pretender (1720-1788) on Good Friday—an ill-omened day for a wedding—1772 at Macerata. She had never seen her husband, but no doubt to a young girl he was a romantic figure and his adventures in Scotland in 1745 most appealing. He had become " de jure " King of England in 1766. Unfortunately, he was now anything but an attractive figure. Failure and disillusionment had for some years caused him to give way to what his brother, Henry, the Cardinal Duke of York, called " the nasty bottle." John Howard, the prison reformer, who at one time lived within half a mile of Fleetwood House, caught sight of Charles Edward in Rome a few years before his marriage and wrote to Lady Whitbread:—" The Pretender passed close by me yesterday and I had a full strong view of him. He had the look of a mere sot, very stupid dull and bending double." Louise was a delightful person and her situation created sympathy. In 1773 Karl Victor von Bonstetten a young Swiss aristocrat arrived in Rome and was soon a frequent guest at the Stuart Palace. He wrote of Louise:—" She was of middle height, fair, with dark blue eyes, a slightly turned-up nose, and a dazzling white English complexion. Her expression was gay and espiègle, and not without a spice of irony on the whole more French than German. She was enough to turn all heads. The Pretender was tall, lean, good-natured, talkative. He liked to have opportunities of speaking English, and was given to talking a great deal about his adventures—interesting enough for a visitor, but not equally so for his intimates, who had probably heard those stories a hundred times over. His young wife laughed heartily at the story of his dressing up in woman's clothes." (The Flora MacDonald episode.) " I was in love with the Queen without admitting it, she was in love with me without telling me." Forty-four years later von Bonstetten could write to her:—" I never pass through the Apostles' Square without looking up at that balcony, at that house where I saw you for the first time."

But it was in 1777 that Count Vittorio Alfieri, the real romance of Louise's life, appeared on the scene. He was then twenty-eight, handsome, with blue eyes, bright red hair, and strong aquiline features. He wore uniform. He did not like the army but he liked the uniform. He was educating himself in literature so that he might be a writer. He described Louise as having " . . . very dark eyes, with a soft fire in them, combined as rarely happens, with a very fair skin and fair hair, giving her beauty a most striking and overwhelming éclat."

Just as no one had raised objection to a girl of nineteen being married by proxy to a man thirty-two years older who turned out to be a brutal sot, so now no one objected to a young man of twenty-eight seeking and obtaining the love of a married woman of twenty-five. As Vernon Lee wrote, " the immoral law had produced the immoral lawlessness." In 1780 Charles Edward celebrated St. Andrew's Day with a drunken debauch which culminated in his attempting to strangle Louise in bed. She thereupon sought refuge

in a convent whence the Pope permitted her to withdraw after a few
months. Charles Edward is said to have offered a reward for Alfieri's
murder. At this time Louise wrote: —" What a cruel thing to expect
one's happiness from the death of another! Oh God! how it degrades
one's soul" In 1784 Charles Edward at last agreed to a separation,
and on 17th August Louise and Alfieri met at the inn of the " Two
Keys " at Colmar.

Four years later Charles Edward died and Alfieri wrote: —
" Although his death left his widow entirely free, and she lost no
friend in her husband; in spite of all I was to my great astonishment
eye-witness of the fact that she was not a little moved by it, and
with a grief neither assumed nor exaggerated; for no artifice ever
entered into that pure and unparalleled nature. And certainly her
husband, despite the wide disparity of their ages, would have found
her an excellent friend and companion, even if she could not have
given him love, had he not embittered her by his continual rude and
rough and drunken treatment. I owe this testimony to the interests
of pure truth."

Louise and Alfieri actually visited London in 1791, and Louise
was received at Court. Horace Walpole wrote: —" The Countess of
Albany is not only in England, in London, but at this very moment,
I believe, in the palace of St. James'—not restored by as rapid a
revolution as the French, but, as was observed last night at supper at
Lady Mount-Edgcumbe's, by that topsy-turvyhood that characterized
the present age. Within these two months Madame du Barry, mistress
of Louis Quinze, has dined with the Lord Mayor of London, and
the Pretender's widow is presented to the Queen of Great Britain! "

Alfieri died on 8th October, 1803, after a very short illnness, in
Louise's words " without fear, without struggle, without knowing it,
like a bird, or a lamp when the oil has failed." He was buried in
Santa Croce, Florence. He had written his own epitaph, " so that
nobody should write a worse one," but it was not used. Louise
engaged Canova to design a monument, which is described by John
Cam Hobhouse in his " Historical Illustrations of the Fourth Canto
of Childe Harold ": —

" The tomb of Alfieri in the Santa Croce, is one of the least
successful productions of Canova. The whole monument is heavy,
and projects itself into the aisle of the church more prominently
than becomes the associate of the more modest but richer sepulchres
of Michael Angelo and Machiavelli. The colossal Cybele of Italy
weeping over a medallion in low relief, shows the difficulty of doing
justice to the mourner and the monument, and may besides be
mistaken for the princess of the house of Stolberg, whose name and
title have left little room on the inscription for Alfieri himself. They
show a little step opposite to the monument, on which the princess
herself periodically contemplates her own work and that of Canova.
The grief of an amiable woman for the loss of an accomplished man,
may be expected to endure; and, to say the truth, the other sex has
too long wanted a ' pendant ' for the twice retold tale of the

Ephesian matron."

Louise, who had always been a great reader and devoted to literature, now established a salon in Florence to which came Chateaubriand, Stendhal, Sismondi, Byron, Madame de Stael, Nelson, Madame de Récamier, Thomas Moore and many others. Lamartine, later to be a visitor to Stoke Newington, described her: " There was now nothing about her which recalled either the queen of an empire or of a heart. She was just a short dumpy woman whose figure had lost all lightness and grace. Her features, also, too thickly rounded preserved no line of ideal beauty; but her eyes had a light, her ash-grey hair a tint, her mouth a welcome, all her face an intelligence and her expression a grace that made one dream of the past, if one could not admire the present. Her courteous speech, her easy manner, her re-assuring familiarity immediately raised one to her level. You could not tell whether she descended to you, or raised you to her, she was so natural and easy."

In August, 1812, Ugo Foscolo arrived in Florence, driven from Milan by political persecution, He had been born in Zante in 1776, the son of a Venetian father, who died while he was a child, and a Greek mother. He had studied at Padua and by the time he arrived at Florence was already famous as the author of the novel, " Jacopo Ortis " and the classic poem, " I Sepolchri." He was a liberal who wished to see Italy freed from Austrian domination. He and Louise were soon on excellent terms. He was thirty-four and she sixty-two. With his red hair and clear cut features he bore a certain resemblance to Alfieri. He seems to have confided all his troubles to her, not least his many love affairs, which invariably turned out unhappily. When absent from Florence he wrote to her: " My friend, and not the friend of my good fortune. I seem to have left home, mother, friends and almost the person dearest to my heart in leaving Florence." And again: " I had in you, mia signora, a friend and a mother; a person, in short, such as no name can express, but such as sufficed to console me in the miseries which are perhaps incurable and interminable."

At one time Foscolo had supported Napoleon and the French but came to oppose them. He also refused to support the Austrians. Disliked and spied on by both sides he decided to go into exile in 1815. Louise misunderstood his motives which were sincere and wrote attributing his conduct to a desire to show off. This letter hurt Foscolo, who replied: " So thus generosity and justice are banished even from nobler souls. Your letter, Signora Contessa, grieves me, and confers upon me, at the same time two advantages: it diminishes suddenly the perpetual nostalgia which I have felt for Florence, and it affords me an occasion to try my strength of spirit . . . "

In the autumn of 1816 Foscolo arrived in England and it was not long before his attitude towards Louise softened and he began writing friendly letters to her once more, but the old relationship was never quite restored. Holland House and Whig society in London, including Samuel Rogers, welcomed him. But he was handicapped by lack of means and a diffidence in asking for help from his many well-to-do acquaintances. In this situation he met Byron's friend John Cam Hobhouse. Byron, while writing the Fourth Canto of " Childe Harold," decided that his work required numerous explanatory and historical notes, together with some account of the more modern Italian poets. Hobhouse undertook to supply these notes, most of which he wrote during the summer of 1817 while visiting Byron in Italy. Neither of the friends, however, felt capable of producing the section required on modern Italian literature, and Hobhouse returned to London, in February, 1818, with this still unwritten. It was on the night of Monday, 23rd, March, 1818, that Hobhouse, dining at Roger Wilbraham's house in Stratton Street, Piccadilly, found himself sitting next to Foscolo and was vastly pleased with him. Almost at once he decided to enlist his help in writing the notes. Foscolo agreed, on condition that he was not mentioned as author, and supplied the " Essay on the Present Literature of Italy," so quickly as to suggest that he already had it written. The " Historical Illustrations of the Fourth Canto of Childe Harold " were published on 28th April, 1818, and Foscolo's " Essay " occupied pages 345 to 484. It must have been somewhat mortifying for Hobhouse to find that the " Essay " attracted more attention than the rest of the book. " My ' Illustrations ' are praised and particularly that part in which I have the least concern," he noted in his diary.

The opening part of the section dealing with Alfieri reads as follows: —

" The life of this Author has been written by himself. His tragedies have been criticised in every European language. There still remain some notices on his death, and some opinions on his other works, which may be new to the English reader.

His connexion with the Countess of Albany is known to all the world, but no one is acquainted with the secret of that long intercourse. If they were ever married, Alfieri and the Countess took as much pains to conceal that fact, as is usually bestowed upon its publicity. Truth might have been spoken on the tomb of the poet, but even there we only find that Louisa, Countess of Albany, was his only love—' quam unice dilexit '—A church, perhaps, was not the place to boast of such a passion; but after every consideration we may conclude, that the Abate Caluso, who wrote the epitaph, and received the last sighs of Alfieri, knew, and did not choose to tell, that his friend was never married to the widow of Charles Edward Stewart—' Tacendo clamat '—his silence is eloquent.

Alfieri, in the langour of a protracted agony, which the presence of Caluso assisted him to support, received the last visit of a priest, who came to confess him, with an affability for which he was not distinguished in the days of his health: but he said to him, ' Have the kindness to look in to-morrow; I trust that death will wait for twenty-four hours.' The eccliastic returned the next day. Alfieri was sitting in his arm-chair and said, ' At present, I fancy, I have but a few minutes to spare,' and turning towards the Abbe, entreated him to bring the Countess to him. No sooner did he see her than he stretched forth his hand, saying, 'Clasp my hand, my dear friend, I die.'

The religious opinion of Alfieri cannot be collected from his writings. His tragedies contain here and there a sarcasm against the Popes, and in his fugitive pieces may be found some epigrams against the monastic orders, but more particularly against the cardinals. Not a word, however, has ever escaped him against the Christian doctrines. It is only upon close inspection that we find, in a treatise on tyranny, that auricular confession, and the indissolubility of marriage, have contributed to the enslavement of Italy. His latter years were divided between a haughty irascibility and a deep melancholy, which afflicted him by turns, to a degree which rendered him scarcely accountable for his actions. Alfieri was then not unfrequently seen in the churches from vespers to sunset, sitting motionless, and apparently wrapt up in listening to the psalms of the monks, as they chanted them from behind the screen of the choir. The way in which he died would, however, lead us to conjecture, that his meditations were not those of religion, and that he chose such a retreat in search of that solemn tranquillity which alone promised him a temporary repose from the relentless furies that preyed upon his heart."

The Countess of Albany was not at all pleased with references to herself, and indeed the book by reason both of its contents and omissions caused great offence in Italian literary circles. It was suspected that Foscolo had had a hand in it. Hobhouse found himself involved in lengthy written arguments and explanations. Byron was highly delighted by this uproar and did all he could to fan the flames. He and Foscolo never met, which is to be regretted, as something amusing would surely have resulted. In one letter, Byron called him "that charlatan, Foscolo," but he was pleased to hear that the latter had praised "The Two Foscari"; " he has more of the antient Greek than of the modern Italian . . . 'tis a wonderful man; and my friends Hobhouse and Rose both swear by him. . . "

Although at times he earned large sums by lecturing, Foscolo was extravagant and always hard-up. By 1824 he was in difficulties, and the last three years of his life must have been bitter ones. Under the names of Marriott, Emerytt and Florian he moved round the outskirts of London getting what temporary work he could.

A letter from William Allen shows how Foscolo came to teach at Fleetwood House: —

"near London 13 of 6th Month June 1826.

W. Allen presents his respects to his Friend Foscolo and has sent his letter to Dr. Pinkerton one of the Secretaries of the British and Foreign Bible Society, though W.A. does not think that the Society will undertake the translation at present. W.A. will be very glad if it shall be in his power to procure some scholars for a private class in the Italian Language in a few weeks time and requests his friend Foscolo to keep him informed from time to time as he may change his lodging where a letter may find him."

The British and Foreign Bible Society can trace no correspondence with Foscolo. The letter is preserved in the Labronica Library at Leghorn in Italy (Mss. Lab. Vol. 46. f. 243).

Louise died on 29th January, 1824, and was buried in Santa Croce. Her death was mourned by all Florence, a town in which she had lived for thirty years and never refused an appeal for help. Alfieri's epitaph in which he described the Countess as buried next to him had to be altered as her tomb is not beside his. In all probability Miss Moline heard of Foscolo discussing Alfieri and his wish to be buried close to his Countess, and confused this with Foscolo's own desires. In 1827 Foscolo was living in a cottage at Turnham Green. He was very hard up and had to keep his expenses down. He said he felt " he could at least die in it like a gentleman." His health failed rapidly and he died in his forty-ninth year. The Marchesa Vitelleschi in " A Court in Exile," says: " Feeling his health failing fast, he testified his wish to be buried under a tree in the fresh and open churchyard at Chiswick." Many years later his body was removed to Italy, and a monument erected in Santa Croce.

$$\boxed{\text{XX}}$$

The school, at which Ugo Foscolo found employment in 1826, had been opened two years previously. There is a note in the "Life and Correspondence of William Allen" under the year 1824 which definitely fixes the date: —

"A female Friend who had for many years been anxious that these important objects (i.e., science, classical literature and the divine teachings) should be combined in the education of youth, opened a boarding school for girls at Stoke Newington in the autumn of this year."

Also, in the Library of the Society of Friends in Euston Road are preserved two manuscript copies of the school prospectus. It is unfortunate that this document was not printed, as many of the Quaker school prospecti issued round about the same time are beautifully printed and illustrated in colour with views of the school buildings. The prospectus for the Fleetwood House school reads as follows: —

"Dear Friend,

Some Friends who have been much interested on the subject of education, have long been desirous of seeing an Establishment in our religious society on a plan in degree differing from any hitherto adopted wherein the children of Friends should not only be liberally instructed in the Elements of useful knowledge, but in which particular attention should be paid to the state of mind of each individual child. It has appeared to them that this can only be accomplished by an arrangement which shall afford a competent Instructor to every ten or twelve pupils. They considered it highly important, in the formation of the habits and character of the rising generation, that the children should be trained in a manner strictly consistent with the Principles of our Profession, that every appearance of religious sensibility should be watched over and encouraged and that particular attention should be bestowed upon the development of kind and benevolent feelings.

With the desire of promoting so important an object it is concluded that a Girls' School shall be established in the neighbourhood of London, and the following friends have taken shares as Proprietors of the Establishment, viz.: —

William Allen	Joseph Foster	Thomas Christy
Grizell Birkbeck	Luke Howard	John Sanderson
Anna Hanbury	Samuel Gurney	Edward Harris
Susanna Corder	W. F. Reynolds	Henry Tylor

The School will be conducted by Susanna Corder, who has for several years past been engaged as Governess of the Female Boarding School at Suir Island in Ireland, and believes it right to devote her attention to the Instruction of Friends' children on the proposed plan.

The number of pupils will at first be limited to *twelve* but may be extended when a young woman with suitable qualifications shall have been educated so as to become competent to assist in superintending and instructing a few more, but in all cases it is deemed essential that the attention of the Teachers should be confined to a small number of children, in order that their dispositions may be carefully studied and their characters more decidedly formed. It is proposed also that a certain number of young women, whose conduct, disposition, and talent may qualify them for the right formation of the youthful mind, should be trained in this Establishment with a view to their becoming private Teachers in the families of Friends or Assistants in schools.

A commodious house has been taken at Stoke Newington and the following Friends have proposed to make an arrangement among themselves for visiting the school as often as it may be deemed requisite and are willing that the Superintendent should apply to them for counsel and support, viz.: —

William Allen	Rebecca Christy
Grizell Birkbeck	Isabella Harris
Tabitha Bevans	Anna Sandeson

The course of Instruction shall comprehend a Grammatical knowledge of the English language, Writing, Arithmetic, Geography, Astronomy and the Use of the Globes, Ancient and Modern History, Elements of Mathematics, of Physics or Experimental Philosophy, Chemistry, Natural History—The French Language and Needlework.

In teaching some of the above branches our Friend, William Allen, has offered not only his assistance but the use of an extensive philosophical apparatus.

Terms £50 per annum, Washing not included.

The Latin, Greek, German and Italian languages and drawing taught if required, on the usual terms.

No Entrance or other extra charge will be made.

The School to be opened the 1st of the 10th month ensuing.

If thou shouldst know of any Friends who may incline to send their children, please to address a line to Susanna Corder, to the care of William Allen, Plough Court, Lombard Street.

The Pupils will be admitted in the order of their application.

On account of the distance from Meeting the Proprietors have made arrangements for the comfortable conveyance of the children without any additional expence to the Parents.

A vacation of six weeks in the summer.

Signed by order of the Proprietors.

EDWARD HARRIS

Stoke Newington 14th of 8th Month 1824."

The proprietors were all either resident in Stoke Newington, mostly living in Paradise Row as part of Church Street was then called, or had very close connections with the district. William Allen's firm was to develop into the great business of Allen and Hanbury. Luke Howard was his first partner and a brilliant pioneer in meteorology. Grizell Birkbeck became Allen's third wife in 1827, and Anna Hanbury must have been of the family later taken into partnership by Allen.

Susanna Corder was born in 1787. She was a delicate child, and from the first deeply religious, often being troubled by such things as the vanity of wearing clothes that were too attractive. She was greatly attached to her mother whom she nursed through a long illness. After her mother's death she felt a definite urge to become a teacher, and quite by chance, in the year 1817, learnt that there was a vacancy at the school at Suir Island, Clonmel, in Ireland. She obtained the appointment and remained in Ireland for seven years.

In 1820 William Allen visited Ireland. He returned on 8th May. He wrote in his diary, his first mention of Susanna Corder: —

"The steamer started at five minutes past nine; there was a great deal of motion, and the wind and rain made it very uncomfortable. Two young women friends were also passengers, viz. Susanna Corder and Sarah Strangman. We arrived at Holyhead at six, and we all dined together at Spencer's Hotel, where S.C. and S.S. are intending to remain until the morning."

Susanna Corder had been much impressed with the educational methods used at the Suir Island school, and on returning to England desired to establish a school run on the same lines. It was fortunate that she came into contact with William Allen, as there is no doubt that he was the driving force behind the establishment of the "Friends'" school in Fleetwood House.

In "Family Memorials: Chiefly the Memoranda Left by Isabella Harris with Some Extacts from the Journals of Her Mother," Not Published, 1869, are to be found three brief glimpses of Susanna Corder: —

"Stoke Newington 7th Month, 1825
. . . Susanna Corder came in this evening: she has been at Harwich with•John and Sarah Grubb, and paid a sweet visit to Mary Proud during her absence; the latter has had another stroke a fortnight ago, which affected one side; but S.C. says she never heard her so clear and powerful (in her ministry) as in an opportunity they had under her roof, in which she said the happiness she enjoyed was wonderful to herself . . .
Thy affectionately attached
ISABELLA HARRIS."

"5th Month 25th 1826.
. . . S. Corder called while we were at supper, and made one in a little opportunity we had afterwards. . . A little after this when our meeting was concluding, S. Corder remarked that she could

not feel satisfied without saying to the dear friends of this family,
that whatever might be their trials permitted, they had abundant
reason to thank God and take courage."

"Twelfth Month 20th 1826.

Today I went to the reading at the girls' school which was a
profitable time to me. I felt it as a table spread in the desert, and
my soul was fed as with dainties I had much union of spirit with
W. Allen who was present. Divine good appeared to flow as oil
from vessel to vessel. What shall I render to God for all his
benefits! For this truly has been a rich repast to me after the long
drought which my soul has sustained."

In "Emma Marshall: A Biographical Sketch" by Beatrice
Marshall it is stated that all the pupils at the school wore the stiff
cardboard Quaker bonnets except one, who suffered from headaches.
The bonnets were specially made by a milliner in Bishopsgate Street
and attracted the jeers of the girls at an adjoining school over the
wall. It may be that at this time both parts of Fleetwood House were
occupied by girls' schools and that those who jeered at the Quaker
bonnets were pupils of the school started by Mrs. Elizabeth Crisp
and later carried on by Miss Jeffries. Miss Beatrice Marshall goes
on to quote her aunt, Miss Mary Martin, a pupil at the school, who
left an interesting account of it. Miss Martin was clearly not
favourably impressed with Sarah Grubb, whom Susanna Corder had
visited at Harwich.

"We were not allowed to sing hymns, only to repeat them.
On Sundays we went to Meeting twice, and before starting had
to repeat either a prophecy and its fulfiment, or portions from a
catechism compiled by Joseph John Gurney, to confirm us in
Friends' principles. There was no lack of ministry, William Allen,
Cornelius Hanbury and some others frequently preaching and
praying. I remember a certain Sarah Grubb who preached. She
filled my young soul with fear and horror. She was like some
weird prophetess, very forbidding and gaunt, who even eschewed a
white lining to her Friends' bonnet. The great events of our school-
life, instead of being theatricals, a concert, or prize-giving, were
a visit to the British Museum, and the Friends' great festival of
Yearly Meeting. It was a gathering of Friends from all parts of
the United Kingdom and from America. There were a set of
queries which had to be read and answered, as to the state of the
Meetings with regard to attendance, 'plainness of speech, behaviour
and apparel,' and other signs of consistency. I shall never forget
the impression the first Meeting I attended at Devonshire House
made upon me, when I was about ten or eleven years old. We
drove up to London in coaches, and most of the girls had relations
who came to Yearly Meeting, so it was a treat for many."

William Beck made some notes in 1890, and these were published
in 1927 as "Church Street." His account bears out that of Miss
Martin especially about the trips the pupils made by coach.

"Friends' connection with these large and ancient premises was of previous date through their large school for girls long presided over by Susanna Corder as its Head Mistress. She was in herself an embodiment of perfection as regards propriety of manner, costume, and doctrine of the mediaeval section of the Friends' Society. Order and decorum were here cultivated in a high degree. The grounds were too extensive to make it necessary for outdoor exercise to be taken beyond the precincts of this favoured spot, rich in groves and bowers with tall elms, evergreen shrubs and shaded walks, but on meeting days when a journey to the city was on hand, for there was at that time no place for assembly of Friends in Stoke Newington, the sight of well filled conveyances with these fair damsels of varied ages, but all similarly attired in the neatest and most delicately coloured costumes, was a very pleasing one."

In 1827, one Joseph Pease, wrote of the school and its wide curriculum some amusing doggerel verses, " A Yearly Meeting Epistle from Friend Joseph in London to his Cousin Anne in the Country." The verses are preserved in manuscript in the Library of the Society of Friends: —

" Dear Coz, in my last (which I sent by Friend P . . .)
I shewed the advantage as well as renown
That our body of Friends cannot fail to acquire
By the Female Establishment 2 miles from Town.

Where the pupils imbibe such astounding variety
Of stores intellectual—I solemnly vow
Since the earliest days of the Quaker Society,
Such achievements by girls were ne'er heard of till now.

No science, no art, in their tribe is a mystery
The path of the earth and the tides of the sea,
Cosmography, Algebra, Chemistry, History,
To those juvenile Blues are a mere A.B.C.

And in languages—oh you'd not credit their skill!
One can scarce name a tongue, Coz, but what they can reason in,
Greek, Hebrew, French, Latin, Italian at will,
With Irish and Welch for occasional seasoning.

Nay more—if our principles did but permit
I doubt not ev'n fortification and gunnery
Might be added with ease as a kind of tit-bit,
To enliven the studies at N[ewingto]n Nunnery.

'Tis true some reports have transpired of caballing
From the fair inmates dreading they elsewhere must roam
Should Hymen take from them the lectures of Allen
The Champion of Colonies settled at home.

The straight path of Truth the dear Girls keep their feet in
And ah! it would do your heart good Cousin Anne
To see them arriving at G[racechurc]h Street Meeting
All snugly packed up, 25 in a van."

The reference to William Allen is clearly to his forthcoming marriage to Grizell Birkbeck, which caused quite a stir among local "Friends," as she was many years his senior. The school was evidently flourishing as its original number of twelve pupils had been more than doubled in three years. Susanna Corder was the author of several books and pamphlets, most of them published anonymously. "A Brief Outline of the Origin Principles and Church Government of the Society of Friends," is a very clearly written pamphlet which evidently achieved great success as it was translated into German in 1847, French in 1851, and Italian in 1867. The "Life of Elizabeth Fry" was actually translated into Japanese in 1894. Other works are a "Memoir of Priscilla Gurney," 1856, "Reasons why Christian Women should exercise the Gifts of the Holy Spirit," translated into French in 1851, "Friendly Cautions addressed to the Advocates of Total Abstinence from all Intoxicating Beverages, by a Total Abstainer," "Christian Instruction in the History, Types and Prophecies of the Old Testament, illustrating those Fundamental Doctrines of the Gospel which are acknowledged by true Christians of every Religious Denomination," 1854, and "Some Remarks on the Prize Essays," 1860.

Mrs. Sophia Elizabeth de Morgan, before her marriage, lived in Defoe's old house with her father, William Frend. From her "Reminiscences" it appears that she sometimes attended William Allen's chemistry lectures, which he gave to Susanna Corder's pupils: —

". . . I made the acquaintance of William Allen, who kindly allowed me to attend the lectures on chemistry which he gave, with experiments, to a class of young girls. . . Mr. Allen's quick perception of facts was greater than his power of following out extensive inferences. He was a good observer and classifier, but stopped at facts and phenomena. In philanthropy the same ready perception and hastiness of inference were apparent. His exceeding benevolence and strong impulse to help the suffering led him occasionally into exaggeration of the evils he opposed; but all good causes need pioneers who overdo their work at first. Without such the work would not be done . . . "

William Allen took a keen interest in the school's progress and noted in his Journal for 16th January, 1826, "The Friends' girls' school at Newington, under the care of Susanna Corder, prospers. I generally attend the readings there on first and fourth-day readings, and they are often times of spiritual refreshment." He sometimes took his telescope so that the pupils could view the stars, and went out of his way to make their studies interesting.

He had an ever increasing opinion of Susanna Corder's abilities.

In 1835 he took her to Lindfield, in Sussex to see his "agricultural community," and from there to the Friends' Quarterly Meeting at Brighton. On the 3rd September, 1837, he was again at Fleetwood House, "Tea at the girls' school and reading afterwards. There was a solemn pause, and I thought I felt that divine goodness was near; I encouraged the dear children to keep up an exercise of mind in our silent meetings, reminding them that though the disciples had toiled all night and caught nothing, yet, when the Master came, and they followed his directions by casting the net at the right side of the ship, they enclosed a great multitude of fishes." In 1842 Allen's health was beginning to fail. He wrote to Susanna Corder, "I believe this illness is sent in mercy to me, to wean me more and more from all things below, and to make me look more steadily to the end of time." He died in the following year at Lindfield, leaving all his manuscripts and papers to his late wife's niece, Lucy Bradshaw, and Susanna Corder.

In 1836 there seems to have been a schism among local Quakers. One John Wilkinson had evidently been expressing unorthodox religious views. He wrote a book in his own defence, "Quakerism Examined: in a reply to the Letter of Samuel Tuke." He finally resigned from the Society of Friends. Susanna Corder was one of the four signatories to a letter addressed to him: —

"Stoke Newington, 28th of 1st Month, 1836.

Dear Friend John Wilkinson,

It is under a feeling of much Christian love and interest, that we believe it to be our duty to inform thee, that for a considerable time past, but more particularly last first-day and this day, thy communications in our meetings have deeply afflicted our minds; and we have much painful evidence that thy ministry has caused great uneasiness to others also.

Under these feelings, we would very tenderly, yet earnestly, express our hope that thou mayst when assembled with us, feel it thy place to remain in silence.

We remain thy sincere friends,

JOHN KITCHING,
ROSAMUND POST,
ISABEL KITCHING,
SUSANNA CORDER."

Soon after the founding of the school Susanna Corder had been appointed to the station of Elder, and no doubt it was in this capacity that she signed the letter to Wilkinson. Her obituary notice in the "Annual Monitor" for 1865 says that at about the same time " she was also appointed a member of the revising committee of the Morning Meeting in which service she continued to be engaged during the remaining fifteen years of her residence near London." This suggests that she ceased to be headmistress of the Fleetwood House school some time during the period 1840-45. William Beck, however, in his book, "Church Street," says that "on the death of

Susanna Corder " the Friends' Girls School moved to " The Laurels," which adjoined the Manor House School, also in Church Street. Beck mentions a family called Thomas as living in " The Laurels," in 1836, but possibly between this year and 1840 they left, for it was at this time, on the incorporation of the Abney Park Cemetery Company, that Fleetwood House lost most of its grounds. These had been one of the house's main attractions as a school, so it is possible that Susanna Corder left when it became necessary for the school to move to new premises. She retired to Chelmsford where she died on 28th February, 1864, aged 76. Perhaps she had come from this district as Corder is a well-known East Anglian name. She herself said, " I have had to pass through evil report and good report; through prosperity and adversity."

In 1865 William Ball wrote in his " Memorials ": —

" Susanna Corder "

" Can Time, to thee, have brought
So soon the eventide?
But all is well with thee,
For thou hast sought
Jesus, the Crucified!

Though ailing oft. and oft
With various suffering tried,
Still hast thou loved thy Lord;
Still hast thou wrought
For him, the Crucified!

Oh, let this golden thought
Gleam on thy eventide,
That thou hast served His cause,
And glory brought
To Him, the Crucified!

P.S. Now Loved One, thou has sought
In Heaven His Sheltering side!
For ever safe with Him
Who loved and bought
Thy soul, the Crucified! "

The usual fate of a great mansion is to end as a school, a boarding house or a tenement. Fashions change, and the type of dwelling desired by one generation is not regarded with favour by the next. Fleetwood House had resounded to the shrill voices of Susanna Corder's schoolchildren, but with her departure these were stilled, and the house entered on its final phase and degenerated into a lodging-house. The formation of a company deprived the house of the grounds which had been its main attraction as a school. In 1836 the Abney estate of over thirty acres was purchased by this company, which was incorporated as the Abney Park Cemetery Company. Four years later the cemetery was opened, and forming part of it were the eight acres of land which had been the garden of Fleetwood House. The great tree, described by Robinson as standing in the ornate garden was now to be found shading the cemetery's ever increasing array of tombstones.

Before describing the last days of Fleetwood House it is of interest to refer to a matter of pure speculation, which will probably never be answered finally one way or the other for lack of evidence. Did Edgar Allan Poe ever enter the house? This great American writer was brought to England as a boy by his foster-parents, and spent three years, from 1817 to 1820, as a boarder at the Manor House School, also in Stoke Newington Church Street, kept by the Rev. John Bransby, M.A. In one of his best stories, "William Wilson," Poe purports to describe the Manor House School. "The house was old and irregular . . . there was really no end to its windings—to its incomprehensible sub-divisions. It was difficult, at any given time, to say with certainty upon which of its stories one happened to be. From each room to every other there were sure to be found three or four steps either in ascent or descent. Then the lateral branches were innumerable—inconceivable—and so returning in upon themselves, that our most exact ideas in regard to the whole mansion were not very far different from those with which we pondered upon infinity. During the five years of my residence here, I was never able to ascertain with precision in what remote locality lay the little sleeping apartment assigned to myself and some eighteen or twenty scholars."

More than one local historian has declared that this description is far better suited to Fleetwood House than to the Manor House School. Poe must often have walked along Church Street and looked at the outside of the house. Whether he ever saw the inside must remain an unsolved mystery.

In 1927 a little book called "Church Street," by William Beck (1823-1907) was published. It was based on notes made by Mr. Beck in 1890, and contains a short description of the house in its final days : —

"Subsequent owners had covered the old brickwork with cement, which from the wear and tear of time acquired a very dingy and forbidding aspect, accentuated by the plain high wall of its forecourt. For some time previous to its demolition the once large mansion had become sub-divided into several tenements, the chief portion being occupied by a family of the name of Mercy, probably like so many another in Stoke Newington of Huguenot extraction. They were highly respectable, but through being in somewhat reduced circumstances, were in the practice of taking in lodgers who occupied different apartments."

On 3rd April, 1872, Mr. S. Arnott went over Fleetwood House, and subsequently wrote to "Notes and Queries": "I this day, in company with a friend, went over the old house on the north side of Church Street . . . once the residence of Lieutenant General Fleetwood. The house is now about to be pulled down to make way for a new street, and is already partially dismantled. . . The house was divided into two in the last century; it contains on the whole about sixty rooms. We observed some remains of panelling, and an early example of a sashed window."

Mr. Arnott's friend was Mr. Edward J. Sage, who was much interested in local antiquarian matters, and he, too, wrote to "Notes and Queries": —

". . . perhaps I may be allowed to add a few particulars to the account he has given of this mansion. I have gone over it several times since that visit; and have, I believe, thoroughly explored it in all its parts. There are considerable remains of . . . early Jacobean oak panelling in and about the kitchen and passages in the eastern part of the house, which appears to be the oldest. There is a fine massive Jacobean staircase of solid oak, painted stone colour, leading from the first floor to the second storey and attics. There is also a very elegant staircase leading from the hall to the first floor; this dates from early in the last century and probably takes the place of one of much earlier date, and I consider this to be continuous with the other. Opening upon this latter staircase is the room, from the ceiling of which, the coat of arms of the Hartopp's was removed. The four corners of the ceiling are also ornamented with heraldic devices. These are as follows: —

(1) The arms of Ulster; (2) a ducal coronet—a part only of the crest of the Hartopps; (3) a coat which I recognised as the arms of Coke of Melbourne; and (4) the crest of the Cokes. . . I have only to add, that the demolition of Fleetwood House is rapidly proceeding, and that some of the more ancient and interesting rooms have been removed. A street of small houses is being carried across the site of the garden, and the materials of the mansion are used as required for the erection of these houses."

And so the great mansion disappears and is soon little but a memory. Few mourned its passing but one, Alexander Andrews wrote: "Stoke Newington, the old picturesque suburb of thirty years ago, has contracted the disease which it resisted longer than

Charles Fleetwood.

Bridget Cromwell-Ireton-Fleetwood.

Deare wyfe I writt vnto you by Dobs the
last Saterday & hope you shall receaue that
letter before this ca to your hands. I
had placed John Mayo in this house: but
I know not out of what consideration hee
changed his mind & desired to returne
home, pretending that hee liked not to liue
in the cittie but rather in the contrie
according to his breeding. So hee put mee
to a new labor both for his returne &
for his contrie imployment wth Sr Fulk
hath offred him if occasion serue. If I
could as safilie disingage my self I should
now ca home wth him: but I am otherwise
bownd for a while as hee can tel you. I
thancke god I haue my health & hope to
breake away about the end of the terme.
the meane tyme I haue bought youre
gownd cloth, & for the children wch I purpose
god willing to send by Dobs this next Saterday
So as you may receaue it at Rosse on thurse
day after. I pray you therfore forget not
to send thither to demand it. I am not
quiet til I heare fro you in regard of that
indisposition wherin I left you. write I pray
you as often as you may specially of youre
health & how youre sowing proceedeth this weather wch hath been here verie extreme wet
euer since my cumming vp. Comend mee to

one frinds at Tordon & delivir this inclosed. pray for delivverance for hence, as I do for your heath & comfort. the Lord most euen his grace begin vs in this world peace in moderate es-

London this wensday your assured louing husband Io. Coke
19th Octb. 1617.

Letter from Sir John Coke to his wife, Marie Coke.

3

THE RIGHT HONOURABLE

S.ᵗ JOHN COKE K.ᵗ

Secretary of State to King Charles the first.

Deare husband we sent yesterday to you by sir Edwarde
Conway we hope you haue receiued, with a letter from sir
Fraunces Coke & another from ye bishop of Exeter And before ye
2 or 3 other letters by Mr Bulloches messinger. Now this
day sir John Worstenam sent this letter hither & desired
to haue it sent speedily to you, & ye other was sent from
Plimmouth to you. I thanke God we all in our family
are in health and I am better this day since the frost
was not so colde. then I was yesterday. I hope well ye you
are well & pray for ye continuance of your health & comfort
yesterday this letter to our John was sent him by the carier
from his Tutor. And this day John sent a letter backe to
him wch I helped him to endite to satisfy him for the
Christian & peaceable death of his brother, & ye none amonge vs
had any thought of any suspicion of blame against Mr Greene
yet because you are so nigh ye vniuersity I thought best to
send his letter to you, if you should finde fit to satisfy him
further in it. . Thus beseeching ye Lord to blesse preserue &
keepe both you & vs frest

Janua: 23

your true louing wife
Marie Coke

Letter from Marie Coke to Sir John Coke.

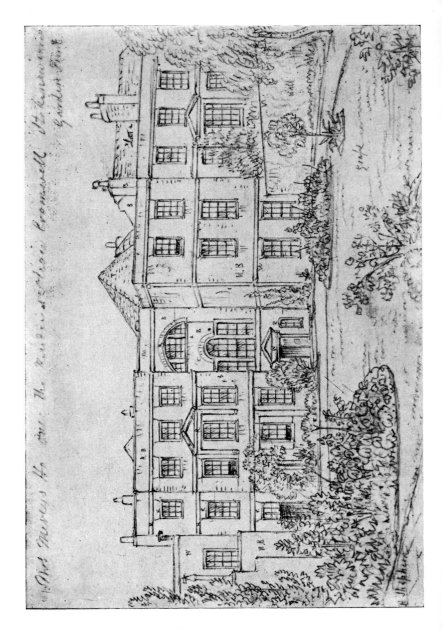

Fleetwood House.

I am given to understand by my kingsman Mr George
Goodman the bearer hereof (who is honest and [illegible])
that he is warned this tearme to appeare before yorselfe
wth others of his Maties most honorable Privy Councell, for
what he knowes not but thinkes it is about the altering of
the feilds of Croft where he is sexton. If soe, then he
conceives it to be upon some misinformation, first because
they have made not inclosure but a husbandly contrivement
of their feilds for the benefitt of the whole towne, poore
lands with inter-removinge as before. Secondly because they
have an order from the Lords of the Councell approvinge of
that wch they have done. Now my request unto yor honour
in his behalfe is that yow will afforde unto him yor honoure
... assistance wth as quicke a dispatch as may be, by reason
he hath left his wife very ... in the countrie fearinge
he shall not finde her alive att his returne. Thus humbly
takinge leave of yor honour (beinge very glad to heare of
the recoverie of my Lord ... after the losse of soe much
bloud ...) remembringe my
humble service to yor honour, and to yor noble Lady
I shall ever rest

Burbmister this
... of Maye 16[26]

Yor humble servant

E[dw] Hartopp

Yor Daughter wth her great Belly (thanked be to god) is very
well, and in good health!

Letter from Sir Edward Hartopp, 2nd Bart. to Sir John Coke.

Elizabeth of Bohemia.

Deare Brother

if this sad ocation hath brought you to
Buckminster I do not question but you will
help what you can with your aduise and
councell I Intreat it allso from you and
further that you and my Cosen Dury will
consider what is to be dun conserning the
funerrall that nothing you two Iudy meete
be neclected as becoms his qualiby and our
duty. through the Lords goodnes your sunn
is in uery good health. and we all at present
with my dear loue to you I remaine

fo 9

if my husband
coms down what
disturbance may be.
I know not pray
consider any
thing that belongs
to my children may be out
of dainger or remoue
if you and my Cosen
Bury thy fitt

your faithfull louing
Sister

Marie Hartopp

Letter from Mary Hartopp to Thomas Coke.

Baron George Fleetwood
Governour of Calmar.
and of the Iste of Oeland.
in Sweden. 1630.
Brother of Sr Wm Fleetwood
of Woodstock, and of
Charles Fleetwood, Lord
Deputy of Ireland.

George Fleetwood.

Bulstrode Whitelocke.

69

Right Hono:ble

I doubt not but my Lieu: Collo: hath given you account of owr Chanselors answer concerning Berkeleyes vers, and I will afsur you it shall not bee the least of my care to put him in minde upon the first aduantage. I cannot as quet speake with my marchant Doctor, but doe howerly expect him and then I will infeur your Lordshipe of eather veceate or medicine, with full directions. Owr Parlament is this day begun, if ought fall in it worth your notis I shall weakely acquainte you.

I must now trouble your Lordshipe in beging your afsistance to procure Mr Avery to fulfill my request in a busines I am now forced to make use of him in: I received letters from my fathor lately, wherein hee acquaints mee hee hath retur= net mee 1000 Rex: Doll: to Mr Nekemiah: Harvis in Hamburge, by Mr Forde of London, or more if I should have occasion to use it, acordng to which adufe I wrote to Mr Harvis to pay the monies to Dobor Stenebruge, but was anfured hee had received noe fuch ordrs for any monies, which forceth mee to make bould with Mr Avery: hee will not refufe mee, but if hee should

163

1640.

Letter from George Fleetwood to Sir Thomas Roe.

CHRISTINA REGINA
SUEC:

A Paris chez Pierre Mariette file rue St Iacques aux colonnes d' Hercule

13

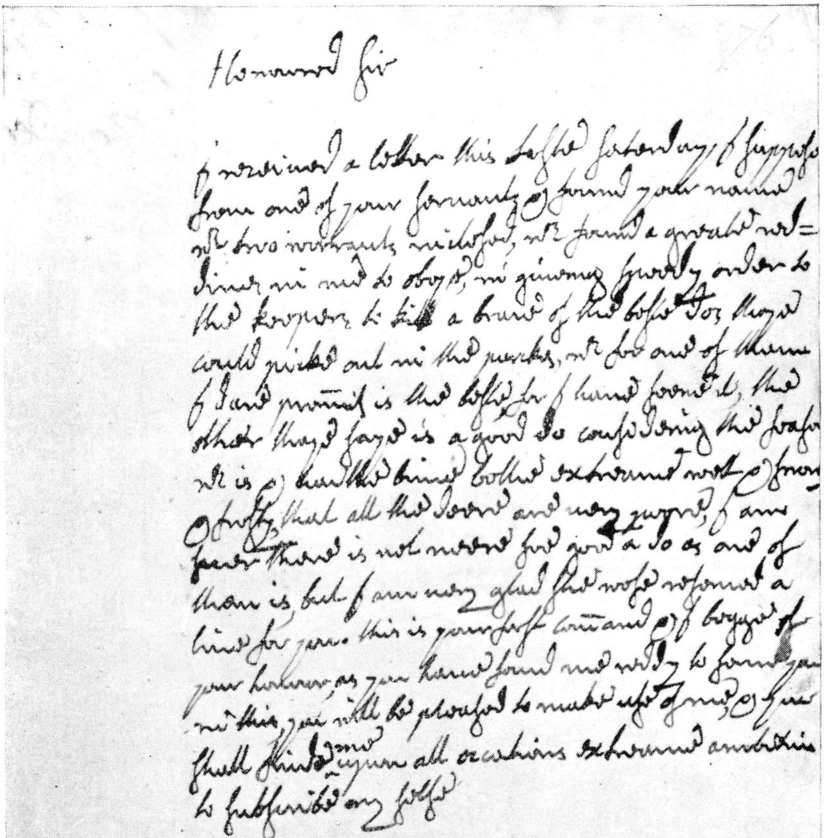

Honoured Sir

I receiued a letter this laste saterday I suppose from one of your seruants & found your name wth two warrants inclosed, wch found a greater obe=dience in me to obey it, in giueing speedy order to the keepers to kill a brace of the beste Does they could picke out in the parke, wch for one of them I dare promise is the beste for I haue seene it, the other they saye is a good Doe considering the season wch is & hath bine latlie extreame wett & frosty, that all the deere are very poore, I am sure there is not more fine good a Doe as one of them is, but I am very glad the were reserued a brace for you. this is your first command & I begge of your honour, as you haue found me ready to serue you in this, you will be pleased to make use of me, & you shall finde me upon all occasions extreame ambitious to subscribe my selfe

Honoured Sir

woodstock parke
this 30th of december

your faithfull friend &
most humble seruant

Will Fleetwood

155

Letter from Sir William Fleetwood to Mr. Secretary Bennett.

Henry Ireton.

Charles Fleetwood.

Bridget Cromwell-Ireton-Fleetwood.

LIEUTENANT GENERAL

FLEETWOOD

In the Possession of Thomas Cook Esq.

Charles Fleetwood.

Bridget Cromwell-Ireton-Fleetwood.

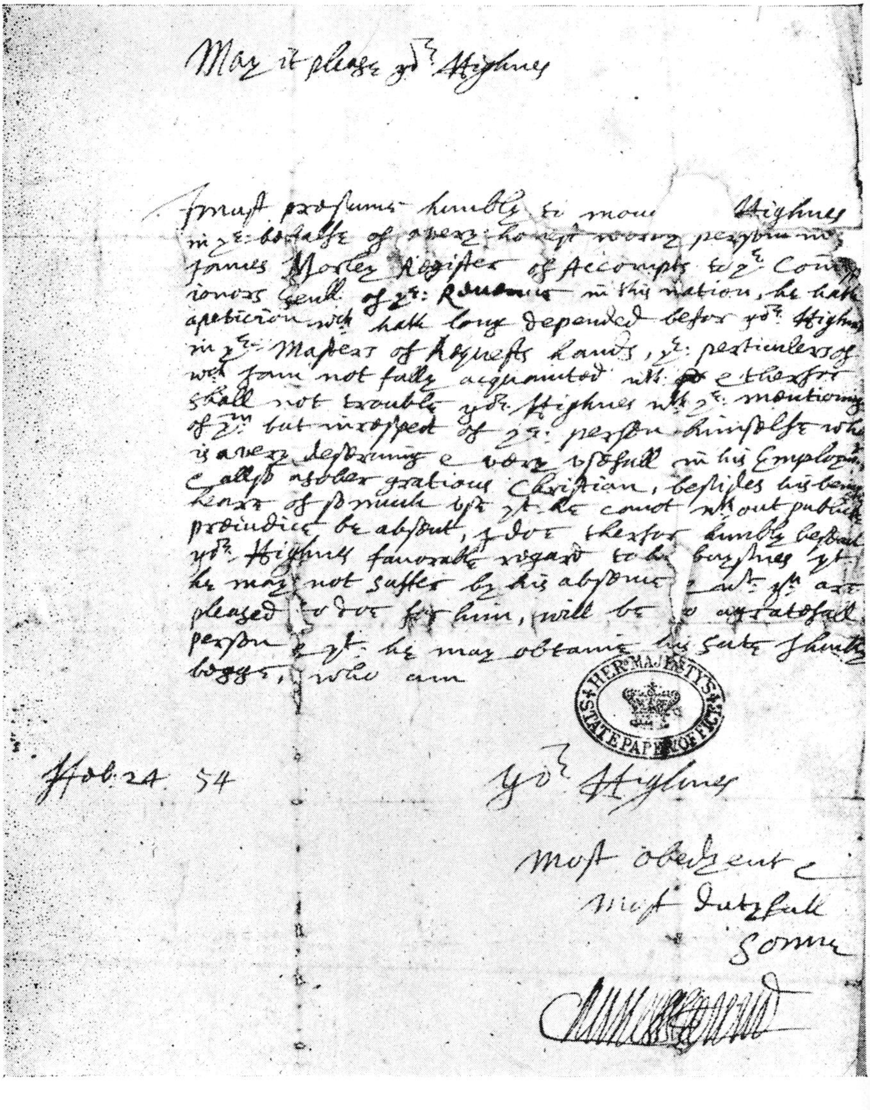
May it please yor Highnes

I must presume humbly to move [yor] Highnes in ye behalfe of a very honest worthy person namely James Morley Register of Accompts to ye Commissioners Genll of ye Revenue in this nation, he hath a peticion wch hath long depended befor yor Highnes in ye Masters of Requests hands, ye perticulers of wch I am not fully acquainted wth & therfore shall not trouble yor Highnes wth ye mentioning of ym but in respect of ye person himselfe who is a very deserving & very usefull in his Employment & allso a sober gratious Christian, besides his being heare of so much use yt he cannot wthout publick prejudice be absent, I doe therfor humbly beseech yor Highnes favorable regard to his busines yt he may not suffer by his absence & wt yu are pleased to doe for him, will be to a gratefull person & yt he may obtaine his sute shortly begge, who am

Feb. 24. 54

Yor Highnes

most obedient &
most dutyfull
Sonne

[illegible]

Letter from Charles Fleetwood to Oliver Cromwell.

Charles or George Fleetwood.

Mrs Lucy Hutchinson.

Charles Fleetwood's Monument in Bunhill Fields.

Dr. John Owen.

Lady Mary Fauconberg.

The Dunbar Medal.

Dr. Isaac Watts.

The Watts Window at Freeby.

A FUNERAL

SERMON

Occasioned by the

DEATH

Of the very Religious

Mrs. *Elizabeth Fleetwood,*

Preach'd at

STOKE NEWINGTON,
June 23, 1728.

By JOHN ASTY.

LONDON:

Printed for JOHN CLARK, and RICHARD
HETT, at the *Bible* and *Crown* in the
Poultry, near *Cheapside.* 1728. (Price 4*d.*)

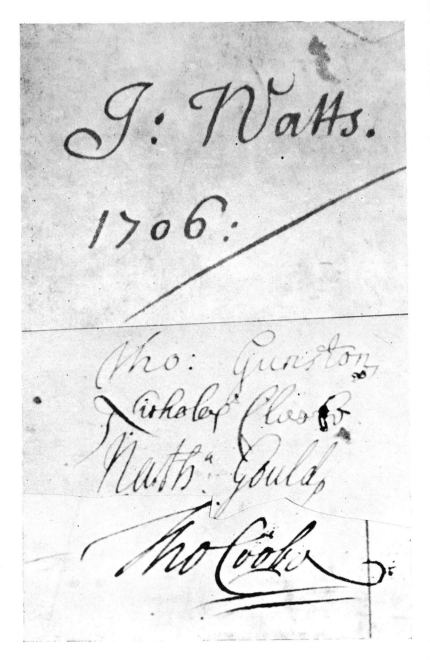

Signatures of Isaac Watts, Thomas Gunston, Sir Nathaniel
Gould and Thomas Cooke.

AN
ESSAY
ON ·THE
PUBLICK DEBTS
Of this KINGDOM.

WHEREIN

The Importance of difcharging them is confidered; the Provifions for that Purpofe by the SINKING FUND, and the Progrefs therein hitherto made, are ftated and explained; the Sufficiency of thofe Provifions are demonftrated; fome general Miftakes about the Nature and Efficacy of this Expedient examined and removed; and the Progrefs of the Sinking Fund defcribed and computed from *Midfummer*, 1727.

To which is fubjoined,

An Enquiry into the General Convenience of reducing farther the Intereft of our Publick Debts below 4 *per Cent. per Annum.*

In a LETTER *to a* MEMBER *of the* HOUSE *of* COMMONS.

LONDON:
Printed for J. PEELE, at *Locke's-Head* in *Pater-nofter-Row.* M,DCC,XXVI.
(Price One Shilling and Six-Pence.)

Title page of Sir Nathaniel Gould's " An Essay on the Public Debts."

Charles XII of Sweden.

Postscript

Since writing the above being well assured that the Resident of Hughley in 1770, and 1771, has been particularly engaged in the Monopoly of Rice complained of in the above ⟶ ⟶ 2 Par⟨?⟩; and although this grievance was of such a degree it appears that the Governor only reprimanded him for it, you are therefore especially to make his conduct one of the immediate objects of your enquiry and if he shale have been a Delinquent in that respect he must be punished in the manner we have ordered other Defaulters to be.

W. Rs

London
18 Decemr 1771

We are
Your loving Friends

Jo. Purling

Robt Gregory
Edwd Wheler
John Roberts
J. Manship
George Cuming
S. Sullivan
Fredk Pigou

Geo Dudley
H. Fletcher
Hurlock
J. Woodhouse
Daniel Wier
Wm James
Geo Michie
Joshua Smith
Peter Dulane Jun
John Harrison
Henry Savage

Postscript of Letter from the East India Company to **Warren**
Hastings, showing the signature of Joseph Hurlock.

The Perrott Monument in Laleham Church.

The Countess of Albany.

Vittorio Alfieri.

Lord Byron.

John Cam Hobhouse.

HISTORICAL ILLUSTRATIONS

OF

THE FOURTH CANTO

OF

CHILDE HAROLD:

CONTAINING

DISSERTATIONS ON THE RUINS OF ROME;

AND

AN ESSAY ON ITALIAN LITERATURE.

BY

JOHN HOBHOUSE, ESQ.

OF TRINITY COLLEGE, CAMBRIDGE, M. A. AND F. R. S.

LONDON:

JOHN MURRAY, ALBEMARLE STREET.

1818.

Title page of Hobhouse's " Illustrations "

Ugo Foscolo.

3.

near London 13 of 6 month June 1826

W. Allen presents his respects to
his Friend Foscolo and has sent
                    O Dr. Pinkerton
his Letter to one of the Secretaries of
the British & Forn Bible Soc.ty — though
W. A does not think that the Society
will undertake the translation at
present — W. A will be very glad if
it shall be in his power to procure
some Scholars for a private class
in the Italian Language in a few
weeks time and requests his Friend
Foscolo to keep him informed from
time to time as he may change
his lodging when a Letter may find
him —

Letter from William Allen to Ugo Foscolo.

William Allen.

An Old mansion, Stokenewington, and I have seen the Residence of General Fairfax.

Fleetwood House.

Esteemed friends,

Thomas Thompson Hon

I write by re-
quest of the friends now
about to go to Ireland
to say that they intend
to lodge in Liverpool to-
morrow night & to
proceed from thence to
Dublin on 7th day

Will you be so
kind as to take care
that two beds be pro-

noted for them & that
they be forwarded to
the parties

With much esteem
your affec'y frd
S Carder

Stoke Newington
9 mo 29 — 1842

Francis Thompson of
pointe to the Cemetery
will kindly accom-
modate with one bed
if he be at home & he

informed — but per
ships Wm Blain will
take the pins in —
short time

Letter from Susanna Corder to Thomas Thompson.

Fleetwood House.

45

Plasterwork from a Fleetwood House ceiling.

Plasterwork from a Fleetwood House ceiling.

The Fleetwood Cabinet.

The Fleetwood Cabinet.

17th Century Arms
(a) The Fleetwoods of Aldwincle
(b) Arms of the Hartopps

any other neighbourhood, and is suffering from a fearful eruption of
bricks and mortar of a very low type and of the most malignant
character . . . and, after allowing Defoe's house to be carted away
as old bricks, without (so far as I know) a more intelligent being to
' make note of it ' than the bricklayer's labourer who pickaxed it,
I am ashamed to let Fleetwood House be ' improved off the face of
the earth ' without letting readers know of its impending fate."

" Malignant " is a strong word with which to brand the harmless
but uninspiring little houses of Fleetwood Street, but it is useless to
pretend that they worthily replaced the great dwelling that had gone,
worn out though it may have been. Its disappearance was a true
reflection of the age. Beauty and distinction, romance and history
were everywhere giving way to utilitarian ugliness. When Fleetwood
House fell, it was more than bricks and mortar that had been pickaxed. History itself had vanished in the dust of the crumbling walls,
walls that had sheltered Fleetwood, Watts, Gould and Foscolo, and
had overheard many a fascinating conversation. Farewell,

> " . . . the glory that was Greece
> And the grandeur that was Rome."*

*Edgar Allan Poe.

APPENDICES

1. Addenda.

2. Hartopp Pedigrees, A, B, and C.

3. Ireton-Fleetwood Pedigrees, D, E, F, and G.

4. Luke Pedigree.

5. Entries in the Stoke Newington Parish Registers.

6. Bibliography.

ADDENDA

(Mainly from " Fleetwood Family Records " by R. W. Buss
and from information given by Miss Louisa Hack.)

1. *Sir Miles Fleetwood, Charles Fleetwood and John Milton.*
Professor Masson in his life of Milton says that Charles Fleetwood
and Milton were friends from boyhood. This is possible. Sir Miles
Fleetwood had a house in Wood Street. He died there in 1641.
Milton was born in Bread Street. Both these streets turned into
Cheapside and were not far from each other.
In 1651 Charles Fleetwood, Sir John Trevor, and Mr. Chaloner,
or any two of them, were appointed a committee, regarding the case
of John Milton who had been ordered to leave his lodgings in
Whitehall, to represent that his duties for the Council required him
to reside nearby.

2. *Register of Admissions to Gray's Inn.*
George Fleetwood (the Swedish Baron), son of Sir Miles Fleet-
wood, on 2nd February, 1619-20.
Charles Fleetwood (Cromwell's deputy), son of Sir Miles Fleet-
wood, on 16th January, 1638-39.
Thomas Fleetwood, younger brother of Sir Miles Fleetwood, on
11th March, 1600-01.
Miles Fleetwood (d. 1688), son of Sir William Fleetwood, on
23rd June, 1648.
Cromwell Fleetwood, second son of Charles Fleetwood, on 19th
April, 1671.

3. *George Fleetwood.*
Was of Lincoln College, Oxford.
Matriculated 9th November, 1621. B.A. 6th February, 1623-24.
He was knighted by Charles I, at Greenwich, on 3rd June, 1632.
The following children of George Fleetwood, Gustaf Miles, born
at Colberg, Pomerania, on 8th August, 1642, George Wilhelm, and
Adolf Jacob, were all naturalised in England on 9th June, 1657.
His wife, Brita Gyllenstjerna, was born at Nynäs on 13th May,
1606. In 1630 she was maid of honour to Queen Maria Eleanora,
and went with her to Germany. In 1634 she became lady of the
bed-chamber to Queen Christina. She died at Jälunda, on 29th
December, 1653, and was buried in Nyköping Ostra Church, on 24th
April, 1654. Her husband was buried in a vault beneath the altar
in the same church. His coat of arms was set up in the choir.

4. *Sir Gerard Fleetwood.*
Younger brother of Sir Miles Fleetwood. Was of Crawley, Hants.
Knighted by James I, at Sir George Farmor's, on 9th July, 1603
(see Foster's " Alumni Oxon " and " Notes and Queries," 1906). He
had four wives: —
   1. Jane Lambert.
   2. Mary Dutton.
   3. Isabel Nevill, previously married to Sir John Harpur (1) and

and Sir Peter Frecheville (2).
    4. Anne (parentage unknown).
He was Ranger of Woodstock Park, 1611, and M.P. for Woodstock
in 1625 and 1626.   During the Civil War he supported the King,
and in 1647 compounded for his delinquency, being fined £570.   By
his second wife he had a son, Dutton Fleetwood, who matriculated at
Queen's College, Oxford, on 11th October, 1639, and was a Colonel
in the Royalist army.   His will dated 26th November, 1657, was
proved on 26th February, 1658, by the executors, his widow Anne,
and his nephew, Sir William (son of Sir Miles).   His will mentions
two daughters.   The date of his death is not known.   He would seem
to have vacated his position at Woodstock in favour of his nephew,
Sir William, before the outbreak of the Civil War, unless both had
positions there.
5. *Sir William Fleetwood.*
    Father of Sir Miles Fleetwood, of Ealing, Middlesex.   Married
Jane Clifton, whose first husband was Hugh Coplestone.   Colonel and
chief captain of the trained men at Ealing in 1588.   Sir Miles
Fleetwood, his eldest son, was baptised at St. James', Clerkenwell,
on 1st October, 1576.
6. *Sir William Fleetwood* (1603-1674).
    Colonel in the Royalist army.   Commander of Array for Nor-
thampton, 1642.   Probably is the William Fleetwood who received
a bullet wound in the leg at the Isle of Rhé in 1627 (Buckingham's
expedition) which lamed him.   Mr. Buss states that his first wife was
Frances Sture.   This conflicts with the present writer's theory that
she was a daughter of Thomas Barley.
7. *William Fleetwood.*
    Son of Sir William Feetwood (1603-1674) by his first wife.   Served
in the Royalist army, but later, perhaps persuaded by his uncle,
Charles Fleetwood, took service under Cromwell.   In Flanders 1657,
and Lieutenant-Colonel of the garrison at Dunkirk.   His will was
proved by his sister Martha Coward, who had been married to
Thomas Milton, nephew of the poet.
8. *Charles Fleetwood.*
    (a) His support of preaching officers involved him in a quarrel
        with his cousin Sir Samuel Luke.
    (b) A copy of Dr. Owen's " Doctrine of Justification by Faith "
        exists bound in blue morocco with the Fleetwood coat of arms
        on the cover, and inscribed, " Ex dono Authoris, July 12th,
        1677." Another hand has added, " Given to Charles Fleet-
        wood, Esq."
    (c) He was frequently directed by the Council of State to report
        on various petitions presented by the East India Company,
        mainly relating to disputes with the Dutch in the Far East.   His
        son, Smith Fleetwood, became a Freeman of the East India
        Company by redemption, on 7th April, 1676.
    (d) His son, Smith Fleetwood, is said by Mr. Buss to have been
        three times married. (See entries in Stoke Newington Registers

for confirmation, at any rate, of a second marriage.)

(e) Charles Fleetwood is said by Mr. Buss to have been born in 1618.

(f) After the death of Charles I rooms were allotted to Charles Fleetwood for his use in Somerset House.

(g) "Like Fleetwood, he cried in the bitterness of his soul that God had hid his face from him"—Macaulay, "Essay on Milton."

(h) In May, 1677, Sir John Reresby visited the Duke and Duchess of Lauderdale at Ham House, near Richmond. The Duchess had been previously married to Sir Lionel Tollemache, the owner of Ham House, and after his death had married John Maitland, second Earl, and first Duke of Lauderdale. A contemporary lampoon refers to her: —

"She is Bess of my heart, she was Bess of old Noll,
She was once Fleetwood's Bess, and she's now of Atholl."

Reresby described her in his Memoirs: —"The next day I went to visit the Duke and Dutchess of Lautherdale, at their fine House at Ham. After Dinner, her Grace entertained me in her Chamber with much Discourse upon Affairs of State. She had been a beautiful Woman, the supposed Mistress of Oliver Cromwell, and at that time a Lady of great Parts."

The suggestion in the lampoon that she had been Fleetwood's mistress (if Charles Fleetwood is intended) is hardly likely to be true from all known accounts of his life and character.

9. *Story by Voltaire.*

"No king was ever more absolute than Cromwell. He would observe, ' that he had preferred governing under the name of protector rather than under that of king, because the English were aware of the limits of the prerogative of a king of England, but knew not the extent of that of a protector.' This was knowing mankind, who are governed by opinion, and whose opinion depends upon a name. He had conceived a profound contempt for the religion to which he owed his success. An anecdote, preserved in the St. John family, sufficiently proves the slight regard he attached to that instrument which had produced such mighty effects in his hands. He was drinking once in company with Ireton, Fleetwood, and St. John, great grandfather of the celebrated Lord Bolingbroke; a bottle of wine was to be uncorked, and the corkscrew fell under the table; they all looked for it, and were unable to find it. In the meantime, a deputation from the Presbyterian churches waited in the antichamber, and an usher announced them. ' Tell them,' said Cromwell, ' that I have retired, and that I am seeking the Lord.' This was the expression employed by the fanatics for going to prayers. Having dismissed the troop of divines, he thus addressed his companions: ' Those fellows think we are seeking the Lord, while we are only seeking a corkscrew '."

10. *Smith Fleetwood.*

"Elen" Fleetwood was the second or third wife of Smith Fleetwood, son of Charles Fleetwood. Her will, dated 30th May, 1727, was proved by William Stiles on 24th July, 1731. She mentions her son Charles, who predeceased her, and daughters, Elizabeth, Frances, Carolina and Jane. She revoked a gift of his father's picture to Charles Fleetwood by a codicil dated 25th November, 1728, as he had died before that date. Mr. Asty, minister of the gospel is also mentioned in the will. Elizabeth Fleetwood's will made in 1710 and proved on 10th August, 1728, also mentions Mr. Asty.

Charles, Elizabeth and Jane Fleetwood were in reality step-children of Ellen Fleetwood, the latter two were the third and sixth daughters of Smith Fleetwood by his first wife, Mary Hartopp. (" Notes and Queries," 1904.)

Elizabeth Fleetwood in her will also mentions her two brothers Charles and Smith. Ellen Fleetwood the *third* wife of Smith Fleetwood was presumably childless.

Charles Fleetwood's will dated 1726 and proved in 1728 shows him to be the owner of Armingland Hall. He left his Norfolk estates to his sister Anne Gosney, and then to his unmarried sisters, Elizabeth, Frances, Carolina and Jane. He also refers to his late brother, Smith Fleetwood. (" Notes and Queries," 1909.)

11. *Mary Carter.*

Is mentioned in her father, Charles Fleetwood's will and in Smith Fleetwood's, dated 25th August, 1697, and proved on 5th May, 1709. Mr. Asty is again mentioned in Smith Fleetwood's will. In a funeral sermon occasioned by the death of the very religious Mrs. Elizabeth Fleetwood preached at Stoke Newington on 23rd June, 1728, Asty says his earliest service in the Ministry was devoted to the Fleetwood family, " wherein I lived many years." (" Notes and Queries," 1904.)

12. *Cromwell Fleetwood.*

Married Elizabeth, only child and heiress of George Nevill by his wife Elizabeth, youngest daughter of Sir Henry Trotter of Shelton Castle, Yorks. Cromwell Fleetwood died intestate. Administration granted to his widow on 27th September, 1688. She died on 26th April, 1692. Her will, dated 23rd May, 1691, mentions " Sister Bendish." There is a large slab in the church of St. Andrew, Little Berkhampstead, bearing this inscription: —

" Here lyeth the Body of Elizabeth
Fleetwood widow
who died the
xxvi of April MDCXCIII
adjacent to ye body of her vertuous husband
Cromwell Feetwood Esq. who died ye 1 June
MDCLXXXVIII this
Elizabeth was sole daughter of
George Nevill Gent and died
without issue."

(" Notes and Queries," 1905.)

There is a discrepancy in the date given for the death of Elizabeth Fleetwood, 1692 and 1693. 1692 is probably correct.

13. *Nathaniel Carter.*
Married Mary, Charles Fleetwood's daughter by his second wife, Bridget. He died in 1722.

14. *The Luke Family.*
(a) Anne Luke, wife of Sir Walter Luke and daughter of Sir Thomas Launcelyn, was nurse to Henry VIII.
(b) " The hero of ' Hudibras ' was a real personage, one Sir Samuel Luke, who had been a captain in the armies of Fairfax and Cromwell "—Voltaire. Samuel Butler at one time was clerk to Sir Samuel Luke and took his old master as model for Sir Hudibras.

15. *The Drydens.*
Sir Edward Hartopp the first baronet " married Mary, daughter of Sir Erasmus Dryden—a family which later on espoused the parliamentary side very warmly "—Miss Louisa Hack.

The Dryden pedigree is as follows: —

John Dryden
|
Sir Erasmus Dryden, Bart.

Sir John Dryden	Another Son	Mary m. Sir Edward Hartopp, 1st Bart.	Erasmus Dryden (d. 1654) m. Mary Pickering (d. 1676) on 21st Oct., 1630, at Pilton near Aldwincle (d. of Henry Pickering, son of Sir Gilbert Pickering) | John Dryden (1631-1700) (The poet)

16. *Sir Edward Hartopp, the second baronet.*
Miss Louisa Hack writes: —" George 7th Earl of Rutland entertained Charles I at Belvoir in July, 1636. The King, while there, knighted Edward Hartopp." This date conflicts with that given by other authorities.

17. *Manor of Braunston.*
Thomas Hartopp sold this manor to the third Earl of Rutland in 1565.

18. *Elizabeth Cholmondeley.*
Daughter of Sir Edward Hartopp, 1st Bart., married Montague Cholmondeley of Easton. After his death she returned to live at Buckminster and died in 1676. She was the last of the Hartopps to be buried in the vault in Buckminster Church. (Miss Louisa Hack.)

19. *An Ancient Sampler.*
Mrs. J. A. Swan of Cambridge, Mass., was the owner of a sampler, which she inherited from her ancestors the Quincy family of Massachusetts. It was inscribed, " Miles Fletwood, Abigail Fletwod, 1654."

20. *The Fleetwood Cabinet.*
This was an " ebony cabinet ornamented with paintings by Old Franks and silver repoussée work," given by Cromwell to his daughter,

Bridget on the occasion of her marriage to Charles Fleetwood. Its ownership can be traced as follows: :

    (a) Bridget Fleetwood (d.1662);

    (b) Her son Cromwell Fleetwood (d.1688);

    (c) His widow, Elizabeth (née Nevill) (d.1692) first cousin to Sarah Burkitt. Elizabeth left legacies to Sarah Burkitt but did not specifically mention the cabinet;

    (d) Sarah Burkitt (d.1729) left the cabinet to her eldest son;

    (e) John Burkitt of Sudbury (d.1775) who left the cabinet to his eldest son;

    (f) John Burkitt (d.1786) who left the cabinet to his youngest son;

    (g) John Burkitt of Sudbury (d.1841 without issue). He left the cabinet to Alexander Horace Burkitt of Sudbury;

    (h) Alexander Horace Burkitt is said to have sold the cabinet to his sister Lydia Augusta, wife of Dr. Edward Rawlins of Bedford (d.1850). She then married James Corcoran of Hammersmith and Dublin;

    (i) Lydia Augusta Corcoran left the cabinet to her husband, James Corcoran;

    (j) James Corcoran (d.1879 without issue) left all his furniture to his niece, Anna Corcoran;

    (k) Anna Corcoran (d. unmarried about 1890) left the cabinet to her brother;

    (l) Edward de Verdon Corcoran of Bedford (d.1900) who left the cabinet to his wife Jeannie (née Andrews) of Dublin;

    (m) Jeannie Corcoran (d.1902) left all her property to her sister;

    (n) Frances Margaret Andrews of Dublin (d.1931);

    (o) A clause in Miss Andrews' will reads: " I bequeath to the Trustees of the National Gallery of Ireland the cabinet known as the ' Fleetwood Cabinet,' which was presented by the nation to the daughter of Oliver Cromwell on her marriage to General Fleetwood. . . ." (" Notes and Queries," 1932.)

21. *Madresfield Court Miniatures.*

Mr. R. W. Buss considers both that by John Hoskins a water colour dated 1647) and that by David Des Granges (oil on copper) to be portraits of Charles Fleetwood. That by David Des Granges, however, is inscribed on the back, " George or Charles Fleetwood." Mr. R. W. Ramsay considers it to be a portrait of George Feetwood.

Readers should compare it with the Swedish portrait of George Fleetwood and the other portraits of Charles Fleetwood.

22. *The Fleetwoods of Aldwincle.*

(Northamptonshire " Notes and Queries," 1905-7, and, "A History of the Church of the Holy Sepulchre, Northampton," by the Rev. J. Charles Cox, LL.D., F.S.A., and the Rev. R. M. Serjeantson, M.A.)

The Fleetwoods of Aldwincle were descended from John de Fletewoode who is known to have been alive in 1404. His fourth son, Henry, of Little Plumpton, Lancs., is referred to as a burgess of Preston in 1397. Henry was still alive in 1424. His son, Edward, married Elizabeth Holland. Their son, William of Heskin, married Helen Standish, and was the father of six children including Thomas, who founded the family of Fleetwood of the Vache, Chalfont St. Giles, Bucks. He was Treasurer of the Mint, M.P. and Sheriff for Bucks and Beds. He died in 1570, aged 52, and was buried at Chalfont St. Giles. He had two wives. From Barbara Francis is descended the family of Fleetwood of Rossal. From Bridget Spring, daughter of Sir John Spring of Lavenham, Suffolk, is descended the Fleetwood family of Aldwincle, through Sir William Fleetwood.

Sir William was of Cranford, Middlesex, and owned the manor of Cardington, Beds. He was Receiver of the Court of Wards and estimated his profits at £15,000 to £16,000 a year (see letter to Sir Robert Cecil). He was knighted at the Charterhouse on 11th May, 1603. He married Jane Clifton. His eldest son, Sir Miles, succeeded him as Receiver of the Court of Wards, having been admitted to Gray's Inn on 9th January, 1587-8. Sir Miles was M.P. for Huntingdon Borough, 1614, Westbury, 1620-21, Bletchingley, 1623-4, but elected to sit for Launceston, Cornwall, Newton-in-Makerfield, Lancs., 1625 and 1625-6, Woodstock, 1627-8, and Hindon, 1640. On 10th September, 1635, he wrote from Aldwincle to Sir John Coke that he and his brother-in-law, Luke, were much prejudiced by Lord Lambert withholding rents due to them in Ireland. Sir Miles married Anne Luke and was the father of : —

1. William, baptised at Cardington, 8th January, 1600, died in infancy.
2. Sir William, baptised at Cardington, 20th July, 1603.
3. Miles, baptised at Cardington, 5th July, 1604.
4. George (the Swedish baron).
5. Charles, baptised at Cardington, 12 April, 1607, and buried at Cople, 24th April, 1608.
6. Charles, Cromwell's son-in-law.
7. Gabriel, buried at Goldrington, Beds, 23rd November, 1630.
8. Roger, of Lincoln College, Oxford. Matriculated 24th October, 1628, aged 14, B.A. 30th April, 1631, incorporated at Cambridge, 1632, canon of Lichfield, 1640, vicar of Hanbury, Staffs, which living he gave up and joined the Royalist army. Prebendary of Bubbenhall.
9. Dorothy, baptised at Cople, 10th February, 1599, married Sir Robert Cooke, who died in 1643.
10. Martha, who married Robert Dukinfield, Governor of Chester.
11. Possibly also Edward, Elizabeth and Anne.

Sir William Fleetwood succeeded his father as Receiver of the Court of Wards, but, being a Royalist, forfeited it to his brother Charles, who, according to Lord Holles' Memoirs, received £3,000 compensation when the Court was abolished. In 1646, after Charles I had left Oxford, Sir William made his submission to Parliament.

" To the honoble Committee, etc. . .

The humble peticion of Sir William ffleetwood, of Alldwinckle, in the county of Northton. Knt. Humbly sheweth that long before these troubles he was and yet is, a servant in Ordinary to his Majestie and thereby necessarily occasioned to wayte upon his Person, which he hath constantly done at Oxford and other places for the space of these fower yeares last past, for which his estate became sequestered.

Now, for as much as he hath taken the Nationall Covenant and Negative Oath and submitted himselfe to the power of the Parliament before the first of May last, he therefore desires that he may be admitted to a reasonable composition for his Delinquency in adhering to the forces raysed against Parliament.

And he shall pray etc.

Will. Fleetwood.

Received primo Decemb. 1646."

Sir William was fined £585, which his brother, Charles, paid for him. Sir William's descendants were:—

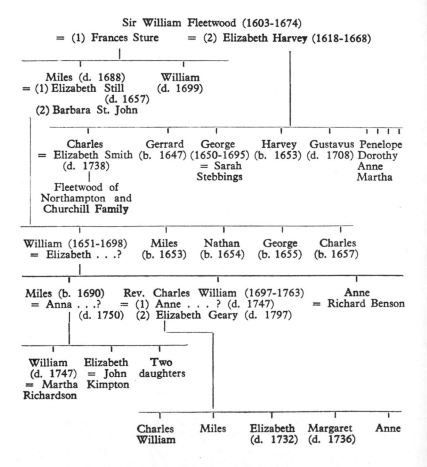

The descendants of Charles Fleetwood and Elizabeth Smith
were: —

Charles Fleetwood = Elizabeth Smith

| Smith Fleetwood (1670-1747) unmarried | Elizabeth (1669-1706) = Samuel Clarke | Margaret (b. 1671) = Thomas Milton | Penelope (1678-1750) = Joseph Churchill | Anne (b. 1674) = Sir Philip Jackson | Barbara Charles Charles (All died young) |

Joseph Churchill (1704-1781) = Mary Ford (d. 1761)   Elizabeth (1710-1794)

| Fleetwood Churchill (1731-1780) | Joseph (b. 1734) = Mary Dixie (d. 1806) | Smith Churchill (1743-1803) = Isabella Mills |

In December, 1668, Sir William Fleetwood lost his wife, Dame Elizabeth Harvey, step-daughter of Sir Francis Harvey, Judge of Common Pleas, who used to speak of her as " little Betty Harvey," and remembered her in his will. She was buried at St. Sepulchre's, Northampton.

> " December . . . the wife of Sir William Fleetwood
> was buried ye 18th Day."

Sir William's children by his first wife, Frances Sture, were: —

(1) *Miles Fleetwood.* He was of Gray's Inn and M.P. for Woodstock, 1658-9, and Northampton, 1677-8, 1679 and 1680-1. He was on friendly terms with Lord Hatton. In 1682 he wrote to him asking for " a warrant for a doe and three bottles of your Lordship's sherry." On 11th December, 1684, he wished to see Lord Hatton and asked him to dine " at ye blew posts in ye haymarket or any other place." Again, in 1686 he asked for half a buck as he had a friend with him. He was buried at All Saints, Aldwincle. " Upon a common stone on the ground in Mr. Spinckes's burial place:

> M. F. Esq.
> July 28
> 1688."

The Spincke family bought Aldwincle from the Fleetwoods in 1699. Miles was twice married, first to Elizabeth Still, and then to Dame Barbara St. John. He was father of: —

(a) *William Fleetwood* of the Middle Temple. He was steward to Lord Hatton for his Court Leets of Higham and Raunds. In 1697 he wrote to Lord Hatton regretting that the gout prevented him waiting on his Lordship, but sending him " a pretty good Jack taken in my Bownetts." He died in 1698.

(b) *Miles Fleetwood,* a member of the Levant Company and Consul at Cairo.

(c) *Charles Fleetwood,* writer to the Hon. East India Company.

(2) *William Fleetwood.*

See Adenda 7.

Sir William Fleetwood had the following children by his second wife, Elizabeth Harvey: —

1. *Charles Fleetwood,* who married Elizabeth, daughter of Matthew Smith of London. On the death of his father he moved to Northampton, and lived in a house in Lady's Lane, the north side. The site of the house and grounds is now occupied by Kerr Street and Park Street. The rate books often mention " Fleetwood's Park." He was a leading man in his parish and his signature in the vestry books usually appears above even that of the vicar. There are several entries in the registers of St. Sepulchre's such as: —

> " A crysome child of Charles Fleetwood, Esq.
> buried ye 18th of January, 1680."

The elder children of this marriage were born at Woodstock Park. In the parish church of St. Sepulchre's there are several monuments relating to Charles Fleetwood and his family.

> " Near this place is interred
> The Body of Elizabeth Relict
> of Charles Fleetwood, Esq.
> who departed this life
> The 24th September, 1738
> Aged 91.
> Near this place also lies interred
> the body of
> Smith Fleetwood Esq.
> Son of the said Charles Fleetwood, Esq.
> and Elizabeth his wife,
> who departed this life,
> The 29th day of June
> 1747, aged 77."

> " Here lyes ye body of
> Barbara Fleetwood
> The daughter of Charles Fleetwood
> and Elizabeth his wife,
> who departed this life
> ye first year of her aige Anno Dom.
> 1676."

"Here lyes ye body of
Charles Fleetwood
the sonne of Charles Fleetwood and
Elizabeth his wife
who departed this life
ye 14th of July, the day after
it was born. Anno Do. 1677."

"Here lyeth the body of
Margaret Smith, who
departed this life the
third of March, 1687
She was the mother of Elizabeth Fleetwood
wife of Charles Fleetwood
of Northampton."

---

2. *Gerrard Fleetwood.*
Baptised at Wootten, Oxon, 29th November, 1647.

3. *George Fleetwood.*
Baptised at Wootten, 29th September, 1650. Of the Inner Temple. Married Sarah Stebbings of Wissett, Suffolk, on 20th July, 1680. Lived at Chediston Hall, Suffolk. Died 1695.

4. *Harvey Fleetwood.*
Baptised at Wootten, 25th February, 1653.

5. *Penelope Fleetwood.*
Baptised at Wootten, 8th November, 1651. Married . . . Browne.

6. *Dorothy Fleetwood.*
Baptised at Wootten, 26th February, 1656. Married (1) Lionel Holle; (2) Henry Bomfield.

7. *Anne Fleetwood.*
Married the Rev. Arthur Humphreys. She died in 1700, leaving a son, Arnold.

8. *Martha Fleetwood.*
Married (1) Thomas Milton, Deputy Clerk of the Crown in Chancery, son of Sir Christopher Milton of Ipswich, and a nephew of the poet; (2) William Coward, M.D., of Ipswich.

9. *Gustavus Fleetwood.*
May have been a son of Sir William's first marriage. His will was proved in 1708. He mentioned in it his brother George and his wife Sarah, and the children of his sisters Penelope, Anne and Dorothy. His wife, Catherine, died in 1736 and was buried at Wandsworth.

The Fleetwood arms are: —

>Per pale nebulée azure and or, six
>martlets countercharged.
>The crest: —
>A wolf statant regardant arg. vulned in the
>shoulder gu.
>The motto: —
>Homo homini lupus.

———

HARTOPP PEDIGREES

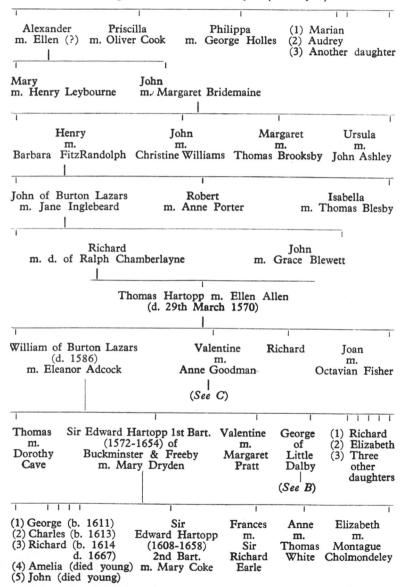

Ralph Hartopp (living in 1377)
m. daughter of Alexander Mayne (or Moyne)

Alexander   Priscilla   Philippa   (1) Marian
m. Ellen (?)   m. Oliver Cook   m. George Holles (2) Audrey
                                                   (3) Another daughter

Mary   John
m. Henry Leybourne   m. Margaret Bridemaine

Henry   John   Margaret   Ursula
m.   m.   m.   m.
Barbara FitzRandolph Christine Williams Thomas Brooksby John Ashley

John of Burton Lazars   Robert   Isabella
m. Jane Inglebeard   m. Anne Porter   m. Thomas Blesby

Richard   John
m. d. of Ralph Chamberlayne   m. Grace Blewett

Thomas Hartopp m. Ellen Allen
(d. 29th March 1570)

William of Burton Lazars   Valentine   Richard   Joan
(d. 1586)   m.   m.
m. Eleanor Adcock   Anne Goodman   Octavian Fisher

(See C)

Thomas   Sir Edward Hartopp 1st Bart. Valentine   George   (1) Richard
m.   (1572-1654) of   m.   of   (2) Elizabeth
Dorothy   Buckminster & Freeby   Margaret   Little   (3) Three
Cave   m. Mary Dryden   Pratt   Dalby   other
                                                                  daughters
                                                     (See B)

(1) George (b. 1611)   Sir   Frances   Anne   Elizabeth
(2) Charles (b. 1613)   Edward Hartopp   m.   m.   m.
(3) Richard (b. 1614   (1608-1658)   Sir   Thomas   Montague
    d. 1667)   2nd Bart.   Richard   White   Cholmondeley
(4) Amelia (died young) m. Mary Coke   Earle
(5) John (died young)

Sir Edward Hartopp 2nd Bart
m. Mary Coke

(1) John (b. & d. 1635) (2) Edward (b. & d. 1636)	Sir John Hartopp 3rd Bart. (1637-1722) m. Elizabeth Fleetwood (d. 1711)	Mary (1639-1681) m. Smith Fleetwood (*See F*)

(1) Charles (b. 1672) (2) Edward (b. 1675) (3) John (b. 1679)	Sir John Hartopp 4th Bart. (1682-1762) m. (1) Sarah Woolfe (d. 1736) (2) Mrs. Sarah Marsh in 1760. (She died in 1763)	Frances (d. 1711) m. Sir Nathaniel Gould (1661-1728)	(1) Anne (d. 1674) (2) Helen (d. 1691) (3) Martha (d. 1739) (4) Bridget (d. 1741) (5) Mary (d. 1749) (6) Elizabeth (d. 1754) (7) Dorothy (d. 1755) (8) Anne (d. 1764)

Elizabeth (1717-1789) m. Timothy Dallowe, M.D. (d. 1775) (no issue)	Sarah (1719-1766) m. Joseph Hurlock (d. 1793) Anne Hurlock m. (in 1777) Edmund Bunny The Cradock- Hartopp Family	Mary (d. 1720) m. Sir Francis St. John	Elizabeth (1700-1763) m. Thomas Cooke (1672(?)-1752)

	Frances	Mary m. Sir John Bernard	Frances (1722- 1728)	Margaret (1726- 1749)

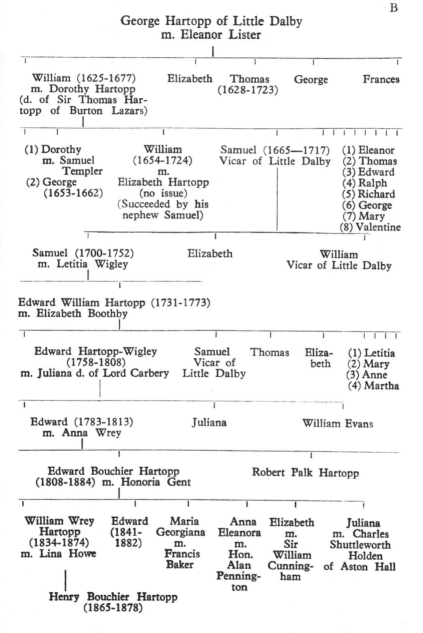

George Hartopp of Little Dalby
m. Eleanor Lister

| William (1625-1677) m. Dorothy Hartopp (d. of Sir Thomas Hartopp of Burton Lazars) | Elizabeth | Thomas (1628-1723) | George | Frances |

| (1) Dorothy m. Samuel Templer (2) George (1653-1662) | William (1654-1724) m. Elizabeth Hartopp (no issue) (Succeeded by his nephew Samuel) | Samuel (1665—1717) Vicar of Little Dalby | (1) Eleanor (2) Thomas (3) Edward (4) Ralph (5) Richard (6) George (7) Mary (8) Valentine |

| Samuel (1700-1752) m. Letitia Wigley | Elizabeth | William Vicar of Little Dalby |

Edward William Hartopp (1731-1773)
m. Elizabeth Boothby

| Edward Hartopp-Wigley (1758-1808) m. Juliana d. of Lord Carbery | Samuel Vicar of Little Dalby | Thomas | Elizabeth | (1) Letitia (2) Mary (3) Anne (4) Martha |

| Edward (1783-1813) m. Anna Wrey | Juliana | William Evans |

| Edward Bouchier Hartopp (1808-1884) m. Honoria Gent | Robert Palk Hartopp |

| William Wrey Hartopp (1834-1874) m. Lina Howe | Edward (1841-1882) | Maria Georgiana m. Francis Baker | Anna Eleanora m. Hon. Alan Pennington | Elizabeth m. Sir William Cunningham | Juliana m. Charles Shuttleworth Holden of Aston Hall |

Henry Bouchier Hartopp
(1865-1878)

N.B.—The two sons and the grandson of Edward Bouchier Hartopp predeceased him leaving his four daughters co-heirs.

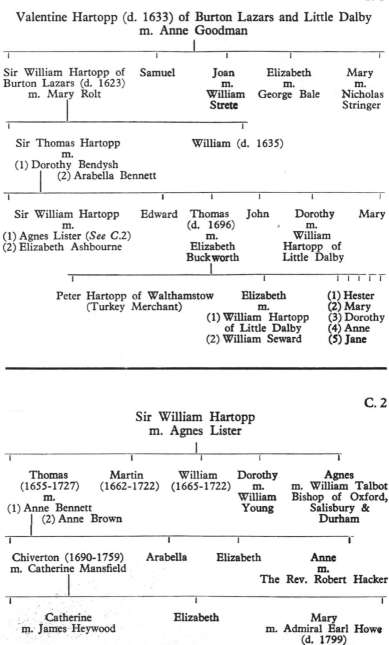

C. 1

Valentine Hartopp (d. 1633) of Burton Lazars and Little Dalby
m. Anne Goodman

Sir William Hartopp of Burton Lazars (d. 1623) m. Mary Rolt   Samuel   Joan m. William Strete   Elizabeth m. George Bale   Mary m. Nicholas Stringer

Sir Thomas Hartopp m. (1) Dorothy Bendysh (2) Arabella Bennett   William (d. 1635)

Sir William Hartopp m. (1) Agnes Lister (See C.2) (2) Elizabeth Ashbourne   Edward   Thomas (d. 1696) m. Elizabeth Buckworth   John   Dorothy m. William Hartopp of Little Dalby   Mary

Peter Hartopp of Walthamstow (Turkey Merchant)   Elizabeth m. (1) William Hartopp of Little Dalby (2) William Seward   (1) Hester (2) Mary (3) Dorothy (4) Anne (5) Jane

C. 2

Sir William Hartopp
m. Agnes Lister

Thomas (1655-1727) m. (1) Anne Bennett (2) Anne Brown   Martin (1662-1722)   William (1665-1722)   Dorothy m. William Young   Agnes m. William Talbot Bishop of Oxford, Salisbury & Durham

Chiverton (1690-1759) m. Catherine Mansfield   Arabella   Elizabeth   Anne m. The Rev. Robert Hacker

Catherine m. James Heywood   Elizabeth   Mary m. Admiral Earl Howe (d. 1799)

MARY HARTOPP'S COKE DESCENT

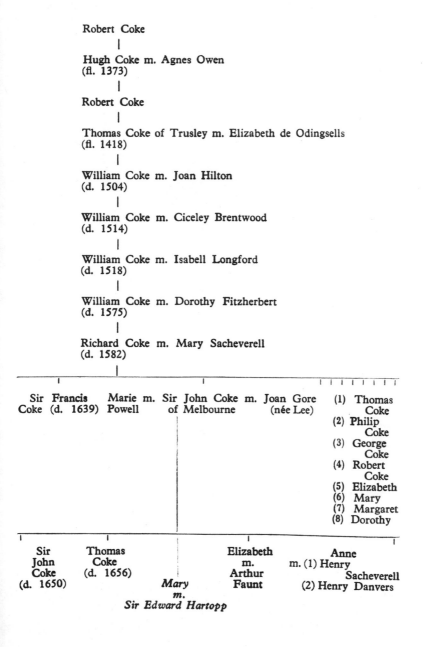

Robert Coke
|
Hugh Coke m. Agnes Owen
(fl. 1373)
|
Robert Coke
|
Thomas Coke of Trusley m. Elizabeth de Odingsells
(fl. 1418)
|
William Coke m. Joan Hilton
(d. 1504)
|
William Coke m. Ciceley Brentwood
(d. 1514)
|
William Coke m. Isabell Longford
(d. 1518)
|
William Coke m. Dorothy Fitzherbert
(d. 1575)
|
Richard Coke m. Mary Sacheverell
(d. 1582)
|

Sir Francis Coke (d. 1639)   Marie m. Powell   Sir John Coke m. of Melbourne   Joan Gore (née Lee)

(1) Thomas Coke
(2) Philip Coke
(3) George Coke
(4) Robert Coke
(5) Elizabeth
(6) Mary
(7) Margaret
(8) Dorothy

Sir John Coke (d. 1650)   Thomas Coke (d. 1656)   Elizabeth m. Arthur Faunt   Anne m. (1) Henry Sacheverell (2) Henry Danvers

Mary
m.
Sir Edward Hartopp

IRETON—FLEETWOOD PEDIGREES

D

E

Henry Ireton (d. 1651) = Bridget Cromwell (d. 1662)

- Henry m. Katherine Powle (no issue)
- Elizabeth m. Thomas Polhill in 1674
- Jane m. Richard Lodge in 1668
- Bridget (d. 1729) m. Thomas Bendysh in 1669 (d. 1707)

Thomas Fleetwood of the Vache
m. (2nd wife) Bridget Spring m. Sir Robert Wingfield (2nd husband)

Sir William Fleetwood of Aldwincle Receiver of the Court of Wards
m. Jane Clifton

Sir Miles Fleetwood (1576-1641) Receiver of the Court of Wards
m. Anne Luke

- Dorothy
- William died in infancy
- Sir William Fleetwood (1603-1674) Comptroller of Woodstock Park Receiver of the Court of Wards Cupbearer to Charles I and Charles II m. (1) Frances Sture (2) Elizabeth Harvey
- Edward
- Miles
- George (1605-1667) m. Brita Gyllenstjerna Descendants in Sweden (*See G*)

(1) Charles (d. 1692) (*See F*)
(2) Gabriel
(3) Charles (b.1607 d.1608)
(4) Roger
(5) Martha

189

F

Charles Fleetwood (d. 1692)

m. (1) Frances Smith m. (2) Bridget Ireton (née Cromwell) (d. 1662)

| (3) Dame Mary Hartopp (no issue)

Smith Fleetwood (1644-1709) m. Mary Hartopp

Elizabeth m. Sir John Hartopp (*See A.2*)

Cromwell Fleetwood (1653-1688) m. Elizabeth Nevill (no issue)

Anne (died young)

Mary m. in 1678 Nathaniel Carter

Charles

Smith (d. 1726) m. Elizabeth Athill

Mary m. Rev. Abraham Coveney

Frances (d. 1749)

Elizabeth (d. 1728)

Carolina (d. 1744)

Anne m. William Gosney

Jane (d. 1761)

Elizabeth (d. 1732) m. Fountain Elwin (d. 1735)

Fleetwood Elwin (died young)

(N.B.—This is the generally accepted pedigree as printed in the older authorities.)

SUGGESTED FLEETWOOD PEDIGREE

Charles Fleetwood (1618-1692)

m. (1) Frances Smith   m. (2) Bridget Ireton   m. (3) Mary Hartopp (no issue)

Smith Fleetwood (1644-1709)
m. (1) Mary Hartopp (d. 1681)
m. (2) Anne (d. 1684)
m. (3) Ellen (d. 1731) (no issue)

Charles (d. 1676)

Elizabeth m. Sir John Hartopp (*See A.2*)

Cromwell Fleetwood (1653-1688) m. Elizabeth Nevill (d. 1692) (no issue)

Anne   other issue (?) (died young)

Mary m. Nathaniel Carter (d. 1722)

Charles died in infancy 1675

Charles of Armingland Hall (d. 1727-1728?)

Smith (d. 1726) m. Elizabeth Athill

Bridget

Mary m. Rev. Abraham Coveney

Frances (d. 1749)

(1) Elizabeth (d. 1728)
(2) Carolina (d. 1744)
(3) Anne m. William Gosney
(4) Jane (d. 1761)

Elizabeth (d. 1732) m. Fountain Elwin (d. 1735)

Fleetwood Elwin (died young)

(N.B.—It is probable that all Smith Fleetwood's children were by his first wife, Mary Hartopp, but not absolutely certain. See Addenda 10. Possibly some of the daughters were older than the two surviving sons.)

G

George Fleetwood (1605-67)
m. Brita Gyllenstjerna

Anna Christina (1641-81)
m.
Kammarherren Gustaf Adolf von Siegroth

Gustaf Miles (1642-1705)
m. friherrinnan Marta Stake

Georg Vilhelm (1644-after 57)

Adolf Jakob (1647-76)
m. friherrinnan Christina Maria Sioblad

Maria Catherina (1649—child before her mother)

Georg Vilhelm (1669-1728)
m.
1. Charlotta Beata Hard af Segerstad.
2. Hedvig Charlotta Rhenberg

Brita Christina (1671-1702)
m.
Erik Svensson Borg, ennobled Drakenfeldt

Carl Hartvig (1675-1729)
m.
friherrinnan Christina Sparre

Adolfina Johanna (1676-1756)
m.
1. friherre Lars Sparre
2. Axel Rutenskold

Brita Magdalena (1670-1755)
m. hauptmannen Johan Westphal ennobled von. W.

Marta Catharina (1671-90)

Anna Christina (1672-1730)

Beata Ebba (1674-1704)

Elisabet Maria (1675-1734)

Georg Miles (1678-1710)
m. friherrinnan Maria Morner

Ingeborg Margareta (1679-1737)

Harald Erik (1681-1709)

Gustaf Adolf (1682-1757)
m. 1. Anna Uggla
2. Martta Reenstierna

Agneta Hellena (1687-1745)

Elsa Eleonora (1686-1734)

Carl Christoffer (1685-1706)

Johan Vilhelm (1683-1695)

LUKE FAMILY PEDIGREE

Sir Walter Luke of Woodend, Cople, Beds

m. Anne (d. 1538) daughter of Sir Thomas Launcelyn

|

Nicholas Luke m. Cecily Wauton

|

John Luke m. Anne Heming

|

Nicholas Luke (d. 4th July, 1613)

m. Margaret daughter of Oliver Lord St. John of Bletsoe

|

Anne Luke (b. 1578)   Sir Oliver Luke
m. Sir Miles Fleetwood   m. Elizabeth Knightley

|

Sir Samuel Luke (d. 1670)

Entries in the Stoke Newington Parish Registers

Baptisms

1672.   Charles Hartop, Esqr, the sone of Sr John Hartop, Kt. and Baronnet, was Borne in the parish of stoak newington, the fift day of June. (Probably baptised in the Puritan form at home).

1689-90. Elizabeth, the Daughter of ffrancis St. John, Esqr, and Mary his wife, was bapt: the 22nd January.

1696-7. Walter, The son of ffrancis St. John, Esqr, was Baptized the 21st January.

1697.   Elizabeth, the D. of Mr. James Gould, bapt. 7th Oc.

Married

1677-8. Mr. Nathaniel Carter of Yearmouth, and Mris. Mary ffleetwood, were Married by Licence the 21st of ffeb. 1677.

1696.   John Allen and Mary Hartopp were Married by Banns the 12th of Nov.

Burials

1673.   Mary Smith, from my Coll. ffleetwood's was buried December the 8th, 1673.

1674.   Mris Ann Hartop, the daughter of Sr John Hartop, Barronet, was buried the 8th day of May.

1675.   Charles ffleetwood, the sone of Mr Smith ffleetwood, was Buried the 14th of May.

1675-6. Edward Hartopp, the son of Sr John Hartopp, was buried the 25th of January.

1676.   Mr Charles ffleetwood, the sone of Esqr ffleetwood, was Buried the 14th of May.

1679.   John, The son of Sr John Hartope, Barronett, was buried ye 28th of May, in Wollen: Church.

1680-1. Mary, The wife of Esqr ffleetwood ye younger, of this parish, was buried ye 21st of January in Wollen: Church. (Daughter of Sir Edward Hartopp and Mary Coke; baptised at Buckminster, April 17th, 1639; married Smith Fleetwood —son and heir of the general—in 1666).

1681.   Bridgett ffleettwood was buried ye 5th of September, in Wollen, according to an act of Parliament in yt Case prouided, as was attested within ye time limited before Justice Cheyney: Church.

1683-4. A still borne child of Mr Smith ffleetwood was buried in Wollen ye 31st of January: Church.

———   Anne ffleettwood, the wife of Mr Smith ffleettwood, was buried the 29th of ffebruary in Wollen: Church.

1691.   Hellen Hartop was buried in Wollen the 8th of December.

1707-8. William Rance, Seruant of Sr John Hartop, bur. 26th Jan.

1708-9.   Smith ffleetwood, Esqr, of the Parish of Armingland, in the County of Norfolk, was byried ye 4th of february. Certified by Erasmus Earle, Esq. J.P for Norfolk.

1711.   Dame Elizabeth Hartopp, was buried in woollen, the 26th day of November, 1711. (Daughter of General Fleetwood by his first wife; married Sir John Hartopp in 1666).

——   Madam Gold was buried in woollen ye 28th of Novr. (Frances, daughter of Sir John Hartopp and Eliz. Fleetwood; wife of Sir Nath. Gould).

1720.   The lady St. John Carried into the Countrey, December 12, 1720.

1722.   Sr John Hartopp, Bart, was buried in the Church, April 11, 1722, and paid Information money. (Buried in linen, for which a fine had to be paid. Baptised at Buckminster, Oct. 31, 1637).

1728.   Elizabeth Fleetwood Buried in A velvett Coffin in ·the Church, and Thomas Price buried in woollen, June 30. (Sic in Reg. Many entries of this kind occur).

——   Sr Nathanel Gould was Caried and buried in the Country, July 30, 1728.

——   Justice Cooke's Daughter was buried in A velvet Coffin, Novm 9th, 1728. (Frances, daughter of Thomas Cooke, Esq. by Eliz., daughter of Sir Nath. Gould. Ob. aged six years).

1730.   My Lady Hartopp was buried in a velvet Coffin, Sept. 22nd. 1730, in the Church.

1731.   Ellen ffleetwood buried in a Velvett Coffin, July 23, 1731.

1738-9.   Feb. 15. Martha Hartopp, in wollen only.

1741.   Jan. 15. Bridgett Hartopp, in linnen.

1744.   April 18. Carolina Fleetwood, in wollen.

1748-9.   Jan. 2. Mary Hartopp.

1749.   April 14. Frances Fleetwood.

——   Dec. 1. Margaret Cook. (Daughter of Thomas and Eliz. Cooke of Fleetwood House. Ob. aged 23 years).

1754.   March 15. Elizabeth Hartopp.

1755.   April 23. Dorothy Hartopp.

1761.   Nov. 7. Jane Fleetwood, in Linnen.

1762.   Jan. 28. Sir John Hartopp, Bart.

1763.   Feb. 3. Elizabeth Cooke, in Linnen. (Daughter of Sir Nath. Gould; widow of Thomas Cooke. Ob. aged 63).

——   April 22. Sarah Hartopp.

1764.   April 6. Ann Hartopp.

1766.   April 4. Sarah Hurlock. (Daughter and co-heiress of Sir John Hartopp, the last baronet, and wife of Joseph Hurlock).

1793.   Aug. 15. Joseph Hurlock, Esqr (of Chelsea), aged 78. (Husband of above Sarah Hurlock: he also lived in Fleetwood House).

Bibliography

Allen, William	— Life and Correspondence of.
Anon (Major Müller)	— Memoirs of Sophia Dorothea, Consort of George I.
Aubrey, John	— Brief Lives.
Aubrey, John	— Miscellanies.
Baxter, F. W.	— Paradise Row. 1924.
Beck, W.	— Church Street. 1927.

Bibliotheca Topographica Brittannica, No. IX.
Calendar of State Papers, Domestic, 1604-1675.
Camden Miscellany, Vol. 1.

Carlyle, T.	— Letters and Speeches of Oliver Cromwell.
Clapham, Sir John	— The Bank of England.
Clarendon	— History of the Great Rebellion.
Clarke	— Glimpses of Ancient Hackney and Stoke Newington.
Coke, Dorothea	— The Last Elizabethan.
Defoe, Daniel	— The Wars of Charles XII of Sweden.
De Morgan, Sophia	— Three Score Years and Ten.

Dictionary of National Biography.

Dutton, the Rev. A. M.	— A Short History of Buckminster Parish Church.
Fletcher, Rev. G. D.	— Leicestershire Pedigrees and Royal Descents.
Foss	— Lives of the Judges.
Foster, William	— A Guide to the India Office Records, 1600-1658.

Gentleman's Magazine for 1752 and 1769.

Hallendorff and Schück	— History of Sweden
Hobhouse, John Cam	— Historical Illustrations of the Fourth Canto of Childe Harold.
Howell, James	— Familiar Letters.
Howell, T. B.	— State Trials.
Hutchinson, Lucy	— Memoirs of Colonel Hutchinson.
Jackson, the Rev. T.	— Stoke Newington.
Lane, Jane	— Titus Oates.
Lindsay, Philip	— For King and Parliament.
Lysons, D.	— Environs of London.
Martyn	— Masters of the Inner Temple.
Milner	— Life and Times of Dr. Isaac Watts.
Milton, John	— Prose Works.
Mitchener, M.	— No Crown for the Queen.
Mitton	— Hackney and Stoke Newington.
Moline, Miss I. P.	— Old Stoke Newington.
Nichols	— Leicestershire.
Noble, Mark	— Memoirs of the Protectorate House of Cromwell.

Notes and Queries (particularly 1872).

Orme, W. — Life of Dr. John Owen.
Pirie, V. — His Majesty of Corsica.
Ramsay, R. W. — Henry Cromwell.
Ramsay, R. W. — Richard Cromwell.
Ramsay, R. W. — Cromwell's Family Circle.
Ramsay, R. W. — Henry Ireton.
Robinson, W. — History of Stoke Newington.
Saintsbury, George — Caroline Poets.
Smith, Logan Pearsall — Life and Letters of Sir Henry Wotton.
Spratling, J. R. — Story of Church Street.
Thurloe, John (ed. Birch) — A Collection of State Papers.
Vaughan, H. M. — The Last Stuart Queen.
Vaughan, H. M. — The Last of the Royal Stuarts.
Vincent, E. R. — Byron, Hobhouse and Foscolo.
Vitelleschi, Marchesa — A Court in Exile.
Voltaire — Charles XII of Sweden.
Walpole, Horace — Letters.
Walpole, Horace — Memoirs of the Reign of George III.
Warner, O. — Captains and Kings.
Watts, Isaac. — Poems and Sermons.
Waylen, J. — House of Cromwell.
Whitelocke, B. — Journal of the Swedish Embassy.
Whitelocke, B. — Memorials.
Whiting, Nathaniel — Old Jacob's Altar Newly Repaired.
Williamson, Hugh Ross — Four Stuart Portraits.
Wood, Anthony à — Athenae Oxonienses.
Wood, Anthony à — Fasti Oxonienses.
Wright, T. — Life of Isaac Watts.

INDEX OF PERSONS.